Martin Luther

Yves Congar

Translated and with a Foreword by
Roger Whittall

Martin Luther

His Faith and His Reform

Yves Congar

Translated and with a Foreword by
Roger Whittall

ATF THEOLOGY
Adelaide
2025

Cover image: Martin Luther © shutterstock.

ISBN
978-1-923385-50-4 Soft
978-1-923385-51-1 Hard
978-1-923385-52-8 Epub
978-1-923385-53-5 PDF

SCAN ME

Published by:

Making a lasting impact
An imprint of the ATF Press Publishing Group
owned by ATF (Australia) Ltd.
PO Box 234
Brompton, SA 5007
Australia
ABN 90 116 359 963
www.atfpress.com

Table of Contents

Abbreviations

BC	*The Book of Concord*, Robert Kolb & Timothy J Wengert, editors (Philadelphia, 2000).
BK	*Die Bekenntnisschriften der evangelisch-lutherischen Kirche* (Göttingen, 1952).
CR	*Corpus Reformatorum* (Berlin, 1863–1900).
DCT	*Dictionnaire de Théologie Catholique* (Paris, 1903–1950)
DSch	*Enchiridion symbolorum*, Heinrich Denzinger & Adolf Schönmetzer, editors, Editio XXXVI emendata, 1973.
ET	English translation
PL	*Patrologiae cursus completus.* Latin JP Migne, editor (Paris, 1844–1890).
Sum. Theol.	Thomas Aquinas, *Summa Theologiae.*
Vg	*Vulgate*
	MARTIN LUTHER'S WRITINGS
LW	*Luther's Works*, 'American Edition' (St Louis & Philadelphia: Concordia & Fortress Press, 1955–.)
WA	*D Martin Luthers Werke*, Kritische Gesamtausgabe (Weimar: Bohlau, 1883–.)
WABr	Briefwechsel (Letters)
WADB	Die Deutsche Bibel
WATr	Tischreden (Table Talk)

Editor's Foreword

In his recent biography of Father Yves Congar, Étienne Fouilloux introduces a comprehensive study of his life through the theme of Congar's 'Four Vocations'.[1] These callings were to the priesthood, to the order of St Dominic, to the study and teaching of ecclesiology, and to the life-long search for ecumenical understanding and the related task of dialogue between Christians. Considered together, these shaped and defined Congar's entire life and work, and stand as the foundations of its enduring substance and achievements. His ecclesiological and ecumenical vocations are especially significant for a consideration of his engagement with the legacy of the German reformer as we have it here in this translation of the collected writings in *Martin Luther, Sa Foi, Sa Réforme.*

Congar published this summary of his research in 1983, as one of the unfinished tasks of a lifetime of study and writing. It draws together his findings on the origins and effects of Luther's theology: his fervent rejection of scholasticism, the medieval sacramental system and the papacy, as well as his heightened awareness of the importance of personal faith that drew Luther into his role as the pre-eminent protestant reformer. He had also made a careful study of Luther's Christology, and his personal struggles, and these are also updated in the additional material in this volume.[2]

On the basis of an extensive reading of his works, Congar saw many positive aspects to Luther's theological enterprise, and admired his spiritual genius. But he also challenged Luther's approach to the

1. Étienne Fouilloux, *Yves Congar : A Life : 1904–1995.* Translated by Patricia Kelly (Adelaide, Australia : ATF Press, 2023).
2. Yves Congar, *Martin Luther. Sa Foi, Sa Réforme. Études de théologie historique* (Paris: Cerf, 1983).

life and teaching of the Church and its reform as representing an 'insufficient' theology based on a too narrow understanding of the sources of Christian faith and practice. Both Congar's admiration and his reservations serve to make this volume a fascinating addition to the wide world of 'Luther Studies'.

Congar's Own Enduring Significance[3]

It is well established that Father Yves Congar, OP (1904–1995), ranks as one of the most important theologians of the mid to late twentieth century. As a key figure in the modern development of Roman Catholic theology, he was an ecclesiologist and advocate for ecumenical engagement with both the protestant and the orthodox Churches. His approach to theological research linked the Scriptures, the established tradition of the Fathers, and the Church's liturgical heritage to contemporary pastoral challenges. His extensive writings, and his active participation in Second Vatican Council had a major influence on the formulations of the Council.[4] Congar's personal experience of war and conflict, his deep commitment to the Roman Catholic Church, and his passion for the ecumenical movement despite the disapproval of the Church's hierarchy, also provide the setting for his extensive engagement with Luther's theology.

The Context for Congar's 'Vocations'[5]

Congar was born in Sedan in 1904, and was living with his family in this region of eastern France when it was invaded by Germany

3. In addition to Fouilloux's biography, see (for example): Aidan Nichols, *Yves Congar*, Outstanding Christian Thinkers (London: Geoffrey Chapman, 1989), 1–13; Flynn, Gabriel, editor, *Yves Congar: Theologian of the Church*, New and expanded edition (Leuven, Belgium: Peeters, 2018). Elizabeth Teresa Groppe, *Yves Congar's Theology of the Holy Spirit*, American Academy of Religion Academy Series (Oxford; New York: Oxford University Press, 2004). Each of these contain further references for the study of Congar's life and work.
4. Gabriel Flynn, 'Yves Congar and Catholic Church Reform', in Flynn, editor *Yves Congar*, 97–131; Timothy Radcliffe, *Congar and Chenu: Friend, Teacher, Brother* (Hindmarsh, South Australia: ATF Theology, 2017).
5. Fouilloux, *Yves Congar*, 1–24, reveals in some detail the circumstances and the many people influencing and guiding Congar through his early years. Yet, at each stage, it appears that he is making his own prayerful decision as to the pathways into which he is being led. Likewise, it was his personal choice to pursue the study of Martin Luther.

in late August 1914 and occupied until 1918. Further early contact with Germany, its people, and the protestant faith came during his compulsory military service in the French-occupied Rhineland in 1924–25. Called to the priesthood, he studied as a seminarian in Paris from 1921 and in 1925 he joined the Dominicans, studying in Belgium at Le Saulchoir. In 1930 Congar was ordained priest, and in 1931 completed his doctorate on 'the unity of the Church', lecturing in ecclesiology from 1932–39, and publishing *Chrétiens désunis* in 1937.[6] During these years, Congar began to support the work of lay chaplaincy groups, including *Jeunesse Ouvrière Chrétienne* ('Young Christian Workers'), and argued the case for 'worker priests'.[7]

Congar served as a military chaplain in the Second World War, including as a prisoner of war: after defying a camp commandant's order not to preach he was imprisoned at Colditz. Returning to teaching after the war, his theological output increased, as did the level of Vatican censure and control of the theologians at Le Saulchoir, who were accused of promoting *nouvelle théologie*.[8] Congar's major work, *Vraie et Fausse Réforme Dans l'Église* (1950), was regarded negatively, and this led to severe restrictions being placed on his publishing activity, which intensified after the publication of his theology of the laity in 1951. In 1954 Congar was forbidden to teach or publish. He had to leave France, and spent the next two years under supervision as he studied privately in Jerusalem, Rome, and Cambridge.[9]

However, he was not without supporters in the hierarchy. In 1956 he was able to return to teaching in Strasbourg, and in 1960, recently-elected Pope John XXIII invited him to participate in preparatory commission for Second Vatican Council. From 1962–1965 Congar

6. Yves Congar, *Chrétiens désunis. Principes d'un 'oecuménisme' catholique* (Paris: Cerf, 1937) = *Divided Christendom*, translated by M Bousfield (London: Geofrey Bles, 1939).
7. Through his contact with Joseph Cardijn, the founder of *JOC*, Congar became involved in the range of lay movements known as 'Specialised Catholic Action'. See Stefan Robert Gigacz, 'Cardijn and Congar at Vatican II', *Interface Theology*, 3/1 (2017): 31–67. See also Fouilloux, *Yves Congar*, 101–102.
8. Jürgen Mettepenningen, 'Yves Congar and the "Monster" of *Nouvelle Théologie*' (*Horizons*, 37, 52–71, 2010).
9. For his own account of these difficult years, see: Yves Congar, *Journal d'un théologien, 1946–1956*, (Paris: Cerf, 2001) = *Journal of a Theologian (1946–56)*, translated by Dennis Minns (Hindmarsh, South Australia: ATF Theology, 2015).

served as *peritus* ('expert') to the Council, which instituted major reforms and renewal in the Church.[10]

In 1965, Congar was appointed to the bilateral Catholic-Lutheran commission, and from 1969–1985, he also served as a member of the Church's *International Theological Commission.* He continued to write and lecture prolifically, and his later work on the Holy Spirit is a major expression of his mature theology.[11]

Congar's Ecclesiology[12]

Yves Congar produced no single, unified work of systematic theology, nor a single, definitive study of ecclesiology to summarise his many books, articles, sermons and lectures. In this he resembles Luther, but the significance of neither theologian is diminished by it. Both wrote and taught prolifically, to promote the reform of the Church and what they understood to be its authentic message. Their thought, as Christian teaching formed by their life-long vocations of active engagement with the life of the Church, commands its own authenticity.

The principles that Congar sets out for Church reform provide significant background to his evaluation of Luther as a reformer, and it is helpful to summarise elements of his own ecclesiology that relate to Luther's teaching. Consistently, Congar taught that the Church is to be considered in its two aspects, that is, as an apostolic institution and as community. In *Vrai et Fausse Réforme Dans l'Église*, he wrote

> [The Church] precedes us by faith, by the sacraments of the faith, and by the exercise of the apostolic authority received from Christ (*cf* Matthew 28:19). Before existing as a community of the faithful [*communauté des fidèles*], the Church exists as an institution [*au titre d'institution*]. That is, it exists first as that ensemble of means by which Christ willed to animate and unite the faithful. These means, which

10. Yves Congar, *My Journal of the Council* (Adelaide: ATF Press, 2012).
11. Yves Congar, *Je crois en l'Esprit Saint,* 3 volumes., (Paris: Cerf, 1979) = *I believe in the Holy Spirit*, translated David Smith (New York: Seabury Press; London: Geoffrey Chapman, 1983).
12. In addition to the works cited above, this summary draws on Gabriel Flynn, 'Yves Congar', in the *Oxford Handbook of Ecclesiology*, edited by Paul Avis (2018), 382–408.

> build and structure the Church, are: the deposit of faith (and principally the revelation of the Holy Trinity); the sacraments of the faith, instituted by Jesus Christ, as the means for being united to the mystery of his passage to the Father; and, finally, the ministries or apostolic powers. These are the elements, we discover, that can generate and form communities to be the Church—as we see in Acts [2:42] and in, for example, Tertullian.[13]

Some of this is close to Luther's understanding of the Church as a community gathered by the Spirit through the Gospel, created and nurtured by the word and the sacraments of grace.[14] Congar also stressed the importance of the Church as communion, and the people of God gathered as a holy community, as an essential aspect of the mystical body of Christ. In *Jalons Pour Une Théologie Du Laïcat*, he was developing what he described as a 'total ecclesiology': a focus on the Church as the whole people of God in Christ Jesus. He writes,

> [A]n entirely clerical Church [*une Église cléricale*] . . . would not be the people of God in the fullness of its truth. Fundamentally, there can be only one sound and sufficient theology of laity, and that is a 'total ecclesiology' [*une ecclésiologie totale*].[15]

But Congar's emphases on apostolic authority (*pouvoirs apostoliques*), 'structure', and tradition suggests that he goes far beyond what Luther believes is essential to the life of the Church. This marks a key divergence in their thought.

Congar was committed to the Roman Catholic Church as divinely instituted; governed and taught by its apostolic hierarchy of priests, bishops, and the pope. Congar's complex understanding of the Church as Christ's 'mystical body' means that this Church becomes

13. Yves Congar, *Vraie et Fausse Réforme Dans l'Église*, 95–96 = *True and False Reform in the Church*, rev. ed., trans. Paul Philibert (Collegeville, MN: Liturgical Press, 2011), 70–71.
14. BK 511–512, BC 355–356 (Martin Luther, *The Small Catechism*, The Apostles' Creed: Third Article).
15. Yves Congar, *Jalons Pour Une Théologie Du Laïcat*, 13 = *Lay People in the Church*, revised edition, translated by Donald Attwater (London: Geoffrey Chapman, 1965), xvi (translation altered).

the 'sacrament of salvation' for the world.[16] As shall be seen, Congar criticises Luther for failing to appreciate the role that this genuine, living tradition continues to play in the structured development of the Church, both in its sacramental core and also for the purpose of its mission to the world. Tradition determines how Scripture, with its interpretation by the Fathers of the Church, is read and applied. For Congar, and his co-workers at Le Saulchoir, this *ressourcement*—the return to the sources—was a key aspect of their revitalisation of Catholic theology.[17]

As with the duality in Congar's approach to the Church's structure and its life, he works similarly to identify the 'true reform' of the Church that also affirms the role of tradition, which provides the sources and the substance of the Church's teaching and life. In *Vraie et Fausse Réforme*, Congar argues that true reform can only be initiated by the prophetic voices that remain within the Church, not those who attack it from the outside. Luther, he writes, falls into that error.[18]

Congar sets out four principles that underpin his approach. The first is the 'Primacy of Charity, and of Pastoral Concerns'.[19] This is the spirit in which reform must be proposed and enacted. Second, the true reformer seeks to 'Remain in Communion with the Whole Church', since reform can never be an end in and of itself, but is always looking to build up the Church in its existing life and structure.[20] True reform is not schismatic, but remains catholic: only in this way can the full truth be grasped, with the 'Centre' having a responsibility to listen to the 'Periphery'. Third, the reformer must 'Have Patience with Delays'.[21] Luther is very much in Congar's sights here![22] Although the prophet/reformer may appear to be persecuted, it is not their place to issue the Church with ultimatums. Neither, however, should Church leaders be 'too patient' with regard to the implementation of necessary reforms. Fourth, Congar proposes that 'Genuine Renewal'

16. Flynn, 'Yves Congar', *OHE*, 395–396.
17. See: Groppe, *Yves Congar's Theology*, 20–21. Also: Flynn, 'Yves Congar', 383–386.
18. Congar, *Vraie et Fausse Réforme*, 241–247 = *True and False Reform*, 160–163.
19. Congar, *Vraie et Fausse Réforme*, 248 = *True and False Reform*, 165.
20. Congar, *Vraie et Fausse Réforme*, 264–265 = *True and False Reform*, 175.
21. Congar, *Vraie et Fausse Réforme*, 306–307 = *True and False Reform*, 201.
22. Congar, *Vraie et Fausse Réforme*, 310–13 =*True and False Reform*, 203–204.

is only achieved 'through a Return to the Principle of Tradition'.[23] This involves adaptation rather than innovation or 'novelty': *ressourcement* means that the Church lives in contact with its 'deepest tradition'. From these principles, Congar is able to evaluate the success or failure of various reform movements in the Church's history.[24] They will also come to reflect his own experience as a theologian–reformer in the Catholic Church, and especially his encounters with the opponents of reform in his Church's hierarchy.[25]

Then, in his revised edition (1968), this evaluation also included a brief look at the reforming work of the Second Vatican Council, which was, in effect, Congar's own reform.[26] The English translation (2011) omitted the section in which Congar analysed the theology of the Protestant reformers in detail.[27] But Congar's evaluation of Luther in relation to his four principles for reform and in his final conclusions was retained. Congar continued to contrast his own, measured approach to what he saw as the violent methods of reformers like Luther, which tore apart the fabric of the Church. In this respect, Congar's work can be distinguished from other, less critical, Catholic evaluations of Luther.[28] But, as will be seen, he based his judgment—both negative and positive—on an extensive reading of Luther's works, and because of this Congar deserves a careful consideration.

23. Congar, *Vraie et Fausse Réforme*, 333–335 = *True and False Reform*, 218.
24. Congar, *Vraie et Fausse Réforme*, 537576 = *True and False Reform*, 228–251 ('Conclusion').
25. Fouilloux, *Yves Congar*, 117–145. The chapter is titled 'A Second Imprisonment?' and describes the circumstances surrounding his censure by Rome and his time of 'exile'.
26. Congar, *Vraie et Fausse Réforme*, second edition (Paris: Éditions du Cerf, 1968), 515–521 = *True and False Reform*, 252–56. This 'Postface' was written in the aftermath of the protests that swept through Paris in May–June 1968.
27. Congar, *Vraie et Fausse Réforme*, 353–536: 'Réforme et Protestantisme'.
28. For a useful survey of Catholic responses to Luther, see Richard Stauffer, *Luther as* Seen *by Catholics* (London: Lutterworth Press, 1967). For an entirely positive study of Luther by a pupil of Congar, see Daniel Olivier, *La foi de Luther. La cause de l'Évangile dans l'Église* (Paris: Editions Beauchesne, 1978) = *Luther's Faith: The Cause of the Gospel in the Church*, translated by John Tonkin, (St. Louis: Concordia, 1982). See also: John Murray Todd, *Martin Luther: A Biographical Study* (Westminster, Md: Newman Press, 1964); Walter Kasper, *Martin Luther: An Ecumenical Perspective* (New York: Paulist Press, 2016).

Congar on Luther

Martin Luther, Sa Foi, Sa Réforme: Introduction

Published in 1983, the quincentenary of Luther's birth, Congar's book gathered the fruits of fifty years of research and gave a Catholic perspective on Luther's continuing ecumenical significance.[29] In it, he revisited his previous work on Luther as a theologian, and his integrity as a reformer.

A balanced approach to Luther was by no means certain, given Congar's background. But his commitment to ecumenical relations and his early fascination with Luther's story led him to seek a more positive direction. The image of Luther as a deeply flawed heretic continued to colour French Catholic perceptions into the early to mid-twentieth century, reflecting the work of writers such as Heinrich Denifle (1844–1905), Hartmann Grisar (1845–1932), and the philosopher, Jacques Maritain (1882–1973). Congar notes that they characterised Luther's personality in terms of mediocrity and subjectivity, marked by pathological tendencies.[30] Congar studied under Maritain and certainly retained reservations regarding Luther's psychology. But he also acknowledges his debt to Joseph Lortz (1887–1975), and others, for a more open response to the challenges presented by Luther.[31] He reflects on his own training in scholastic theology, in the school of Aquinas, and how strongly Luther had rejected a canonical, hierarchical view of the Church and its teaching.[32]

Congar mentions how his early visits to German towns associated with Luther sparked his interest in his life and theology. The first stages of his exploration came to fruition in *Vraie et Fausse Réforme Dans l'Église*, which firmly rejected the approach of Luther, Calvin, and the other Protestant reformers. He felt that they had not only

29. Congar, *Martin Luther*, 6–11, Introduction. For an informed Catholic account of Congar's work on Luther, see Joseph Famerée, 'Yves Congar, lecteur de Luther' in *En 500 Après Martin Luther. Reception et conflits d'interpretation (1517–2017)*, edited Stéphane-Marie Morgain (Turnhout: Brepols Publishers, 2018), 189–201. Famerée summarises this book and also *Vraie et Fausse Réforme* in relation to Luther. He emphasises Congar's positive ecumenical conclusions.

30. Congar, *Martin Luther*, 7. Page references in these notes are to the original French edition.

31. Congar, *Martin Luther*, 8. Joseph Lortz, *Die Reformation in Deutschland*, third edition (Freiburg im Breisgau: Herder, 1949).

32. Congar, *Martin Luther*, 9.

sought to improve the life of the Church, but had attacked 'essential elements of its structure'.[33] However by the 1980s, after many years of ecumenical dialogue, and in the light of the work of Catholic colleagues throughout Europe, he was ready to produce a summation of Luther's life and theology from a more balanced perspective.

Congar now acknowledged the problematic state of the late medieval Church, and also his personal concerns for the Church in his own day. He had by now read extensively in Luther's theology, well beyond the Reformation treatises of 1520, and also in many Protestant, as well as Catholic, interpreters of Luther.[34] He introduces his study with a historical judgment that is typically forthright and expressive:

> The Reformation is primarily 'Luther'. It was through him that the first crater opened up in the solid crust of the Western Christian world. The burning lava that came out of it is not exhausted.[35]

Despite this judgment that Luther violently disrupted—disrupts!—the Church, Congar commented positively about a number of aspects of Luther's work and spirituality. He applauds his personal faith and commitment to the word, to the gospel, and to the cause of Christ in the Church. He acknowledges that, moving beyond the negative perceptions of the past, the Church has much to learn from Luther.[36]

But Congar's own theological convictions are not set aside. He warns in his introduction that Luther 'has misunderstood and denied several articles of the Catholic faith (. . . .) For all his greatness (*grandeur*), Luther may not be the ultimate measure of Christianity

33. Congar, *Martin Luther*, 15. See Congar, *Vraie et Fausse Réforme*, 353–536.
34. He quotes Karl Holl, Walter Link and Hans Preuss; others include (for example) Martin Brecht, Leif Crane, Bernhard Lohse, and Steven Ozment. He also uses extensively the work of Henri Strohl (1874–1959), a French protestant historian who lectured in the Faculty of Theology of the University of Strasbourg from 1919 to 1945.
35. 'La Réforme, c'est d'abord Luther. C'est par lui que le premier cratère s'est ouvert dans la croûte solide du monde chrétien d'Occident. La lave brûlante qui, en est sortie n'est pas épuisée'. Congar, *Martin Luther*, 7.
36. Congar, *Martin Luther*, 8. He describes Luther's theological *richesses*—his 'wealth', abundance.

and ecclesiality even for the Lutherans themselves'.[37] However, with a personal commitment to the cause of ecumenical reconciliation, Congar seeks rapprochement with the 'Christian Luther', just as some modern Lutherans now come close to the 'catholicism of the undivided Church (*catholicisme de l'Eglise indivise*)'. In this reconciliation, says Congar, 'it is Jesus Christ who must be victorious, he, his gospel, and his Apostles'.[38]

Martin Luther: *'Sa Foi'*

Throughout Congar's studies, references and direct quotations from Luther abound, from the early and later writings, from the *Dictata super Psalterium* to the final *Vorlesung über Genesis*. This is a significant feature of this enquiry, revealing the depth of his encounter with Luther's writing. Further citations come from Luther's early correspondence, and his *Tischreden* (table-talk).Having undertaken his own reading of Luther, Congar does not often rely on quotations lifted from the secondary sources.[39] In his chronology of Luther's life, he lists over twenty-five significant works.[40]

The initial dispute over indulgences, Congar writes, was based on the profoundly personal nature of Luther's spiritual experience, and its impact on his theology.[41] It was, he says, 'the opposition he encountered [that] led Luther to extend and to radicalise his reformist ideas (*propos reformate*)'.[42] So he briefly walks through Luther's early

37. Congar, *Martin Luther*, 9. He notes,'Voir par exemple JS Preus, "La discussion luthérienne sur Luther"', in *Concilium*, 118 (1976): 91–98.

38. 'C'est Jésus-Christ qui doit être vainqueur, lui, son Évangile et ses Apôtres', Congar, *Martin Luther*, 9–10.

39. Congar, *Martin Luther*, 11. Congar provided his own translations of Luther, which are reproduced in the text that follows. Luther's writings are therefore cited according to their Latin and German titles from *WA*, with indicative references to their English sources (*LW*), where available. Thus, in the first sections on Luther's 'discovery of Christ', he includes references to (for example) *Vorlesung über den Römerbrief* (1515–1516), *Sermo de digno praeparatione cordis pro suscipiendo sacramento eucharistiae* (1518), *Sermo de poenitentia* (1518), *Acta Augustana* (1518), *Predigt über das 2. Buch Moses* (1525), *Disputation gegen die Antinomer* (1527), *Vorlesung über den 1. Johannesbrief* (1527), *Enarratio Psalmorum LI* (1538), *Das 16. und 17. Kapitel Johannes gepredigt und ausgelegt* (1538).

40. Congar, *Martin Luther*, 13–14.

41. Congar, *Martin Luther*, 16.

42. Congar, *Martin Luther*, 16.

experiences, from his entry into the monastery in 1505, and his search for a gracious God—which, Congar observes, is evident in the first lectures on the Psalms, and precedes his engagement with the problem of *justitia Dei* in Romans 1:17.[43] It was Luther's 'personal discovery' of God's mercy, and the faith that clings to Christ's righteousness, that led him to question the Church's penitential practices.[44] This discovery, says Congar, 'will drive everything else'.[45] In this connection, Congar notes the influence of 'the doctors of conscience and life' on the early Luther, namely Tauler, Gerson, and Ss. Bernard and Bonaventure.[46] This spiritual orientation led to Luther's development as a reformer.

Congar distinguishes three decisive moments for the 'young Luther'. First, there is his reaction against scholasticism, and its use of philosophy to determine theology. Subsequently, he opposed the preaching of indulgences, justified by canonical and papal authority. And thirdly, there is his opposition to the papacy itself, and its ecclesiology. Common to these stages is Luther's personal commitment to the 'sovereign word of God' (*Parole souveraine de Dieu*).[47]

Luther's attack on scholastic theology is clearly significant for Congar, reflecting his own antecedents as a Dominican theologian. He explores this in a consideration of Luther's early physical transfer from Erfurt to Wittenberg, which also involved his movement from Aristotle to Christ, from philosophy to Biblical theology.[48] Luther, he says,

> . . . found [*a (re)trouvé*] Christ in Paul, especially in Romans and Galatians, but also more broadly in Scripture. To extend this discovery to the Church, to draw the consequences and applications from it, to fight to the death against that which is contrary to it, to criticise and even reject that which is

43. Congar, *Martin Luther*, 16–17.
44. Congar, *Martin Luther*, 17–18. He quotes extensively from Luther's letter to Spenlein, WA Br 1:35–36 (1516) (see LW 48:11–14) and notes parallels in the *Sermo de poenitentia*, WA 1:322,9–10 (1518).
45. Congar, *Martin Luther*, 17.
46. Congar, *Martin Luther*, 18.
47. Congar, *Martin Luther*, 18.
48. Congar, *Martin Luther*, 18–21. Congar quotes Luther's letters in the years 1509–1518, and his farewell to scholasticism in the dedication to *Operationes in Psalmos* (1519–1521), WA 5:21,37–22,21(see LW 14:283–284).

> not in conformity with it, and on the other hand to create communities and ministers [*communautés et ministres*] in conformity with this truth: this is Luther's reform, 'The Reformation'. This is what we shall see.[49]

The early sections of the book focus on this 'rediscovery' of Christ in some detail, and he begins with identifying the heart of Luther's theology. As others have done, Congar finds this in Luther's commentary on Psalm 51:

> A later text expresses the deep conviction by which Luther's journey is summed up, this passage from the commentary on Psalm 51 of 1532: 'What theology properly speaks of is human beings guilty of sin and lost, and God justifying and saving sinful people. Anything other than this that is sought or discussed in theology is error and poison'.[50]

Congar will refer to this quotation twice more in his study. Its significance here is its expression of Luther's view that God can be known only in terms of the revealed relationship. This means that—beyond philosophy—God is to be known primarily through Christ's humanity, his suffering and his cross. Congar also cites texts from *Dictata super Psalterium* (1513–1515), and the later *Genesis-Vorlesung* (1535–1545), as well as *De Servo Arbitrio* (1525), and the *Disputatio Heidelbergae habita* (1518).[51] He acknowledges that Luther does not innovate here:

> It was a traditional conviction that God could only be reached and known through Christ, that is, through the humanity of Christ. Testimonies to this abound. It was at least affirmed in principle, without being applied as consistently as Luther.[52]

For Luther, this approach to God is on the basis of faith alone, notes Congar, and it is this 'personal faith' (*La 'Foi Spéciale'—fides apprehensiva*) that is most telling as the basis for Luther's 'new theology'. Congar explores the first expressions of this 'discovery' and

---

49. Congar, *Martin Luther*, 21.
50. Congar, *Martin Luther*, 21–22. WA 40,2:328,17 (compare LW12:311).
51. Congar, *Martin Luther*, 22–24.
52. Congar, *Martin Luther*, 23–24.

highlights its development by reference to Luther's early statements on the efficacy of the sacraments.[53] He notes that this is the critical point identified by Cardinal Cajetan (1469–1534), in his interviews with Luther at Augsburg in 1518.[54] Debating the role of faith in the sacrament of penance, Cajetan sounds the alarm, stating that if Luther's view prevailed, 'that would be to make another Church'. Congar agrees. Luther has over-personalised the sacraments, displacing the authority of the Church's instituted ministry with the individual's apprehension of grace offered in the effective word of God.[55] The heart of faith here, for Luther, is the conviction that God's promise is 'for me' (*pro me*). Congar traces this idea at some length through Luther's early writings.[56]

In the next, related, section, Congar explores Luther's rejection of scholasticism and his creation of a 'new theology'.[57] He traces this movement from the very early lectures on the *Sentences* (1509), through to Luther's debates with Cajetan and Johann Eck (1486–1543), and beyond. Congar quotes extensively, to demonstrate Luther's rejection of the language and concepts of philosophy, and his commitment to a Scriptural presentation of faith and of Christology.[58] Luther, he says,

53. Congar, *Martin Luther*, 26–28. Citations from *In epistolam St Pauli ad Galatas commentarius* (1519), *Sermo de digno praeparatione cordis pro suscipiendo sacramento eucharistiae* (1518), *Sermo de poenitentia* (1518), *Resolutiones disputationum de indulgentiarum virtute* (1518).
54. See: *Acta Augustana* (1518), WA 2:6–26 (see LW 31:253–292). Brecht, *Luther* 1: 246–265.
55. Congar, *Martin Luther*, 28. Martin Brecht notes that Cajetan came to this realisation as he prepared for Luther's hearing, *Luther* 1:250. This is confirmed by J Wicks, *Cajetan responds* (Catholic University of America Press, 1978), 43 and 55. In 55n17 Wicks spells out how this encounter indeed led to a 'new Church'.
56. Congar, *Martin Luther*, 29–31. He also cites here *ad Galatas commentarius* (1535). Congar, it seems, accepts a relatively early date for Luther's theological 'breakthrough'. See Martin Brecht, *Luther* 1:221–237, for a detailed discussion of the dating for Luther's reformatory discovery.
57. Congar, *Martin Luther*, 31–49. The section has the following headings: '(Retrouver le Christ) dans l'Écriture et les Pères'; 'Critique de la Scolastique'; 'Création d'une nouvelle théologie et d'un nouveau langage'.
58. Congar, *Martin* Luther, 34–35, where he quotes at length from Luther on the 'expectant creation' (Romans 8:19), WA 56:371, 2–27 (1515–16), (see LW 25:360–361), and from the *Disputation de sententia:'Verbum caro factum est'*(1539), WA 39:2–5 (see LW 73:254–257), as well as a number of other sources.

> . . . contrasted two realms, that of this world and that of God, just as there were two justices, one *coram hominibus* [in human eyes] and the other *coram Deo* [in God's eyes]. Nature, reason, rights and laws are part of what is valid *coram hominibus*, only the word and the promise are valid *coram Deo*. *Theo*–logy could only exist in a discourse made from God's point of view, normed by his Word, that is, in concrete terms, by the Scriptures.[59]

This distinction, it will be seen, also applies for Luther when he considers the reality of the Church, and it is a key point of contention for Congar. Here, after again citing the *Commentary on Psalm 51*, on theology's unique subject matter, he quotes Luther's *Vorlesung über Genesis*, to the effect that 'the terms and language must correspond to the *subiectum*: that is to say, to the reality in question. A new reality requires a new language, a new grammar'.[60]

Congar has a fundamental problem with Luther's position. He agrees this 'new theology' requires careful reading, on Luther's own terms, and that his own position *vis-à-vis* Luther's Christology has needed revision in this regard.[61] But theological debate, says Congar, does require the use of human reason, and that means using the language of logic and philosophy. In fact, Luther himself does this, and claimed some superiority over his opponents in the sphere of logical argumentation, yet still contends that theology's 'new language' requires the rejection of philosophy.[62] Congar counters,

> Hadn't the Sorbonne defined that the same truth applies to philosophy and theology? This is what Luther could not admit. He admitted the usefulness of dialectic for exercising the mind, as a scholarly and pedagogical utility. He did not posit an absolute heterogeneity between reason exercised on the human level and the same powers, for we have no other, exercised in faith: the same reason operates on the level of creation and redemption.[63]

59. Congar, *Martin Luther*, 41.
60. Congar, *Martin Luther*, 41. This is Congar's summary of WA 42:195,3–21 on Genesis 4:7 (see LW 1:263–264); his footnote contains the complete passage in Latin and in French translation.
61. Congar, *Martin Luther*, 42–43.
62. Congar, *Martin Luther*, 43–46.
63. Congar, *Martin Luther*, 47. He notes a letter to Spalatin, 22 February 1518, where Luther complains about the harm done to theology by scholastic theology, WA Br 1:149,11–12 (see LW 48:56–59).

In this battle, Congar says, Luther fought against two enemies, Aristotle and the Pope. The early culmination of his struggle, in the Leipzig Debate with Johann Eck (1519), meant that Luther 'had to radicalise his positions and his opposition'. He now sees the antichrist at work in the papal condemnation of his cause, and in December 1520, 'as a Christian and as a sworn doctor of Sacred Scripture', he publicly burns both the papal bull, and the books of canon law, as a sign of his defiance.[64] This conflict is one of the defining moments of Luther's reform journey. Congar ends this section by summarising the position Luther had reached:

> Rome herself condemns him as a heretic. Since Gregory VII at least, she considered all those who opposed her decisions to be heretics. Luther did not accept this view. Since one is made a Christian by faith in the word of God [*par le foi en la Parole de Dieu*], only by contradicting it would one be a heretic. Far from opposing it, he was faithful to it. He challenged the normative character of papal decisions in the order of faith [*dans l'ordre de la foi*]. For him, it was the Papists, 'Thomists', and others, who were heretics![65]

This has set the scene, establishing how Luther stakes everything on the word and faith, and Congar is now ready to consider Luther's reform agenda, and to evaluate his view of the Church—including its priesthood.

Martin Luther: *'Sa Réforme'*, and his flawed Ecclesiology

The third part of Congar's investigation considers Luther's 'Réforme et son Église'.[66] Congar refers again to his earlier study in *Vraie et Fausse Réforme Dans l'Église*, presenting the paradox between Luther's stated commitment to the Church of Rome, repeated on a number of occasions before 1521, and his rejection of the papacy as the Antichrist, together with his conviction of the heretical nature of

64. Congar, *Martin Luther*, 48: *Quare Pontificis Romani et discipulorum eius Libri a D. Martino Luthero combusti sunt*, WA 7:161–182 (see LW 31:379–395).
65. Congar, *Martin Luther*, 48–49. Congar notes, once again, the significant publications of 1519–20 (nn97–99), and includes *Adversus execrabilem Antichristi bullam* (1520), WA 6:597–612.
66. *Martin Luther*, 49–81.

scholastic theology. Congar writes, 'there can be no doubt that Luther would have preferred a reform of the Roman Church, according to the Gospel, without a schism (*sans rupture*)'.[67]

Pursuing that thought, he looks at the elements of Luther's early career that represent this struggle. Congar sees Luther's sense of divine calling, his vocation as a doctor of the Church, as a major factor in the equation. He was engaged in a reform of theology, particularly the teaching of justification.[68] But Luther takes this too far says Congar, noting his '***cavalière***' letter of dedication to Pope Leo X, prefacing *De libertate christiana*, with its insistence on the right of Christians to judge doctrine on the basis of the word alone.[69]

Luther struggled with this, Congar says, citing the famous instance where the reformer accuses himself, 'are you alone wise?'[70] But when Erasmus counselled moderation, Luther rejects the advice, because he considers his struggle represents the battle between Christ and Satan.[71] Although he confesses in 1527 that, had he known what sects would emerge from his protest, 'I would not have dared to begin [this]'.[72]

Luther's principle of reform was the primacy of God's word, and he fought against its abuse in the Church by the false teachings of works, laws, heresies, superstitions.[73] So Congar muses on how schism might indeed have been avoided if the Church had listened more carefully: Luther's reform was initially 'a reform of teaching and preaching [*de l'enseignement et de la* ***prédication***] in conformity with this fundamental truth: Jesus Christ is the Saviour, and he alone'.[74] He notes Luther's reform programmes, as they are presented in the *An den christlichen Adel deutscher Nation* (1520) and the *Vermahnung an die Geistlichen . . . zu Augsburg* (1530). It was about correcting abuses on the basis of God's word; this was Luther's reminiscence in the *Genesis-Vorlesung*, how the first act of reformation was to 'cleanse doctrine'.[75]

67. *Martin Luther*, 50.
68. Congar, *Martin Luther*, 52.
69. Congar, *Martin Luther*, 53: WA 7: 43,33–37 (1520), (compare LW 31:335).
70. Congar cites *Vom Mißbrauch der Messen* (1522), WA 8:482,32 (compare LW 36:134).
71. Congar, *Martin Luther*, 53.
72. Congar, *Martin Luther*, 54: *Annotationes in ep. Pauli ad Titam* (1527), WA 25:10,18 (compare LW 29:8).
73. Congar, *Martin Luther*, 54–55.
74. Congar, *Martin Luther*, 56.
75. Congar, *Martin Luther*, 56–57. WA 44:170, 35 (see LW 6:230).

'All of this', says Congar, forms the basis on which Luther proceeded with 'his' reformation. The details of the reforms themselves are not his concern at this point:

> What is most important for my research is that, in Luther's eyes, everything depends on doctrinal truth and must begin with the word. For the word (The Word) makes the Church. The Church is *creatura verbi divini*. Luther repeats that the word has done everything; it overthrew the papacy, it will change the world, but not without painful crises.[76]

This is the key point here for Congar's evaluation, not just of Luther's reform, but also of his critique of Luther's ecclesiology. Luther's reform agenda quickly spilled over into outright opposition to the Roman Church and its hierarchy, and this is contrary to Congar's principles for true reform. It shows Luther's lack of patience, and more than that, his lack of commitment to the Church in its divine constitution.

The papacy, and the curia, oppose his reform, says Luther, thus they must be opposed to the gospel. In *Von den Konzillis und Kirchen* (1539), Luther places the situation in the hands of 'our Lord Christ'.[77] If the Pope opposes the Gospel, he opposes Christ, and is therefore the Antichrist. Congar traces the early development in Luther's attitude to the papacy, agreeing with Danish psychiatrist, Paul Reiter, that 'Luther has fulfilled his psychosis on the character of the Pope'. This, again, is a significant feature of Congar's evaluation of Luther: what he has read leads him to conclude that Luther's aggressive outbursts cannot be explained away and must be included in any account of Luther as a reformer.[78]

For Congar, the turning-point is marked by the publication of the *De captivitate Babylonica* late in 1520.[79] He sees that Luther's limitation of the Church's sacramental system to Baptism, Penance,

76. Congar, *Martin Luther*, 57: 'Car la parole (la Parole) fait l'eglise'. He cites from *Resolutiones Lutherianae super propositionibus suis Lipsiae disputatis* (1519), WA 2:430,6; also *De servo arbitrio* (1525), WA 8:626,26–8 (see LW 33:52).

77. Congar, *Martin Luther*, 57–58. WA 50:512,13–18 (see LW 41:11).

78. Congar, *Martin Luther*, 58. PJ Reiter, *Martin Luthers Umwelt, Charakter und Psychose* (Copenhagen, 1937), 1:385. Congar highlights this issue in two lengthy footnotes (58n138–39). His detailed study of *Luther's Anguish* is included in this book as 'Study Four'.

79. Congar follows J Lortz in this suggestion (48n42).

and the Lord's Supper is especially significant in its rejection of the sacrament of orders. He notes a flaw in Luther's anti-papal argument here—the Orthodox Churches also share this sacrament. But, Congar admits, Luther's reform proposal is not intentionally negative and destructive. There is *le* vécu *luthérien* (Lutheran 'lived experience') at work here in relation to the sacraments. It made possible the creation of new communities, which endure today.[80]

But, he says, the conflict also led Luther to propose the existence of two Churches within the Christian world, one true, the other false. He had not, he believed, been excommunicated by the true Church![81] Luther follows Augustine here, tracing the Church's biblical roots to the two brothers, Abel and Cain, in the *Genesis-Vorlesung*.[82] In Luther, the distinction is made on the basis of faith, adherence to the word. Congar further documents this dichotomy with references to *De captivitate Babylonica, Von den Papstum zu Rom, Responsio ad Catharini, Von den Konziliis und Kirchen*, and *Wider Hans Worst*. He then adds Luther's two Catechisms, and the *Confessio Augustana*, with their identification of the Church with the communion of saints, and true believers.[83]

Congar notes that this is Luther's preferred language for the Church: 'He liked to describe the Church as 'Christendom', '*congregatio sanctorum*', the flock of Christ, which recognises and follows his voice'.[84] Other terms noted include, 'the faithful people', 'the kingdom of faith', and 'the assembly of all believing Christians on earth'. Congar records multiple occurrences of these terms in the *Dictata super Psalterium, Praelectiones . . . in Joel*, and *Von den Papstum zu Rom*. This list is limited, but many other sources had already been noted.

The false, papal Church, on the other hand, 'is based on reason, and human laws'. This is because 'the Romans founded the most beautiful juridical structures and laws'. Congar records Luther's view here—which is markedly different to his own—without further comment.[85]

80. Congar, *Martin Luther*, 59 (emphasis added).
81. Congar, *Martin Luther*, 59. He notes Luther's claim, from *Das 16. Kapitel St Johannes gepredigt* (1538), WA 46:8,3–8, (see LW 24:306).
82. Congar, *Martin Luther*, 59: WA 42:187,13–20 (see LW 1:252).
83. Congar, *Martin Luther*, 59–60. His notes are again extensive, 59n144–47.
84. Congar, *Martin Luther*, 60: 'Il aime définir l'Église comme 'christianisme', '*congregatio sanctorum*', troupeau du Christ, qui reconnaît et suit sa voix'.
85. Congar, *Martin Luther*, 60. He quotes from the *Vorlesung über Genesis*, WA 43:386,21 (see LW 4:347).

For Luther, the true Church is the 'domain of faith', and is therefore hidden, invisible. But, in this world, there are its visible signs: the preached Gospel, Baptism, and the Eucharist. Where the signs are, there are the saints. On this basis, he was able to 'create, nurture, and organise Churches'. Leaving aside his theological judgments, Congar acknowledges what Luther achieved in this regard, on the basis of his preaching and writing. He makes a blunt comparison: 'If the Papacy has educated the West by its decretals, Luther was like the pope of the new Church, born of his reform'.[86]

Congar here returns to his chief point, which is the validity of Luther's ecclesiology as the basis for reform. He states that his own earlier view, analysing what he sees as Luther's false dichotomy, has needed some revision from his original evaluation in *Vraie et Fausse Réforme*. However, given that in 1983 he reproduces the following summary in full, he believes that his argument still carried some weight. He explains,

> In my 1947–1950 study of Luther's ecclesiology, I based my reading very largely on the opposition between the outer and the inner, with two sets of ideas of interdependent or equivalent:
> ***Exterior*** = corporeal = visible / reason = nature = the first 'carnal' birth = *jura politica, disciplina, leges* = *res, loca, corpora*;
> ***Interior*** = spiritual = invisible = faith = second birth, the word and vocation = the Spirit, from God's own being.
>
> It seemed to me that Luther had already dissociated the pure *Act of God* (the Holy Spirit), internally through faith, and the external means of grace which, taken in themselves, i.e. isolated from faith, are purely human and carnal.[87]

Congar acknowledges, 'I felt this made a satisfactory ecclesiology impossible (. . .) [but], I had not taken sufficient account of the fact that, for [Luther], the external means are also from God (from Christ)'.[88] He has now taken note of Luther's repeated assertions that the sacraments instituted by Christ are tangible means of grace and are essential for the life of the Church.

86. Congar, *Martin Luther*, 61.
87. Congar, *Martin Luther*, 62. See *Vraie et Fausse Réforme*, 383 (1968, 346–7).
88. Congar, *Martin Luther*, 62.

But this revised opinion is not explored in great detail. Rather, Congar again identifies Luther's primary emphasis on the role of faith in relation to the sacraments, and how this features in his debate with Cajetan regarding their efficacy: the precise meaning of *ex opere operato*. Against this, he says, is Luther's rejection of Donatism, and then also his frequent acceptance of the papal Church as 'Church'.[89]

He affirms Luther's statements that true faith, and the faithful, were present in the Roman Church and this reveals that the means of grace, the preached word and the sacraments, were at work in it. At some length, Congar notes *Von der Wiedertaufe* (1528) and *Von der Winkelmesse und Pfaffenweihe* (1533), as two sources for this re-evaluation.[90] He says that this leads him

> to recognise the positive place given by Luther to the external means of grace [*moyens externes de grâce*] in the Church, which come from Christ. They also provide a basis for the very important thesis that Luther really did not want to found a new Church, but to purify the existing one: 'we do not want to abolish your Gospel [*votre Evangile*] . . . but to purify and polish it like a dirty and spoiled mirror'.[91]

Yet this purification is 'radical', because, Congar says, for Luther 'faith in Christ, our only salvation, is perverted by practices and a clerical structure which stifles the freedom of faith [*la liberté de la foi*]'.[92] Luther's reform programme can be seen in four essential texts, says Congar. He lists *An den christlichen Adel deutscher Nation, and De captivitate Babylonica*, both from 1520. Less often noted are Luther's *Responsio ad Catharini* (1521), and the *Vermahnung an die Geistlichen versammelt auf dem Reichstag zu Augsburg* (1530). Congar immediately adds a fifth, *Die Schmalkaldische Artikel* (1537), because of its importance in relation to the proposed Council of the Church, planned for Mantua.[93]

---

89. Congar, *Martin Luther*, 62–63.
90. Congar, *Martin Luther*, 63–64. WA 26:147,13–18 (see LW 40:231–32); WA 38:221, 18–35 (see LW 38:177–78).
91. Congar, *Martin Luther*, 64. *Das fünfte, sechste und siebente Kapitel Matthaei gepredigt und ausgelegt* (1530), WA 32:357,8 (see LW 21:70).
92. Congar, *Martin Luther*, 64.
93. Congar, *Martin Luther*, 64n162 outlines Luther's three categories for these articles: those in which agreement exists, those where no concessions can be made, and those open for discussion.

Congar affirms the justice and reasonableness of many of Luther's reforms, his elevation of Scripture, and the correction of abuses in the Church including the dominant role of the papacy and the curia. Congar states that many of these have been subsequently amended. Luther, he says, 'is often right' (*Luther a souvent raison*).[94]

Dogmatic questions, such as those raised in *De captivitate Babylonica,* are more problematic for Congar. He agrees with Luther that the laity should be receiving both bread and wine in the Eucharist, but there remain other contentious issues. He notes Luther's definition of a sacrament ('a promise addressed to our faith, accompanied by a sensible sign'), and his relegation of confirmation, marriage, clerical order, and extreme unction to the category of 'ceremonies accompanied by prayers', lacking the word of promise and not requiring faith.[95]

Ordination (the sacrament of orders) receives more attention, both in Luther and in Congar's analysis. Here he introduces Luther's view of the common priesthood:

> In truth [for Luther], every Christian is a priest. Luther even goes so far as to say that every Christian is a bishop and a pope [*tout chrétien est* évêque *et pape*], which is hardly consistent with the distinction he makes between priestly dignity and ministry or office [*dignité sacerdotale et ministère ou fonction*]. This shows that he understands the 'universal priesthood' [*le 'sacerdoce universel'*] individually, not corporately and within the (mystical) Body of Christ the High Priest.[96]

Congar agrees that in practice, and in some of his later writing, Luther remained more 'catholic' in regard to the ordering of the Church's

94. Congar, *Martin Luther*, 65–66.
95. Congar, *Martin Luther*, 66–67. For Luther's own definitions in *The Babylonian Captivity*, see WA 6: 501,33–8 ('one single sacrament . . . three sacramental signs'); and then, noting in each case the lack of a definitive (Christ-given) instituting promise for confirmation (WA 6:550,7–13 = LW 36:92; marriage (WA 6:550,25–7 = LW 36:92; ordination (WA 6:560,21–3 = LW 36:106–7; and unction (WA 6:568,11–14 = LW 36:122).
96. Congar, *Martin Luther*, 67. For Christians as 'bishops and popes', see WA 6:408,11–13 (= LW 44:129). For a recent study, see Roger Whittall, *We are all priests. The boundaries and horizons of Martin Luther's Common Priesthood* (Philadelphia: Lexington-Fortress, 2023).

ministry than his Reformation writings of 1520 might suggest. But 'ordination' is, for Congar, a decisive issue in his evaluation, and so *De captivitate Babylonica* marks the schism between Luther and the Roman Church. On the common priesthood, Congar only quotes from that writing, and *An den christlichen Adel deutscher Nation.* Luther's view of the Church continues to be a stumbling-block for Congar, here as it relates to the priesthood. His summary expresses this more broadly, in conjunction with Luther's view of theology, and its sources:

> Luther took Scripture as his normative reference. He accepted the Fathers and the ancient councils insofar as they were in conformity with Scripture. This does not amount to what we and the Orthodox call 'Tradition', which presupposes an awareness of the Church as a mystery, as a union of the visible and the invisible, the earthly and the heavenly. This seems to me to be inadequate [*insuffisante*] in Luther.[97]

He continues to commend Luther's deep expression of faith in Christ; but at the same time believes that, coupled with an emphasis on corrupt human nature, it 'reduced his principle of interpretation too much'. His theology 'reduced the angle of vision of Christianity lived in the Church [*christianisme vécu en Eglise*]'.[98] Congar judges that Luther's focus on the word and faith, justification and personal salvation—coupled to his own experience and volatile temperament—leads him to characterise everything in black and white terms, in opposing the 'true Church and the false'. This is especially true in viewing the papacy as antichrist, and in an obsession with the corrupt structures of Church and priesthood:

> Under these conditions, Luther seriously upset the balance of important realities held in organic synthesis by the undivided Church [*l'Église indivise*]. The balance, that is, of the mutual

97. Congar, *Martin Luther*, 67. For an ecumenical study, see 'Living Word, Living Tradition' (Adelaide: Australian Lutheran-Roman Catholic Dialogue, 2011), which (*inter alia*) considers significant issues such as the transmission of 'authoritative teaching'in the Church, 22–4. This Dialogue did not, however, directly address the matter of the Church's sacraments, or its 'structure'. See further, https://www.alrcdialogue.org/
98. Congar, *Martin Luther*, 67–68.

> relationship of realities such as Scripture—Tradition—Church, *ecclesia* and the authority of ordained pastors [*autorité des pasteurs ordonnés*], the community and its ministers, faith and sacrament, various components of the sacraments (for example penance), law [*droit*] and the tyrannical exercise of authority, pope and council.[99]

This summarises Congar's challenge to the way in which Luther arrived at his view of the Church. He repeats his earlier quotation from Cardinal Cajetan and assigns to it prophetic significance, that 'this would be to make another Church'.[100]

Martin Luther, *Sa Foi, Sa Réforme*: Conclusion

In the final section of this study, Congar draws together the lessons of his reading of Luther, in both positive and negative aspects.[101] He also includes some reflections on the reforms of the Second Vatican Council. He begins by again acknowledging the long-standing abuses that needed correcting in the medieval Church, and how Luther stood as the culmination of many reform attempts, and brought to them the light of the Gospel, as well as the energy of his own forceful personality.[102] He expresses his reservations, once again, about what he sees as Luther's self-actuating theological limitations. Congar aligns himself with the response of Eck and Cajetan, against Luther's 'new language' (*son nouveau langage*). As a Catholic theologian trained in the 'great school of the masters' (*grande école des maîtres*), he says, 'I still react somewhat in this way'.[103]

But he finds much that is positive in Luther's Gospel-focus.[104] And, for the third time, he quotes from the commentary on *Psalm 51*: that for Luther the prime subject of theology is 'humanity, guilty of sin and lost, and God who justifies and saves the human sinner'.

99. Congar, *Martin Luther*, 68.
100. See nn52–53 above.
101. Congar, *Martin Luther*, 68–81.
102. Congar, *Martin Luther*, 68–72.
103. Congar, *Martin Luther*, 73.
104. Congar, *Martin Luther*, 73–74. He selects three sources: *Resolutiones disputationum de indulgentiarum virtute* (1518), WA 1:616,20–1 (see LW 31:230); *Weinachtspostille* (1522), WA 10,1,1:13 (see LW 35:120–21); and *Epistel St Petri gepredigt und ausgelegt* (1523), WA 12:259,8–10 (see LW 30:3).

This may be an understanding grounded first of all on the individual's relationship with God their Saviour, but Congar adds that Luther did not leave this insight to stand alone, to be taken in isolation:

> It is in the light of these great fundamental perceptions that Luther applies himself to rethink and formulate the whole of Christianity [*l'ensemble du christianisme*]: faith, Christological-soteriology, sacraments, ministry, Church.[105]

This means, however, that a significant 'negative' remains for Congar, and it is a critical issue: that of Luther's elevation of Scripture to overrule the Fathers, and the Roman Catholic Church. Luther tended to see views that opposed his own reading of Scripture as satanic and, '[m]any things were attributed to Satan!'[106] So Congar cautions:

> This is where, while recognising the greatness and validity of Luther's intention, I cannot follow him in his exercise of it. The intention was to establish as a principle of reform the sovereignty of God's word. It was applied in the sense of '*Scriptura sola*', which I believe we must reject. We cannot accept the divide that an extreme pessimism has put between nature (creation) and grace (redemption).[107]

So against what for Luther and his fellow reformers was a basic principle of their reform Congar brings to bear the perspective of his own ecclesiology, and his positive view of tradition. He asks,

> And is Scripture, or rather the Word, the only gift [*le seul don*] that God has given us for the existence of a Church that is the Body of Christ? The Church as the sacrament of Christ, the sacrament of salvation, is made up of gifts [*est faite de dons*], of instituted means of grace, which have been established as such, without their institution necessarily being attested in Scripture. It is true that this consideration can be abused.[108]

105. Congar, *Martin Luther*, 74.
106. Congar, *Martin Luther*, 75. He cites WA 8:418,1, *De abroganda missa privata*: Luther states that the 'sacrificing priesthood' is 'an addition of the devil'; (c.f. LW 36:142).
107. Congar, *Martin Luther*, 75.
108. Congar, *Martin Luther*, 75.

Congar has acknowledged Luther's 'greatness': his achievement in recalling the Church of his day to the fundamentals of faith in Christ as Saviour, and the correction of abuses. He affirms Luther's focus on the word, and his commitment to Holy Scripture, over against the limitations of the medieval scholastic theology in which he was trained. However, Congar still agrees with Cajetan's judgment on the consequences of Luther's teaching on the word and faith: 'it would be to make another Church'.

Therefore, he does not shy away from leaving his readers with unanswered questions in regard to Luther. To a large extent, Congar's judgment is left hanging, suspended on this paradox between Luther's 'greatness', and his 'insufficiency'. He cannot accept the limitations on Church life and teaching proposed by Luther in, for example, *De captivitate Babylonica*, especially in relation to the sacrament of orders. He feels that Luther would have done better to allow himself a broader vision of the developmental history of the Church, to have listened to the voices of the pre-medieval Church, and the Church before the division between East and West. Early on, Luther had protested his rejection of heretics, those who divide the Church, but had fallen prey to his own emotions and misunderstandings in rejecting the papacy. This led him to declare the opposition of a true and a false Church.[109] That happens, paradoxically, even while he had been able to acknowledge the many authentic elements in the papal Church.[110]

Then briefly—but significantly—Congar considers the alternative opportunities for Church reform, from the Council of Trent onwards, and also the suggestion that Lutheranism represents an 'interim Church'.[111] He reflects on the Second Vatican Council in which he himself played a major role, and quotes Kristen Skydsgaard's summary of positive signs of reform at the Council from an ecumenical Lutheran perspective.[112] 'Since the Council', Congar says, 'we have

109. Congar, *Martin Luther*, 76. WA 51:487,3 *Wider Hans Worst* (1541) (see LW 41:199).
110. Congar, *Martin Luther*, 77. *Von der Wiedertaufe an zwei Pfarrherrn* (1528) WA 26:147,13–18; 148, 5–7 (see LW 40:230–1).
111. Congar, *Martin Luther*, 78.
112. Congar, *Martin Luther*, 78–9. Kristen E. Skydsgaard, 'La Réformation en tam qu'événement œcuménique', in Œcumenica (1969), 238.

experienced this christological concentration in the sacred liturgy and in the proclamation of the word of God'.[113]

But then, evaluating the Council by Luther's standards, and his own, Congar states that for all its achievements, there remained a limited adoption of christological and scriptural norms for Church reform. 'In these circumstances', he says,

> we still need to be challenged by Luther [*interpellés par Luther*], especially if his voice no longer has the violence of his antipapal hatred, which is absolutely unacceptable, but rather carries fraternal accents of dialogue.[114]

So, as Congar suggests in his final paragraphs, the Reformation remains unfinished—eschatological—business, for both Protestants and Catholics. Catholics cannot expect a simple 'return to Rome', because '[t]he Reformers were religious geniuses who expressed original and profound aspects of Christianity'. They created 'a form of Christianity that has been lived (*a été vécue*) for centuries in ecclesial communities'.[115] The task of reconciliation continues, and Congar points to his own recent work, *Diversités et Communion*, as an exploration of its complexity.[116] He concludes his study with a story that summarises the challenges and the opportunities inherent in the Catholic encounter with protestant reform. Would the events of the sixteenth century—reproduced today—bring about the same Church-dividing result?[117]

Studies Two, Three, and Four

In addition to the broad-based examination of Luther's faith and reform, three further studies take up specific aspects of Congar's engagement with Luther, indicating further how his view of the

113. Congar, *Martin Luther*, 80.
114. Congar, *Martin Luther*, 80.
115. Congar, *Martin Luther*, 80.
116. Congar, *Martin Luther*, 81. Yves Congar, *Diversités et Communion*, (Paris: Cerf, 1982) = *Diversity and Communion*. Translated John Bowden (London: SCM Press, 1984). Forty plus years later the ecumenical conversations continue, including the work of the *Australian Lutheran-Roman Catholic Theological Dialogue*. See https://www.alrcdialogue.org/
117. Congar, *Martin Luther*, 81.

reformer developed in his later years. These follow on from a brief note on the reforms of the Fifth Lateran Council (1512–1517).

The two updated studies on the Eucharist ('Study Two') and Luther's Christology ('Study Three') first appeared as articles in the *Revue des Sciences philosophiques et théologiques* in 1982. An earlier study of 'Luther's Anguish' appeared in the same *Revue* in 1976, and is here the concluding essay, presented with a brief addition that takes account of recent Catholic accounts sympathetic to Luther.

In keeping with the main work, the first two connected studies continue Congar's thorough methodology, evaluating Luther's theology on the basis of a wide reading of the primary sources in the context of Congar's own understanding of the historical development of Catholic teaching. He is considering Luther's re-shaping of that teaching according to his new theological language and a focus on his 'discovery' of the essential gospel – the ways in which it represents legitimate development, or, a deviation from authentic tradition. Early on (1950) Congar had identified Luther's Christology as being marked by an approach that emphasises the primacy of God's work in Christ (*Alleinwirksamkeit*) and thus downplays the element of free-will operative in Christ's humanity. For Congar, this is limiting factor for a Catholic Christology that confesses Christ as 'true God, true man'.

Here, he begins with the eucharist, because of its important christological (and ecclesiological) connections – and also (one suspects) because it is an aspect of Luther's teaching that casts a deep shadow over Catholic fundamentals.[118] Early on, Congar says, Luther's teaching is orthodox, but quickly introduces controversial elements when in 1520 the reforming agenda of *The Babylonian Captivity* questions transubstantiation and the sacrifice of the mass, as well as demanding the cup for the laity and the ending of 'private'masses. Luther emphasises the teaching of Scripture here, rather than the tradition of the Church.

The essay's central focus is on Luther's debates with the radical reformers (Karlstadt, Zwingli, *et al*), with whom he disagrees violently over the question of Christ's presence in the communion elements of bread and wine. Several of Luther's major writings are examined by Congar here, including *The Adoration of the Sacrament* (1523) and

118. Congar, *Martin Luther*, 85–103.

Against the Heavenly Prophets (1525). Key factors included Luther's emphasis on union with Christ, through faith, and the centrality of the personal assurance of the forgiveness of sins for understanding the purpose of the sacrament. Congar questions the narrowness of Luther's focus, and the absence of a communal, ecclesial dimension to his later teaching on the significance of Christ's body.[119]

But Christology is central to Luther's disagreements with those he sometimes calls *significatista*. Christ's word, 'this *is* my body'cannot mean 'this *signifies* my body'. He draws in parallel arguments from classical teaching on Christ's incarnation, and the ubiquity of the Godhead, and God's word. For Luther, however, the Scriptural promises of Christ's presence are decisive, against arguments that he characterises as the elevation of human reason over the Word.

Congar traces this conflict through the *Marburg Colloquy* of 1529, and the way in which it soured relationships between the reformers throughout Luther's lifetime. Luther's realist teaching emphasises the unity of Christ's person, and the 'communication of attributes' by which the properties of Christ's divinity are seen to be at work in and through his humanity. Through the vehicle of the later *Formula of Concord* (1580), this became enshrined in Lutheran theology.

And then, after *The Diet of Augsburg* (1530), the issues of sacramental memorial (remembrance) and sacrifice mean that Luther again engages in controversy with his Catholic counterparts. Congar returns to a theme from his first study to explain a key difference that arises from Luther's focus on Christ's presence through the word and faith, in contrast to the thinking of his Catholic opponents:

> We should not forget, however, the very great realism that Luther puts into what he calls *fides Christi*: in the faith that responds to the proclamation or preaching, there takes place that actualisation of redemption through the cross that the Catholic tradition of East and West sees realised sacramentally in the liturgical celebration of the Eucharist.[120]

Luther, Congar repeats, seems to lack an understanding of the significance of the sacrament in relation to Christ's 'Mystical Body'. And yet, this study concludes with the observation that Luther's

119. Congar, *Martin Luther*, 90–98.
120. Congar, *Martin Luther*, 102.

teaching, uniting Eucharist and Incarnation, is able to preserve both the real presence and the integrity of Christ's person as God and man.

The second of these studies ('New Insights into Luther's Christology') first appeared alongside the essay on the eucharist, and develops the themes of Luther's 'rejection of scholasticism and his discovery of *fides Christi*'.[121] Congar considers in some detail how the 'new language' unites both themes in Luther's approach to the person of Christ. Here he considers the insights of writers including Wilfried Joest, Marc Lienhard, Reinhard Schwarz, Theobald Beer, and Albert Michel. But Congar draws most heavily on Luther's own writings, quoting extensively throughout. His major sources include the *Confession concerning Christ's Supper* (1528), *On the Councils and the Church* (1539), and the Christological *Disputations* of 1540. And then—because of the nature of the investigation here—Congar also compares and contrasts aspects of Luther's teaching with that of the Church Fathers, notably Augustine because of his commonly assumed importance for Luther.

The mystery of Christ requires new terminology in Luther's teaching, because he sees it as a new (Scriptural) reality.[122] That reality is Christ himself, who is God the Saviour. Luther's focus here is not on the Trinity (he largely follows classic trinitarian formulations), but on the unity of the divine and human natures in Christ's person. Divinity is all important, because without it there is no salvation, no saviour. This means that Luther does not shy away from statements like God suffers, God dies.

In considering Christ's person, Congar says, Luther's interest lies in the 'what' rather than the 'how' or the mode of the union. This leads, as a number of scholars have noted, to imprecision and even ambiguity in Luther's formulations.[123] The language of 'mixture' of properties is one example. Even where Luther follows the traditional (scholastic) teaching, the imperative to move away from their terms into a more simple Biblical language can lead to confusion. This is perhaps still true in the *Disputations*, where Luther upholds the decisions of the great Councils, while avoiding their reasoning. Overall, Congar largely acknowledges the orthodoxy of Luther's statements, but does

121. Congar, *Martin Luther*, 105–133.
122. Congar, *Martin Luther*, 106–107.
123. Congar, *Martin Luther*, 111.

not draw back from criticism where he feels that Luther has moved across acceptable boundaries into unsafe theological territory. He questions the lack of traditional concepts such as the 'supplicant' in Luther's teaching—the support provided for the humanity of Jesus from the eternal person of the Word. Luther rather relies on the theme of the 'joyful exchange' between the human sinner and justice of Christ. Congar also has reservations about the terminology of the 'communication of attributes' (*communicatio idiomatum*), which—following Luther—became the standard Lutheran formula in Christology and in discussions over the nature of Christ's presence in the eucharist.

Congar sees some justification in the development of these expressions in the on-going debate with Zwingli, who had countered Luther's arguments by proposing the use of 'alloiosis' (figures of speech) against an insistence on the real exchange of divine and human properties in Christ's person. But he also warns that

> It is undeniable that the Lutheran conception of the *communicatio idiomata* evokes statements of a monophysitic flavour. Luther, whose Alexandrian inspiration has struck me often, over many years, is very close to St Cyril of Alexandria. Also in his affirmation that *God* suffered.[124]

He insists—*contra* Luther—that it is necessary to distinguish 'what belongs to God and what belongs to the humanity of Christ in the work of Redemption'. He examines this by quoting from Luther at some length, especially from the 1535 commentary *ad Galatas*. This entire sectionis a detailed analysis of Luther's Christology, with Congar's explanations and responses, and it repays careful reading.[125] It examines both divinity and humanity, inter-woven with the characteristic theme of faith's response to God's work in Christ. Congar concludes that for Luther, 'In the realm of salvation, of what is *coram Deo*, God alone works effectively in Christ, who is inseparably God'.

Congar's final conclusion to this study first invokes Thomas Aquinas (his own 'teacher') to offer what he see as a more balanced, orthodox Christology. He then examines how close Luther is to his own master, Augustine, revisiting the questions that he raised in his

---

124. Congar, *Christologie*, 120.
125. Congar, *Christologie*, 114–127.

original study in 1950. At some points—including the communication of attributes—there is a close proximity with Luther. At others, where Augustine speaks of the perfect obedience of the human Jesus, and his role in our redemption, Congar confesses to being 'a little unclear' and the question of a connection is left unanswered.[126]

At the beginning of the study on the 'Eucharist', he warned that it was 'no more than a documentary essay and a suggestion'. That may be so, but Congar's essays are full of relevant detail and carefully selected sources, meaning that his 'suggestions' are always based on his own insightful reading and analysis, and his grasp of the historical perspectives in modern Catholic theology.

The final essay (Study Four) is titled, *On 'Luther's Anguish'*.[127] Here, Congar engages with three writers who have examined Luther's life from the perspectives of modern psychology and psychiatry. The term 'anguish' (*angoisse*) may seem imprecise in everyday speech, but in medical terms it does indicate a stage of mental suffering which includes fright, feelings of distress, anxiety, depression, grief and/or psychosomatic physical symptoms. There are certainly episodes from throughout Luther's life that match this description; Congar also has in view Luther's outbursts of anger, particularly what he describes as the reformer's 'pathological hatred of the papacy' (see also p56–57). He is concerned to discover the roots of this condition but, as will be seen, from a theological perspective how far Luther's early anguish can be seen as a prelude to his reformatory discovery and his emerging understanding of *fides Christi* ('special faith').

The study begins with a brief reference to psychiatrist Paul Reiter's, *Martin Luthers Umwelt, Charakter und Psychose*, whose investigation into the reformer's childhood environment proposed that it led to a manic-depressive pyschosis, with episodes of extreme agitation and anger later in life.

American psychoanalyst-historian Erik Erikson, in *Young Man Luther*, probed deeply (and somewhat imaginatively) into Luther's fraught relationship with his father and to a lesser extent with his mother. Then, the crises of the thunderstorm and of monastic life reveal the stages of the struggle between destructive and constructive forces as young Martin's search for identity is fulfilled as he became the man and reformer 'Luther'. Congar concludes,

126. Congar, *Christologie*, 133.
127. Congar, *Angoisse*, 135–150.

> For someone who, like me, is interested in Luther's theological positions, knowing, moreover, that they are linked to his personal destiny and experience, Erikson's work is somewhat disappointing.[128]

More promising, from Congar's point of view, is Roland Dalbiez's *Luther's Anguish*, which seeks to explain the origins of the disjunction between Luther's doctrine and classical Catholic teaching. He argues that Luther's anguish arises from personal guilt for sin, and that he escapes from this self-destructive situation 'by making his own justification the object of his faith'.[129]

Congar examines Dalbiez's evidence for Augustine's influence over Luther on the question of the 'guilt of involuntary inclinations'. Dalbiez makes a coherent argument for this, using Luther's scholastic antecedents, but Congar finds this less than persuasive. Not least, this is because Luther has rather more to say on sin, (and contrition) than that which is contained in a narrow focus on one element in the whole dynamic of salvation. And Luther, clearly, was not bound by the scholastic arguments—indeed, he strongly rejects them. Congar suggests that Dalbiez would have done well to study more closely what Luther has to say in his *Römervorlesung* of 1516, and illustrates this in some detail.[130] He concludes this examination,

> Therefore I could not write, as Roland Dalbiez does (. . .): 'The texts of Luther that we have quoted are sufficient to establish that the Reformer built the three stages of his theological system starting from the necessary guilt of natural temptation'. No. He built them from his experience as an anguished and scrupulous man whose conscience was not appeased by the search for virtuous action and perfection.[131]

Neither does he find the related idea of 'forensic justification' to be an adequate presentation of Luther's teaching, nor a confirmation of Dalbiez's thesis regarding the guilt of 'undesired sin'. While there are clear points of difference between Luther and Catholic theology, Luther does teach the necessity for a personal struggle against sin and

128. Congar, *Angoisse*, 137.
129. Congar, *Angoisse*, 138.
130. Congar, *Angoisse*, 141–144.
131. Congar, *Angoisse*, 144.

for growth in faith and love, based on the 'exchange' in which Christ offers his own righteousness (justice) in return for our sin. Congar finds points here that 'very significantly diminish the difference or opposition between Luther and Catholicism'.[132]

Congar concludes by applauding Dalbiez's intention in investigating Luther in the way that he does: 'his questions and insights are invaluable'. But, he says, the net needed to be cast wider than scholasticism to Luther's other contexts, 'biblical, Pauline, Augustinian, as well as his own exacerbated experience'.[133]

The original essay was written in 1976, and in 1982 Congar adds two final paragraphs offering two works on Luther that he had recently read. The first, by Father Daniel Olivier comes from one of Congar's own students, whose *Luther's Faith. The Cause of the Gospel in the Church* (1978, English translation, 1982) presents a positive evaluation that highlights the 'victory of [special] faith' in Luther's teaching. Olivier denies any role for 'anguish' in Luther's development. Congar suggests that the questions raised merit further in depth study. He then notes 'the magnificent *Martin Luther*' published in 1982 by Peter Manns, who was a student of Joseph Lortz. Manns, Congar says, seems to him to have understood very well what Luther is saying about sin and salvation in his early interpretation of the Epistle to the Romans.[134]

This final study provides a fitting conclusion to Congar's collection of his writings on Luther. It seeks answers but leaves open the contentious area of Luther's psychology (often avoided by Luther scholars), and then highlights once more the central importance of the key issue for getting to grips with the reformer's life and thought, his motivation for reform that is summed up in the pregnant phrase 'Luther's faith'.

Editorial Note

This translation of Congar's final writings on Luther preserves the theological language and expression of the original as far as possible. I have endeavoured to let Congar's unique, Catholic voice speak clearly, without Lutheran interpolations! There has been some

132. Congar, *Angoisse*, 147.
133. Congar, *Angoisse*, 149.
134. Congar, *Angoisse*, 149–150.

rationalisation of his notes, where he used a mixture of standard footnotes and textual additions to indicate his sources. He provided his own translations of Luther's original German and Latin, and these have been preserved in the English version, adding a reference to the standard 'American edition' of Luther's Works (LW) where it exists. Footnoted references have been expanded where possible, to provide publishers' names as well as date and place. Where Congar provided Luther's original (Latin) text, this has usually been included in the footnotes, rather than in the main body. Any errors or omissions are the fault of this editor / translator alone.

Roger Whittall, *Adelaide, South Australia.*

Eastertide, 2025.

Author's Introduction

What is the meaning of the Reformation in God's plan? This question was put to me one evening by a Catholic student in Strasbourg; but who (except God!) can boast of having an adequate answer? The realisation of this limitation led the Second Vatican Council to use this formula, a negative turn of phrase that truly expresses a positive appreciation respectful of the mystery of Providence:

> These disunited Churches and communities are by no means devoid of meaning and value in the mystery of salvation (*Unítatis redintegratio*, 3, 4).

The Reformation is primarily 'Luther'. It was through him that the first crater opened up in the solid crust of the Western Christian world. The burning lava that came out of it is not exhausted. We are not talking here about the Lutheran Churches, nor the peoples who have received from them their Christian heritage. Every year books are published on Luther and his reform that could fill a library shelf. And now, for the five hundredth anniversary of his birth, November 10, 1483, how many more books, symposia, exhibitions, conferences will there be? In the Federal Republic of Germany alone, which has only a few Luther-sites (Heidelberg, Worms, Coburg), there are several events each month, from January 1982 to February 1984.

What will happen in France? Until recently, and perhaps still here and there like patches of snow that remain in spring in sheltered places, the image of Luther among the French Catholics continues to be that promoted by Denifle, Grisar, Paquier, Cristiani, Maritain. For them, Luther's errors were prominent, but his person and his life were presented in terms of mediocrity (Denifle), pathological sickness (Grisar), and subjectivity (Maritain).

It's true that Luther carried all this within him, but also so much richness! Thank God: for the last fifty years or so, Catholic historians and theologians have been practising a more truthful approach. There were precursors, Abbé Huvelin, von Hügel, closer to us FX Kiefl (1917), S Merkle (1929), but the change is mainly due to Joseph Lortz (1939), and J Hessen (1939 and 1947). In French, in addition to the translation of Lortz, I should mention Daniel Olivier, whose solidly-detailed book really gets to the heart of the matter, and also Jared Wicks, who is discreetly and reliably accurate, as well as the history documented by Richard Stauffer.[1]

My personal interest in Luther, a kind of attraction, goes back quite a long way. A photograph from 1925 in front of a monument in Worms already bears witness to this. In 1931 I had the opportunity to visit the main Luther-sites: Eisleben, Erfurt, the Wartburg, twice Wittenberg. The authorities, thanks to Mme Schlütter-Hermkes, had even given me permission to open the museum showcases in the buildings where Luther lived. With a sandwich in my pocket, I spent a full day there; I have had in my hand books, objects that Luther had touched; I took notes and thought I had made a discovery that had (in fact) been known for a long time and was of only minor significance.

Since then I have often returned to Luther, in studies, courses, articles, lectures. I have done my best to keep abreast of studies whose weight and technicality have often surpassed me. I never stopped learning. It should not be surprising that this book revisits two studies from 1950, on Luther's Christology and on 'True and False Reform'.

All my life I have maintained the conviction that one truth cannot be contrary to another truth. We need to acknowledge every truth, wherever and from whomever it comes, and try to make room for it in an enveloping organism of which many elements will probably escape us. Thomas Aquinas was an incomparable model and teacher in this respect. This also has its limits, perhaps even its dangers.

1. Joseph Lortz, *la Réforme de Luther* (Paris: Cerf, 1970-1971) 3 volumes; Daniel Olivier, *la Foi de Luther. La cause de l'Évangile dans l'Église* (Paris: Beauchesne, 1978); Jared Wicks, 'Luther', in *Dictionary de Spiritualité* (Paris: Beauchesne, 1976), IX, 1206–1243; Richard Stauffer, *Luther vu par les catholiques* (Paris: Delachaux-Niestlé, 1961); *le Catholicisme à la découverte de Luther* (Paris: Delachaux-Niestlé, 1966). For the record, Yves Congar, 'Luther vu par les catholiques ou de l'utilité de faire l'histoire de l'histoire', in *Revue des Sciences philosophiques et théologiques*, 34 (1950): 507–508 (reprinted in *Chrétiens en dialogue* (Cerf, 1964), 437–451).

I do not regret having been trained in the school of Aquinas: he brought me both order and openness. But now, in the autumn of my life, after a lot of work and a little learning, I realise that Scholasticism could be a prison for the spirit and that it has diminished, in my Church, the possibilities of receiving certain truths. For a long time I have been—and I am still in part—a prisoner of a systematic ideal due to my Scholastic training. This is clear in my approach to Luther's Christology. But that is precisely what Luther rejected. He had the conviction, the evidence even, that he could only be *Christian* by emerging intellectually and existentially from the scholastic, canonical, hierarchical system of the old Church. In so doing, he has taken on a formidable responsibility for the rupture that ecumenism now seeks to redeem. I am a Catholic and I love my Church. I know the vitality it had in the sixteenth century, despite its many weaknesses. I know that Luther misunderstood and denied several articles of the Catholic faith.

In ecumenical dialogue, his followers are rediscovering the evangelical character of many of these articles. The unilateralism of the 'most authentic perceptions' must also be overcome. For all his greatness, Luther may not be the ultimate measure of Christianity and ecclesiality even for the Lutherans themselves.[2] Let truth be our teacher! We are getting closer to the Christian Luther; the Lutherans are getting closer to the catholicism of the undivided Church. It is Jesus Christ who must be victorious, he, his gospel, and his Apostles.

I am aware of the limited value of the studies that make up this volume. I am a great believer in history, and I practise it, but I am a dogmatician, not a historian. The notes show that there is history here. It's not just out of a mania for references that I have multiplied them. It was necessary to work on texts. But for it to be fully history, there would have to be an evocation of the contexts, the events, the characters, the socio-political reality, and so on. All this is to be found in the stories themselves. Recently I have read Martin Brecht's *Martin Luther. Sein Weg zur Reformation 1483–1521* (Stuttgart, 1981). This is about ideas and doctrines which, at their level, also made history. Even at this level of ideas, the studies gathered here remain extremely particular, and therefore partial.

2. See, for example, James S Preus, 'La discussion luthérienne sur Luther', in *Concilium*, 12/10 (1976): 91–98. All of 12/10 is on the reception of Luther.

This is how, in particular, I have described the evolution or process by which the Augustinian brother became Martin Luther. Luther scholars are still divided over how to understand, let alone date, the appearance of the 'reforming' principle in Luther. Many, today, lean towards the spring of 1518. Reflection on the ideas involved in the indulgences dispute, extended by Luther to a theology of conversion and justification, and then the criticism and opposition encountered, would have led Luther to radicalise the perceptions he had formed and to realise, with its consequences, the idea that the Gospel is the justice of Jesus Christ, credited to our account, through faith.

I offer these studies to seekers of truth in this centenary year. I dedicate them to the memory of friends who have helped me to understand Luther better: Lucien Febvre, Etienne Gilson, Robert Grosche, and Joseph Lortz.

Brother Yves M-J CONGAR

NOTES:

The French translation of Luther's texts is my own, with no lack of appreciation for the 17 volumes of Luther's works published in Geneva by *Labor et Fides* since 1957.

The two updated studies on Luther's view of the Eucharist ('Study Two') and his Christology ('Study Three') first appeared as articles in the *Revue des Sciences philosophiques et théologiques*, 66 (1982), 169–180 and 180–198.

An unpublished study on Luther the Reformer was subsequently written, and the study of 'Luther's Anguish' first appeared in the *Revue des Sciences philosophiques et théologiques*, 60 (1976), 638–648 ('Study Four').

Chronological References

Congar's listing of Luther's writings in this chronology has been expanded to include further works discussed in the text, with their shorter English titles. Full references are provided in the text.

1384: Death of John Wyclif. Death of Gerard Groote; origins of the Brethren of the Common Life.

1415: Execution of John Huss at the Council of Constance.

1431–1449: Council of Basel, in schism with the Pope after 1437.

1483: Birth of Luther at Eisleben (baptised Martin on 11 November).

1489: Death of Wessel Gansfort.

1497: Death of Gabriel Biel at Tübingen.

1498: Execution of Savonarola.

1501: Luther enrolled as student of Jodocus Trutfetter in Erfurt:, 1501–1505.

1502: Foundation of the University of Wittenberg. Staupitz is the dean.

1503–1513: Pope Julius II; in 1506 begins the construction of Saint Peters in Rome; 1507: sale of its indulgence begins; bull of Leo X, 31 March 1515.

1505, 7 January: Luther, 'Master of Arts'; **17 July**, enters novitiate with the Augustinians of Erfurt.

1508: Luther sent to Wittenberg.

1512, 18 October: Luther, 'Doctor'. *First Lectures on the Psalms*, 1513–1515; *Lectures on Romans*, 1515–1516; *On Galatians*, 1516–1517; *On Hebrews*, 1517–1518.

1512–1517: Fifth Lateran Council.

1513–1521: Pope Leo X (in whom Luther had put some hope).

1517, 4 September: *Ninety-seven Theses against Scholastic Theology.*

1517, 31 October: *Ninety-five Theses against Indulgences.*

1518, April: Luther at the Heidelberg Chapter. *The Heidelberg Disputation* (Luther's *theologia crucis*).

1518, June: Opening in Rome of a heresy trial against Luther.

1518, August: Melanchthon comes to Wittenberg.

1518, October: Appearance before the legate Cajetan at Augsburg.

1519, June–July: Leipzig Disputation, with Johann Eck.

1520, 15 June: Bull *Exsurge Domine* condemns Luther's errors, and gives him 60 days to recant. Luther: *Against the Roman Papacy.*

1520, August–November: The 'Reformation Writings': *Appeal to the Christian Nobility*; *On the Babylonian Captivity of the Church*; *The Liberty of a Christian.*

1520, 10 December: Luther publicly burned the papal bull and the decretals.

1521, 3 January: Excommunication of Luther.

1521, 15 April: The Sorbonne condemns Luther's doctrines.

1521, 17–18 April: Luther at Worms before the young Charles V and the Diet of the Empire.

1521, 4 May – 1 March 1522: Luther takes refuge in the Wartburg. Translates the New Testament. Writes *The Misuse of the Mass; Response to Ambrosius Catherinus* etc.

1524–1528: Treatises against the teachings of Zwingli and Oecolampadius on the Eucharist.

1525: Peasants' War. Luther's Marriage. Luther: *Against the Heavenly Prophets*; *The Freedom of the Will.*

1529: Luther: *Large* and *Small Catechisms.*

1529, 1–4 October: Marburg Colloquy with Zwingli and Oecolampadius on the Eucharist.

1530, June: Diet of Augsburg. *Augsburg Confession*, written by Melanchthon. Luther at Coburg Castle, writes *Exhortation to all Clergy Assembled at Augsburg.*

1531: Luther's third, great *Commentary on Galatians* (published 1535).

1532: *Lecture on Psalm 51*

1537: *Smalcald Articles*

1538–1545: *Lectures on Genesis*

1539: *On the Councils and the Church*

1540: *Disputations on the Divinity and Humanity of Christ*

1541, April–May: Colloquy of Ratisbon.

1545, 13 December: Opening of the Council of Trent.

1546, 18 February: Death of Luther at Eisleben.

Luther the Reformer. *Return to a Former Study.*

In 1950, when I dealt with the theme of 'true and false reform in the Church', I distinguished between reforms that were concerned with the life of the Church, i.e. the concrete and historical achievements of its being, and reforms that affected what I called its structure. This last term, which is somewhat vague, has been criticised from various quarters. By it I meant the fundamental constitution of the Church and the formally dogmatised religious and doctrinal tradition. Failures at the level of 'life' could take on the density and gravity of a 'state of affairs', even in the order of doctrines as they reigned in the Church as a whole at a given time. This was the case in the sixteenth century, even though Christianity in the West had a vitality that enabled it to supply two religious worlds with fervent people and exceptional personalities. I believed that the Protestant Reformers had not only attacked the state of things, but essential elements of the structure. I proposed an interpretation of their ecclesiology and of that which seemed to me to be involved in Protestantism in general. Since then, I have not ceased to study and learn, and today I am better able to highlight positive elements. As far as Luther is concerned, I do not intend to repeat here all the material contained in the forty-five pages of 1950. I would simply like to give a better account of Luther's vision and commitment as a reformer. That in itself is ambitious, excessively so, and I seek your forgiveness!

Reform is undertaken when a situation appears unacceptable: either because it is ill-adapted to what is needed, which is the least dramatic if not the least urgent; or because there is something truly scandalous and intolerable, a betrayal of truth, of justice. This absolutely has to change. This is what Luther saw in 1517 with the matter of indulgences, which involved a conception of penance and sin, and therefore a certain theology of nature and grace. The opposition he encountered led Luther to extend and to radicalise his reformist ideas. This is what we shall see. But his initial reaction had been preceded and prepared for by years of rather dramatic personal development. The story is already well known but it is essential to recall it briefly.

Luther entered the convent on 17 July 1505. In Erfurt and then in Wittenberg, for several years he experienced spiritual anguish stemming from an acute awareness of the impossibility of being what God's holiness demands of us: How can I find a favourable God, a God of grace?[1] How can I be accepted before God, in his eyes, *coram Deo*? God's justice was frightening, and Luther was afraid of it. On this subject, he often quoted either the verse of St Paul, Romans 1:17, 'in him (in the Gospel) the justice of God is revealed', or those of Psalms 31:2 (Vg 30) and 71:2 (Vg 70), 'in your justice set me free, deliver me'.[2]

In his anguish, from which personal efforts, asceticism and observances did not release him, Luther had indeed received consoling words. An older brother had told him to hope: our salvation lies in faith in God.[3] Is it the same [faith]? An old man had directed his thoughts to 'I believe in the forgiveness of sins'.[4] His superior and friend Staupitz had opened his mind to the true nature of penance, in the sense of *metanoia* (radical conversion of heart).[5]

1. Preaching of 1534 on Holy Baptism (Matthew 3:13–17): WA 37:661, 20–34.
2. Lutheran scholars have focused on the text of Romans, but Luther refers at least as much to the text of the Psalms. I accept, at least for my personal understanding of the meaning of 'justice of God', the explanation of Erich Vogelsang, *Die Anfänge von Luthers Christologie*, (Berlin-Leipzig: de Gruyter, 1929): 40ff. It was shortly before commenting on Ps 71 (70) that Luther came up with his interpretation: *iustitia Dei* is not only the justice that God gives us out of mercy, but it is Christ, *tropologice est fides Christi*. This takes us back to the autumn of 1514. This date is still debated. Some say 1518. See Ernst Bizer, *Fides ex auditu. Eine Untersuchung über die Entdeckung der Gerechtigkeit Gottes durch Martin Luther*, (Neukirchen: Neukirchener Verlag, 1958). The reforming principle is not only to have recognised the meaning of *iustitia Dei*, but also to have applied it personally!
3. WATr 4:4362. Compare WA 40/2:411,30f.
4. Testimony of Melanchthon, *Corpus Reformatorum*, 6:159.
5. Compare letter of 30 May 1518 sending him his *Resolutiones disputationum de indulgentiarum virtute*, for transmission to Leo X: WA 1:525. And also WABr 3:155 (letter of 17 September 1523); Luther speaks of Staupitz as the one 'through whom, at first, the light of the Gospel began to pierce my darkness'.

Luther needed a radical solution. He found it in his personal discovery of the meaning of *iustitia Dei*: not the justice of the judge who punishes sinners, but the mercy of God who grants me forgiveness and justice in Christ. That's what the Gospel was all about: by faith, Christ in me, my salvation, my justice. All we had to do was give ourselves over to him, renouncing all support for what we are and can do. From then on, it is Christ who is my righteousness, thanks to faith: a righteousness that is not mine, and which Luther calls *extranea, non domestica* ('external, not personal'). This is the discovery that will drive everything else.

Luther expressed this admirably in the advice he gave his friend Spenlein on 8 April 1516:

> So, my sweet brother, learn Christ, and Christ crucified; learn to sing to him and, despairing of yourself, to say to him: You, Lord Jesus, are my righteousness and I am your sin; you have taken what is mine and given me what is yours; you took on what you were not and gave me what I was not. Take care never to aspire to such purity that you no longer wish to consider yourself a sinner, or rather to be one. For Christ dwells only in sinners. He came down from heaven, where he dwelt with the righteous, only to dwell with sinners (. . .) So it is in him alone and through a despair of yourself and your works, full of trust, that you will find peace (*per fiducialem desperationem tui et operum tuorum*). Learn from him that, just as he has taken you and made your sins his own, he has also made his righteousness yours.[6]

This text expresses a spiritual attitude that Luther had also found to some extent in Tauler, Gerson, Bernard and Bonaventure, the 'doctors of conscience and life', *lebemeister* as opposed to *leremeister* (scholastics), from whom he also distanced himself in matters of Christian anthropology. But Luther's spiritual attitude developed into a truly 'reforming' theology. It was against the state of affairs in theology and in the Church, this second application having followed Luther's protest against the preaching of indulgences.

We can distinguish three 'moments' that, in my opinion, conditioned Luther's commitment as a reformer: 1. the reaction against

---

6. WABr 1:35–36; see LW 48:12–13, *To George Spenlein*. Compare the *Sermo de poenitentia*, Spring 1518: WA 1:322,9–10.

Scholasticism, to be specifically 'Christian', against the domination of reason; 2. the reaction against the preaching of indulgences and against the justification of indulgences by the authority of canonical texts and the Pope; 3. the criticism of the papacy and papal ecclesiology. And, through these three moments, intimate contact with Scripture, the sovereign Word of God.

Criticism of the prevailing theology preceded that of indulgences. In fact, the *Disputatio contra scholasticam theologiam* of 4 September 1517 predates the 'Ninety-five Theses' (*Disputatio pro declaratíone virtutis indulgentiarum*) of 31 October. But this is just a marker. Luther's criticism came from further back.

Criticism of Scholasticism. *A New Theology*

At the Faculty of Arts in Erfurt, Luther had been trained in the nominalistic philosophy of Occam and the theology of Gabriel Biel; he would name as his masters, Jodocus Trutfetter and Bartholomaeus Arnoldi d'Usingen, for whom he retained a great deal of respect, *tui Gabrielistae*.[7] Sent in 1508 to the young University of Wittenberg (founded in 1502), he first taught Aristotle's dialectics and ethics! It is easy to understand why he wrote to John Braun, a friend from Eisenach, on 17 March 1509:

> If you want news of my health, I am well, thank God, except that studying is difficult [*violentum*] for me, especially philosophy, which I have always been keen to change for theology, by which I mean that theology which searches out the kernel of the nut, the germ [*moelle*] of the wheat and the marrow of the bone.[8]

It is a remarkable text. '*Violentum*' means contrary to my inclination, my desire, my nature. Luther wanted to be a theologian, not a philosophiser. In the margin of a text in the *Collectarium* of Biel, he noted in 1516: 'Nature. It would be better to say God. For thus

7. Letter of October 1516 to Jean Lang, from Erfurt: WABr 1:65,19.
8. '*Quod si statum meum nosse desideras, bene habeo Dei gratia, nisi quod violentum est studium maxime philosophiae, quam ego ab initio libentissime mutarim theologia, ea inquam theologia quae nucleum nucis et medullam tritici et medullam Ossium scrutatur*'. WABr 1:17,40f. Not in LW, but see Margaret A CURRIE, *The Letters of Martin Luther* (London: Macmillan, 1908), 2–3.

we philosophise and cease to speak theology'.[9] And it was not just any theology that Luther would exchange for philosophy, but that theology which went to the heart of the nut, to the finest part of the wheat and the marrow of the bones. This theology was the one that enabled us to find Christ, and Christ my Saviour, beneath the letter of the Scriptures, in the writings of the Fathers and spiritual authors (Tauler, the *Theologia Deutsch*, Gerson).

Scholasticism learned nothing from this and its theologians understood nothing of it:

> I am close to swearing that there is not a single scholastic theologian who has understood a single chapter of Gospel or Bible, especially those of Leipzig. More than this: not even a single chapter of Aristotle the philosopher.[10]

---

9. '*Melius diceret deus. Sic philosophamur, ut theologisare cessemus*'. Hermann Degering, *Luthers Handbemerkungen zu Gabriel Biels Collectorium* (Weimar: Bohlau, 1933), 11.
10. '*Prope est, ut iurem nullum esse theologum scholasticum, qui unum capitulum Evangelii vel bibliae intelligat, praesertim Lipsensem, imo ne philosophi Aristotelis unum capitulum.*' Letter of 24 March 1518 to JS Egranus against Dungersheim, of Leipzig, who attacked Luther: WABr 1:158,38ff. Compare, in 1519, *Resolutiones lutheranae super propositionibus suis Lipsiae disputatis*: 'What others have learned in scholastic theology is their business. As for me, I know and I proclaim that I have learned only ignorance of sin, of justice, of baptism and of the whole Christian life, and nothing about the power of God, the work of God, the grace of God, the justice of God, faith, hope and charity. In short, not only did I learn nothing (I had to put up with it), but I learned only things to be unlearned that were absolutely contrary to the Divine Letters. I'm surprised if others have learned better. If they exist, I naively congratulate them. For me, what I had lost there, I have now found again in Paul'. (*Quae quod alii in Theologia scholastica didicerint, ipsi viderint. Ego scio et confiteor, nec aliud nihil didicisse quàm ignorantiàm peccati, iustitiae, baptismi et totius Christianae vitae, nec quid virtus dei, gratia dei, iustitia dei, fides, opes, charitas sit. Breviter non solùm nihil didici (quod ferendùm erat), sed non nisi dediscenda didici, omnino contraria divinis literis. Miror autem, si alii felicius didicerint. Qui si aliquí sint, candide eis gratulor. Ego tùm amiseram illic, nunc in Paulo reperi*), WA 2:414,22–28. Note this remark by Stephen Ozment: 'The failure of the late medieval Church to provide a theology and spirituality that could satisfy and discipline religious hearts and minds was the most important religious precondition of the Reformation': *The Age of Reform 1250–1550. An intellectual and religious history of late medieval and reformation Europe* (New Haven-London: Yale University Press, 1980), 208.

Luther often wondered, with friends, what profit they had derived from philosophy, and they concluded: 'none'.[11] He had also written to Spalatin on 15 February 1518:

> If you ask me to tell you for which articles logic is necessary to theology, I will answer you: for none, because Christ has no need of human creations. The science and wisdom of this world is foolishness in the sight of God, and the soul must be stripped of the trappings of philosophy if it is to see Christ.[12]

Luther's dedication of his *Operationes in Psalmos* to Frederick of Saxony on 27 March 1519 was an unapologetic farewell to Scholasticism: he had studied it, it was a waste of time, he wanted nothing more to do with it! He was now devoted to true theology, that of Scripture.[13] A little later, he said it again: in scholastic theology he had learned nothing but ignorance of sin, justice, baptism, the Christian life, and the work of God, grace. 'I had lost Christ there', he says, 'but now I have found him again in Paul'.[14]

Luther had indeed found Christ again in Paul, especially in Romans and Galatians, but also more broadly in Scripture. To extend this discovery to the Church, to draw the consequences and applications from it, to fight to the death against that which is contrary to it, to criticise and even reject that which is not in conformity with it, and on the other hand to create communities and ministers in conformity with this truth: this is Luther's reform, 'The Reformation'. This is what we shall see.

1. Finding Christ

A later text expresses the deep conviction by which Luther's journey is summed up, this passage from the commentary on Psalm 51 of 1532:

---

11. Letter of 22 February 1518 to Spalatin: WABr 1:150,17f. See LW 48:57, *Letter to George Spalatin.*
12. '*Dum rogas ut tibi ostendam quibus in locis logica theologiae sit necessaria, tibi respondebo; in nullo locorum, quia Christus non indiget figmentis humanis. Hominum scientia et sapientia huius mundi est apud Deum stultitia, et exspolianda est anima philosophicis praestigiis, quae Christum videre vult*', WABr 1:143,81–85.
13. WA 5:21f. See LW 14:283–284, *Preface to Works on the First Twenty-two Psalms.*
14. '*Ego Christum amiseram illic, nunc in Paulo reperi*', August 1519: *Resolutiones super propositiones Lipsiae disputatis*, WA 2:414. Compare: 'In matters of the soul, we do not live by Aristotle or reason, but there is only one teacher, Christ', 1518: *Ad dialogum Prieriatis responsio*, WA 1:648,36–38.

> What theology properly speaks of is human beings guilty of sin and lost, and God justifying and saving sinful people. Anything other than this that is sought or discussed in theology is error and poison.[15]

It is also in this late text, which we know expresses all of Luther's research, that he tells us what God he knows and what *theo*-logy knows:

> God, I understand him 'in relation', the God we adore, to whom we turn our faces, to whom we give thanks, whom we invoke as the author of all good, the corporeal and the spiritual (. . .) We must be careful not to take anything away from the facts through which God has manifested himself. If you distance yourself from this God, whom we place in the category of 'relation', and if you speculate on a God placed in the category of 'substance' or 'quality', you will be crushed by the majesty; if (you place him) in the category of 'quality', you will be consumed. For 'God is a consuming fire', and 'he dwells in inaccessible light' (Hebrews 12:29; 1 Timothy 6:16).[16]

There is a God-in-Godself, one might say an ontology of God: that is for God alone. Luther only wants to know God *for us*. We must leave God *in natura et maiestate sua* and only know him incarnate in Jesus Christ.[17] In philosophy, we learned from Aristotle to speak and discuss things 'boldly and with many words' (*loquaciter et audacter*).

---

15. '*Theologiae proprium subiectum est homo peccati reus ac perditus et Deus iustificans ac salvator hominis peccatoris. Quicquid extra hoc subiectum in Theologia quaeritur aut disputatur est error et venenum*': WA 40/2:328,17. See LW 12:311, *The Commentary on Psalm 51.*
16. *Genesis-Vorlesung* (begun 3 June 1535, continued until 17 November 1545): '*Deum autem intelligo relative Deum adoratum, ad quem vertimus faciem, cui gratias agimus, quem invocamus tanquam authorem omnium bonorum corporalium et spiritualium Cavendum autem hoc est, ne quid vel addas, vel adimas iis, quibus Deus se manifestavit. Quod si a Deo hoc, quem ponimus in praedicamento relationis, discesseris, et scrutatus fueris Deum in praedicamento substanciae vel qualitatis, opprimeris a maiestate: Si quaesiveris in praedicamento qualitatis, consumeris. Est enim Deus ignis consumens and Habitans lucem inaccessibilem*': WA 42:635,5–26; see LW 3:122, *Lectures on Genesis.* Compare WA 42:646,29f. for the exclusion of the category of substance.
17. *De servo arbitrio* (1525): WA 18:655,14; see LW 33:93, *The Bondage of the Will*; also *Disputationem gegen die Antinomer*, 18 December 1537: WA 39/1:370,13; see LW 73:76, *The First Antinomian Disputation.*

And one would be tempted, as the Scholastics do, to approach divine things *eandem loquacitatem et audaciam.*[18] It is against this that Luther argues. He would know God only in the humiliation of the Incarnation and the Cross. But even when it comes to the latter, it is Christ 'for us' to which Luther binds himself. This famous text has often been quoted:

> Christ has two natures. What business is that of mine? If he bears this magnificent and consoling name of Christ, it is because of the ministry and the task he has taken upon himself: this is what gives him his name. That he is by nature both man and God is for himself. But that he consecrated his ministry, that he poured out his love to become my Saviour and my Redeemer, that is where I find my consolation and my good (. . .) Believing in Christ does not mean that Christ is a person who is both man and God, which is of no use to anyone; it means that this person is Christ, that is to say that for us he came forth from God and came into the world: it is from this office that he derives his name.[19]

This view determines and explains Luther's Christology, of which these lines give quite a good account:

> Humanity and divinity are indeed separate in themselves and in substance, because humanity had a beginning in time. But as regards the object offered to our commitment (of faith), they absolutely cannot be separated from Christ, but are one and the same person.[20]

18. *Dictata super Psalterium* (1513–1515): WA 3:382,19f; see LW 10:322, *The First Lectures on the Psalms.*
19. *Predigten über das 2. Buch Mose* (Allegoria des 12. Kapitels): 30 April 1525, WA 16:217; see LW 62:169, *Exposition of Several Chapters of the Second Book of Moses.* Compare the sermon of 1 April 1521 on Luke 24:13f., WA 9:566,24f.
20. '*Separata quidam sunt humanitas et divinitas in se quantum ad substantiam, quia humanitas coepit in tempore. At quantum ad obiectum, ut ipsi adhaereamus, a Christo separari minime possunt, sed sunt una persona*', *Vorlesung über den I.Johannesbrief* (1527): WA 48:315,15-18; *compare* LW 30:222 (based on the published edition of Luther's *Lectures on 1 John*).

It was a traditional conviction that God could only be reached and known through Christ, that is, through the humanity of Christ. Testimonies to this abound. It was affirmed at least in principle, without being applied as consistently as Luther. This is what he said:

> We should also note that [the writer to the *Hebrews*] mentions Christ's humanity before his divinity, thus approving this rule of a faithful knowledge of God. This humanity is in fact our ladder by which we gain access to the knowledge of God, Genesis 28 and John 6: 'No one comes to the Father except through me'. And again: 'I am the door'. Anyone who wants to rise in a healthy way to the love and knowledge of God must leave behind the human and metaphysical rules for getting to know the divinity and begin by training oneself in the humanity of Christ. It is indeed the most impious temerity for man to seek another way by using the views of his own mind, where God himself has humbled himself.[21]

In theses 19 and 20 of the important *Disputatio Heidelbergae habita* ('Heidelberg Disputation') on the *theologia crucis*, 26 April 1518, Luther said:

> 19. He does not deserve the title of theologian who thinks he understands the invisible reality of God from the things he has made. 20. But only one who understands the visible and 'less-important' things of God (*visibilia et posteriora Dei*) by considering them through Christ's suffering and the cross.

Which was explained thus: The invisible reality of God is God's power, divinity, wisdom, justice, goodness, etc. What is visible is humanity, weakness, folly; and Luther went on to quote 1 Corinthians 1:21 and 25, adding: 'It is neither sufficient nor profitable to know God in glory and majesty if we do not know him in the humility and ignominy of the cross (. . .) In John 14, when Philip said, according to a theology of glory: 'Show us the Father', Christ immediately set aside the trivial thought of seeking God elsewhere, saying: 'Philip, he who has seen

21. *Vorlesung über den Hebräerbrief* (Scholia), 1517: WA 57/3:99,1–10. See LW 29:111, *Lectures on Hebrews*.

me has seen my Father'. It is in Christ crucified, then, that we find true theology and knowledge of God'.[22]

Christ himself is conformed to God: he is his own work. But he corresponds to what God is only in glory; God has given him to us in the opposite form of death and the descent into hell.[23] This is the theme dear to Luther of the revelation and communication of God *sub contraria specia* ('under a contrary aspect'). God reveals himself by hiding himself, he justifies by condemning; he gives life through death; he dwells in sinners; he exercises his *opus proprium* in an *opus alienum* (his own work in the forms of an alien work not corresponding to him) (. . .) This condition of his work is found in us: it is by emptying ourselves that we are filled.[24] And this is the unforgettable text of the *Scolia* on Rom 15:15–16:

> Only the lost sheep is sought, only the captive is set free, only the poor is enriched, only the crippled is strengthened, only the humble is exalted, what was empty is filled, what was not is built (. . .) It is impossible, then, for a man with his own righteousness to be filled with the righteousness of God, who fills only those who hunger and thirst. Man, satiated with his own truth and justice, is not capable of the truth and justice of God, which only emptiness and formlessness can receive. So let us say to God: 'O how gladly we shall be empty, that you

22. WA1:361–362. See LW31:53, *The Heidelberg Disputation*. Compare Joseph E Vercrusse, *'Luther's theology of the Cross in the time of the Heidelberg Disputation'*, in *Gregorianum*, 57 (1976): 523–548. Two related texts can be added: from the *ad Galatas commentarius*, 1531–1535: 'True Christian theology, I often repeat, does not speak of God in his majesty, like Moses and other teachings, but of Christ born of the Virgin, our mediator and pontiff' (*Christiana autem et vera theologia, ut saepe moneo, non ingerit Deum in maiestate, ut Moses et aliae doctrinae, sed Christum natum ex virgine, mediatorem et pontificem nostrum*): WA 40/1:77,11f.; see LW 26:28 *Lectures on Galatians*. And from the sermon of 2 March 1538 on *John 2:18–22*: 'Whoever wishes to seek God apart from Christ finds a God as he is in Moses, namely a devouring fire' (*Wer ausser Christo Gott suchen will, der findet einen Gott, wie im Mose stehet, der ist ein verzerend Fewer*): WA 46:761; see LW22:249, *Sermons on the Gospel of John*.
23. *Vorlesung über den Römerbrief* (1515–1516): WA 56:377,4f; see LW 25:366, *Lectures on Romans*.
24. 'We are capable of his works and purposes when our works and purposes cease and we become purely passive with regard to God' (*Capaces autem tunc sumus operum et consiliorum eius, quando nostra consilia cessant et opera quiescunt et efficimur pure passivi respectu Dei*): WA 56:375,22f.; see LW 25:365, *Romans*.

> may be full in us! Weak, that your strength may dwell in me! Sinners, that you may be justified in me! Fools, that you may be my wisdom! Unjust, that you may be my justice![25]

This again is the *fiducialis desperatio sui* of the letter to Spenlein (see p9n6 above). What responds to this coming of God to us in Christ is faith. Luther specifies two values, which for him are absolutely decisive: the *pro me* aspect, which gives what he calls *fides apprehensiva* (or *particularis, specialis*);[26] and the notion of *fides Christi*. The idea of personalised or particularised faith was announced in 1517–1518 in the *Vorlesung über den Hebräerbrief* as a thesis of sacramental theology:

> Consequently: no one obtains grace because he is absolved, or baptised, or receives communion, or is anointed, but because he believes he obtains grace while he is absolved, baptised, received communion, or anointed. For this well-known maxim is true, 'It is not the sacrament that justifies, but faith in the sacrament', and this text of St Augustine: 'It justifies not because one does it, but because one believes'.[27]
>
> Yet more: it is not enough to believe that he was poured out for the remission of sins if they do not believe that he was poured out for the remission of *their* sins.[28]

During Eastertide 1518, probably on 1 April, Luther preached on the proper preparation for receiving the Eucharist. He says: 'Fifth, be careful to approach with full faith, at least as far as possible, having the most assured confidence in yourself, you will receive grace.

25. WA 56:218; see LW 25:204, *Romans.*
26. '*Fides particularis, specialis*', *Acta Augustana*, Nov. 1518: WA 2:15f; see LW 31:272–274, *Proceedings at Augsburg*. For 'Fides apprehensiva', the *Disputatio* of 11 and 14 September 1535: WA 39/1:45 (thesis 12); see LW 34:110, *Theses concerning Faith and Law.*
27. '*Inde fit ut nullus consequatur graciam, quia absolvitur aut baptizatur aut communicatur aut inungitur, sed quia credit sic absolvendo, baptizando, communicando, inungendo se consequi graciam. Verum enim est illud vulgatissimum et probatissimum dictum "Non sacramentum, sed fides sacramentí iustificat". Et illud B. Augustini: "Iustificat, non quia fit, sed quia creditur"*': WA 57/3:169,23–170,4; see LW 29:172, *The Lectures on Hebrews* (1518).
28. '*Imo nec hoc satis est credere effusum esse in remissionem peccatorum, nisi in eorum ipsorum peccatorum remissionem effusum crediderint*': WA 57/3:208,29–209,2; see LW 29:210, *Hebrews.*

Indeed, you will receive according to the exact measure in which you believe you will receive, according to what Christ says in Mark 11:24 (Matthew 8:13)'.[29]

No doubt shortly before Easter, Luther preached his *Sermo de Poenitentia*, which was immediately published in Wittenberg. In it he rigorously analysed the dispositions of the faithful who confess. He maintained that faith in the fact of being absolved is the only effective condition for true absolution:

> Believe strongly that you are absolved and you will be absolved in truth (. . .) If by impossibility, the one who confesses does not have contrition, or that the priest does not absolve seriously but as a joke, if in spite of that he believes himself to be absolved, he is truly absolved . . .. Faith is the only condition, it is not the sacrament, but *fides sacramenti*: the sacraments are a sign of grace *if you believe*, that is all.[30]

At the end of May of the same year, Luther wrote his *Resolutiones disputationum de indulgentiarum virtute.* Conclusio VII reads:

> And why does Christ say: 'To whomsoever you forgive sins, they shall be forgiven', if not because they are not forgiven to any individual if, when the priest forgives, he does not believe that they are forgiven to him? (. . .) Christ knew that a conscience already justified by grace would vomit out grace through its anxiety if it did not have the help of faith in the presence of grace through the ministry of the priest; moreover, that sin would remain if it did not believe that it had been forgiven. Indeed the remission of sin and the gift of grace are not enough, we must also believe that it is remitted.[31]

29. *'Quinto, id cura cum plena aut saltem possibili fide accedas certissime confidens tete gratiam consecuturum. Tantum enim accipies quantum credis te accepturum, sicut Christus ait'*: WA 1:331,5–7.
30. *Sermo de Poenitentia, 'Crede fortifer te absolutum, et absolutus vere eris (. . .). Esto per impossibile, quod confessus non sit contritus, aut sacerdos non serio sed ioco absolvat, si tamen credat sese absolutum verissime est absolutus'*: WA 1:323,23–324,23.
31. *'Item cur dixit Christus: Quorum remiseritis peccata, remittuntur eis, nisi quod non sunt remissa ulli, nisi remittente sacerdote credat sibi remitti? (. . .) Scivit (Christus) quod conscientia iam iustificata per gratiam sua trepiditate evomeret gratiam, nisi sucurreretur ei per fidem de gratie praesentia ministerio sacerdotis, immo peccatum maneret, nisi remissum crederet. Non enim sufficit remissio peccati et gratiae donatio, sed oportet etiam credere esse remissum:* WA 1:543,14–24; see LW 31:104, *Explanations of the Ninety-five Theses.*

As legate in Germany, Cardinal Cajetan had become aware of the *Sermo de Poenitentia* and the *Resolutiones* when he arrived in Augsburg. Cajetan discussed them in his treatise written on 26 September 1518, '*Utrum ad fructuosam absolutionem in sacramento poenitentiae exigatur fides qua poenitens credat certissime se esse absolutum a Deo?*'[32]

This is where, with regard to the role that is both decisive and exclusive given to 'special faith' in the sacrament, Cajetan sounds the alarm: 'That would be to make another Church.'[33] According to Cajetan, this would mean introducing the specific emphasis concerning 'me' into the object of infused faith, and therefore into Revelation. Now the Church is formed by this infused faith in what has been revealed. This was only possible for Luther because this special faith was addressed to the Word of God, which is absolutely efficacious in what it proclaims or promises.

This question of special faith was one of the two points raised in the interviews between Cajetan and Luther in October 1518. Luther explained and justified his position in the *Acta Augustana* of November 1518. Even (or especially) after Jacques Maritain, Paul Hacker and Roland Dalbiez, Luther's special faith should be studied.[34]

When a Catholic reads 'What you loose on earth will be loosed in heaven', he sees in it the institution of sacramental power. It is necessary to believe, by personal faith, in the efficacy of the word that brought about this institution. From then on, if one approaches the sacrament with the requisite dispositions, one is forgiven. For Luther, it is necessary to believe not only in the efficacy of Christ's word-promise, but also that this promise concerns me. For Luther, this reality is concrete: faith is not merely an intellectual conviction, but an absolute trust in the person of Christ, who is given to me by God in this very faith.

---

32. '*Whether for fruitful reception of absolution in the sacrament of penance one must have that faith by which the penitent believes with full certitude that he is absolved by God?*', Jared Wicks, *Cajetan Responds* (Washington: Catholic University of America Press 1978), 49.
33. Deservedly, this relationship between Cajetan and Luther has been much studied. I will mention only Gerhard Hening, *Cajetan und Luther. Ein Beitrag zur Begegnung von Thomismus und Reformation*, (Stuttgart: Calwer Verlag, 1966); Otto Herman Pesch, 'Das heisst eine neue Kirche bauen', in *Fesgabe H Fries* (Graz: Verlag Styria 1972), 645–661 Wicks, *Cajetan responds*.
34. WA 2:13,6–16,5; see LW 31:270–274, *Proceedings at Augsburg*. See further, n39 below.

This position of Luther's was essential and central to him. It was part of his vision of salvation and revelation, in which we encounter only what God is for me, and of his conception of the Christian faith. He distinguished it from 'historical faith', the acceptance of a purely objective and neutral fact.[35] It is this *pro me* that is essential to the Lutheran faith.[36] Luther had found the way out of his anguish over salvation: faith, provided that it is—as an absolute and tested certainty—the appropriation of what, in Christ, is for me. Luther loved to repeat: 'Me, for me!'

Commenting on Galatians 2:20, he writes: 'Therefore read these words "me" and "for me" with great energy and accustom yourselves to take this 'me' with confident faith and apply it to yourselves. Do not doubt that you belong to the number of those who speak this "me".'[37]

As we have seen, this *pro me* accords with a conception of faith as something other than adherence of the spirit, namely the transplantation into us of the justice of Christ, or even of Christ himself. This is what Luther puts in the formula *fides Christi*, as early as 1513–1515 (*Dictata super Psalterium*, WA 3, 4). We also

---

35. Thus *De libertate christiana*, Autumn 1520: WA 7:58,31f, with this consideration: 'He must be preached with the aim of promoting faith in him: that he not only be Christ, but that he be Christ for you, for me' (*Oportet autem ut eo fine praedicatur, quo fides in eum promoveatur, ut non tantum sit Christus, sed tibi et mihi sit Christus*); see LW 31:257, *Treatise on Christian Liberty.*

36. This theme is central to the study by Paul Hacker, *Das Ich im Glauben bei Martin Luther* (Graz: Verlag Styria 1966). Hacker links other chapters of Luther's theology to it. For him, this is the principle of other errors, which he sets out to denounce and criticise. Although not insignificant, Hacker's study was poorly received on the Lutheran side (Albrecht Peters, in *Theologische Lizeraturzeitung*, 93 (1968): 589–592) and received considerable criticism on the Catholic side (Otto Pesch, in *Theologische Revue*, 64 (1968): 51–56). At least Hacker read Luther seriously. Jacques Maritain speaks of 'the advent of the self' in relation to Luther in *Trois Réformateurs* (Paris: Plon-Nourrit, 1925), but this pamphlet cannot claim any historical value, even if it quotes texts. [Editor's note: Congar continues this discussion, in 'Study Four' below].

37. WA 40/1:299,29f; see LW 26:179, *Galatians* (1535). Compare the enthusiastic 'for me! for me!' of *Wider die himmlischen Propheten* (1525), on the subject of the Eucharist: WA 18:195,35; see LW 40:206, *Against the Heavenly Prophets*. Hacker criticises Luther for using the singular, 'I', 'me', where there is the plural, 'we'. But he himself cites texts in which Luther switches from the *pro me* to the *pro nobis*, and vice versa, for example. *ad Galatas* (1519): WA 2:458,20–28, see LW 27:172; the *Disputatio* of 11 and 14 September 1535: WA 35/1:45,16 and 46,7.

find formulae such as 'It is in the faith of / in Christ that the sins are forgiven'; 'Christ or the faith in / of Christ'; 'it is in the faith in / of Christ that everything is given to us'.[38]

What Christ is personally, we are through this faith: 'Christ is not in his person our justice, peace, mercy, our salvation as the effective source of all this, but it is the faith of Christ through which we have justice and peace'.[39]

Often, instead of 'effective', Luther says *tropologice*, by transfer and application to us, as in the explanation of Psalm 71 (72), where we have seen that his new understanding of *iustitia* is acquired: 'Justice is faith in/of Christ by transfer (Romans 1: *the justice of God is revealed in him*)'. We cannot overemphasise the powerful realism with which, for Luther, Christ is in me through faith.[40]

The theme of 'joyful exchange' obviously takes its place in this highly significant context: Christ becomes my justice because he became my sin. There is a transition from one theme to the other: the '*pro me*' directs the joyful exchange.[41]

---

38. '*in fide Christi remittuntur peccata*', WA 3:175,8 (LW 10:146); '*Christus seu fides Christi*', WA3:649,16 (LW 11:146); 'in fide Christi omnia nobis donantur', WA 4:215,14 (*Gloss*, not in LW).
39. '*Christus non dicitur iustitia, pax, misericordia, salus nostra in persona sua nisi effective, sed fides Christi, qua iustificamur, pacificamur*': WA 4:19 on Psalm 84, see LW 11:174. Likewise, the gloss (not in LW): 'All that Christ the Head has done and suffered, faith in Christ does and suffers in his faithful.' WA 4:264,29 (*Quaecumque Christus caput agit et assus est . . . fides Christi agit et patitur in suis fidelibus*). Luther uses many expressions that link our union with Christ to faith, in line with the traditional theology of the mystical body. Compare for example, in *ad Galatas* (1519), WA 2:504,6*ff*. (LW 27:241); WA 2:535,24 (LW 27:289), 'To believe in Christ is to put him on, to become one with him' (*Credere enim in Christum est eum induere, unum cum eo fieri*); and the *Sermo de duplici iustitia* (1519): WA 2:146,15*ff*, see LW 31: 297–299, *Two Kinds of Righteousness*; and again *Galatians* (1535): WA 40/1:285,5, '[be] as one person', (*quasi una personna*), see LW 26:168; WA 40/1:285,24f. 'cemented to Christ' (*conglutineris Christo*), see *again* LW 26:168, *Galatians* (1535). Wilfried Joest *Ontologie der Person bei Luther*, (Göttingen: Vandenhoeck & Ruprecht, 1967), 365*ff*, has brought together a number of texts on this '*fides Christi, fides apprehensiva Christum*', drawn in particular from the *Theses on Faith and Law* of 1535, WA 39/1:44–62, see LW34:105–132, and the *ad Galatas* lectures and commentaries (both 1517–1519 and 1531–1535), etc.
40. '*Iustitia tropologice est fides Christi*'. 'Romans 1, Iustitia dei revelatur in eo': WA 3:463,1. See LW 10:404, *Psalm 72*. For another important text, see *Galatians*, 1535: WA 40/1,228; see LW 26:129–130.
41. Also, *Operationes in Psalmos* (1519–1521): WA 5:311, on *Psalm 9*.

Finding Christ in Scripture and the Fathers

Criticism of Scholasticism. Creation of a new theology and a new language

Henri Strohl notes that in the sixteenth century, 'the authority of Holy Scripture was not in question. It was not a dogma officially defined by the Church, but it was an indisputable axiom'.[1] It has remained so. It is true that in the twelfth and thirteenth centuries an activity of rational discussion had developed to the point of taking on a fairly large autonomy. Without questioning the authority of Scripture, this discussion by-passed the sacred text.[2]

Luther never followed this path. He practised classical hermeneutics (the four senses) in the *Dictata super Psalterium* of 1513–1515, giving priority to the literal sense and the tropological sense. From then on, he looked for and saw Christ, Christ crucified, Christ for us.[3] The scholastics professed the absolute primacy of Scripture; Luther testifies that he had received it from his Occamist

1. Henri Strohl, *la Pensée de la Réforme* (Manuels et Précis de théologie, XXXII) (Neuchâtel-Paris: Delachaux et Niestlé, 1951), 63.
2. Ceslaus Spicq, *Esquisse d'une histoire de l'exégèse latine au Moyen* Age (Bibl. thomiste, XXVI) (Paris: J Vrin, 1944), 64–69. See also Freidrich Kropatscheck, *Das Schriftprinzip der lutherischen Kirche* (I. Die Vorgeschichte. Das Erbe des Mittelalters) (Leipzig: A. Deichertsche, 1904); Paul de Vooght, *les Sources de la doctrine chrétienne après les théologiens du XIVe siècle* (Paris: Desclée de Brouwer, 1954); Henri de Lubac, *Exégèse médiévale. Les quatre sens de l'Ecriture*, I/l (Paris: Aubier 1959), especially 56–74; last but not least Hermann Schussler, *Der Primat der Heiligen Schrift als theologisches und kanonistisches Problem im Spätmittelalter,* Veröffentlichungen des Instituts für Europäische Geschichte, 86 (Wiesbaden: Steiner, 1977).
3. *Dictata super Psalterium*: WA 3:41f.(LW 10:48, *Psalm 4:1*); WA 3:597f. (LW 11:88–89, *Psalm 78:69*); WA 4:153 (LW 11:304, *Psalm 102:5*). 'It is beyond

masters themselves.[4] But he had detached himself from them and from the doctors who not only did not adhere to the pure Word of God, adding to it or substituting new opinions, but despised Scripture and said, if we are to believe Luther: 'What Bible! The Bible? The Bible is a book of heretics, we have to read the doctors!'[5]

Luther's reaction was indicated in 1509, in his marginal glosses on the Sentences. What is sought and found in Scripture is very different from what is sought and found in philosophy: 'It is not a question of physical or logical definition, but theological. If we ask: What is Christ? The logician would answer: he is a person, etc. But the theologian says: he is a stone, the cornerstone, etc.'[6]

From then on Luther referred to Scripture as the supreme norm:

> For my part, although more than one illustrious doctor thinks like this, nevertheless, because they do not have Scripture for themselves but only human traditions, whereas I have Scripture on this point (. . .) this allows me to say with the Apostle: 'If an angel from heaven, that is, a teacher in the Church, teaches anything else, let him be anathema'.[7]
>
> We must believe and profess faith in the words of Scripture and match our words to them, not the other way round.[8]

So there is a question of terms and categories. Words do not have the same meaning in philosophy, in Aristotle or Porphyry, and in Scripture, which is the source of our faith. Thus *substantia*,[9]

---

question that all Scripture is directed to Christ alone', *Von Menschenlehre zu meiden*, 1522: WA 10/2:73,16; see LW 35:132, *Avoiding the Doctrines of Men.*

4. Letter of 9 May 1518 to Trutfetter: WABr 1:171–172.
5. 'Was Biblia, Biblia? Biblia ist ein Ketzer buch, man mus die Doctores lesen', *Vermahnung an die Geistlichen*, 1530: WA30/3:300; see LW34:27, *Exhortation to all Clergy Assembled at Augsburg.*
6. '*Non est itaque determinatio phisica vel logica, sed theologica. Sicut quasi diceretur: Quid est Christus? respondet logicus: est persona, etc, theologus autem: est petra, lapis angularis, etc*'. WA9:91,22, *Luthers Handbemerkungen zu den Sentenzen des Petrus Lombardus*, Bk3: Dist.23.
7. '*Ego autem, licet multi inclyti doctores sic sentiant, tamen quia non habent pro se scripturam sed solum humanas traditiones, et ego in ista opinione habeo scripturam . . . ideo dico cum Apostolo: 'Si angelus de coelo, id est doctor in ecclesia aliud docuerit, anathema sit*'. *Handbemerkungen zu den Sentenzen*, WA9:46,16, Bk1: Dist.20.
8. '*Credere oportet et verbis scripturae fidem profiteri et linguam illis aptare et non econtra*'. *Handbemerkungen zu den Sentenzen*, WA 9:84,7 (Bk3 Dist.4).
9. *Dictata super Psalterium*, on Psalm 68 (69), WA 3:419–420; see LW 10:355–356.

intellectus,[10] *corpus.*[11] In faith and Scripture, *verbum* is identical to *caro*, which would be absurd and impossible in Porphyry and in philosophy.[12] In the *Dictata super Psalterium* of 1513–1515, Luther shows himself to be very aware of the difference in interest and language: philosophy deals with visible things, faith with invisible ones.[13] Philosophy seeks quiddity. Faith does not.[14] Faith does not need to carry away the spoils of philosophy; this is the traditional theme of the spoils of the Egyptians. She is like the strong woman, 'in whom her husband puts his trust'.[15]

Wilhelm Link has shown that it was in commenting on the Epistle to the Romans, in 1515–1516, that Luther detached himself from the influence of his Occamist masters, although he retained a certain doctrine of freedom, of a progressive movement and of a preparation for grace.[16] Luther goes so far as to quote Aristotle! But even here his perspective is different; Luther gives absolute primacy to God's point of view, to his initiative. This is the meaning of his many statements:

> It is clear that the Apostle does not speak of the law in a metaphysical or moral way, but in a spiritual and theological way (. . .)The Apostle's way of speaking and the metaphysical or moral way are contrary.[17]

10. *Dictata*, on Psalm 31, WA 3:176,3; see LW 10:147–148; on Psalm 73 (74), WA 3:507–508; see LW 10:452.
11. Letter of 22 February 1518 to Spalatin, WABr 1:27*ff*. Here Luther expresses the general principle of the absolute difference between the two 'languages'. See LW 48:8–11.
12. Examples given in the *Christological Disputations* of 11 January 1539, WA 39/2:3, thesis 1 (see LW 38:239), and 28 February 1540: WA 39/2: 94, thesis 20 (see LW 73:255); also WA 39/2:103,121 (LW 73:264,280, *Disputation on the Word became Flesh*).
13. *Dictata* on Psalm 73 (74), WA3:507–508; see LW 10:452.
14. *Dictata* on Psalm 103 (104); WA4:188,10; see LW 11:339.
15. *Dictata* on Psalm 68 (69); WA3:420,11f; see LW 10:356.
16. Wilhelm Link, *Das Ringen Luthers um die Freiheit der Theologie von der Philosophie* (München: C. Kaiser, 1940, reprinted 1955). For the ideas of progressive movement (same invocation of Aristotle!), preparation for grace, 158–160. As noted above (10n7), a letter of October 1516 to Jean Lang, Erfurt, speaks of 'your followers of Gabriel [Biel]' (*tui Gabrielistae*), thus showing that Luther had intellectually left the theology of Biel, represented in Erfurt by Trutfetter and Bartholemaeus d`Usingen, his former teachers (WABr 1:65,19).
17. 'Patet, itaque, quod Apostolus non metaphysice neque moraliter de lege loquitur, sed spiritualiter et theologice(. . .)Modus loquendi Apostoli et modus metaphysicus seu moralis sunt contrarii', *Vorlesung über den Römerbrief*, 1515–1516, WA 56:334,3 and 14; see LW 25:325, *Lectures on Romans*.

Because, in philosophical logic, the sinful act is removed and the person remains the same, whereas in Christian salvation, the person is changed but the sin remains. It will only be totally eliminated eschatologically. But philosophy knows only present things. I cannot grow weary of quoting Luther's commentary on Romans 8:19, *Expectatio creaturae*:

> The Apostle reasons about things and appreciates them differently from philosophers and metaphysicians. For the philosophers drown their gaze in the presence of things in such a way that they consider only their quiddities and qualities. The Apostle, on the other hand, turns our gaze from the consideration of the presence of things, their essence and their accidents, to what they are called to become. For he does not say 'the essence' or 'the operation' of the creature, or 'the action', 'the passion', 'the movement', but using a surprising and theological term, he says 'the expectation of the creature', so that, when the spirit hears that the creature is waiting, it is no longer tending and seeking towards the creature itself, but towards what it is waiting for. Alas, we remain deeply and unfortunately attached to predicaments and quiddities; how many silly metaphysical opinions are we drawn into! When will we have the feeling and the evidence that we have lost ourselves in so many vain searches and have neglected better things? We are constantly acting to prove Seneca right: We ignore necessary things because we have studied superfluous ones. Better: we are ignorant of the things that lead to salvation because we have studied the things that lead to damnation.[18]

18. '*Aliter Apostolus de rebus philosophatur et sapit quam philosophi et metaphysici. Quia philosophi oculum ita in presentiam rerum ímmergunt, ut solum quidditates et qualitates earum speculentur, Apostolus autem oculos nostros revocat ab intuitu rerum presentíum, ab essentia et accidentibus earum, et dirigit in eas, secundum quod future sunt. Non enim dicit "Essentia" Vel "operatio" creature seu "actio" et "passio" et "motus", Sed novo et miro vocabulo et theologico dicít "Expectatio Creature", Ut eo ipso, cum animus audit Creaturam expectare, non ipsam creaturam amplius, Sed quid creatura expectet, intendat et querat. Sed heu, quam profunde et noxie heremus in predicamentis et quidditatibus, quot stultis opinionibus in metaphysica Involvimur! Quando sapiemus et videbimus, quod tam preciosum tempus tam vanis studiis perdimus et meliora negligimus? Semper agimus, ut fit verum in nobis, quod Seneca ait: "Necessaria ignoramus, quia superflua didicimus, Immo Salutaria ignoramus, quia damnabilia didicimus"*': WA56:371,2-17 (LW25:360)

> For myself, I think I owe to the Lord this office of crying out against philosophy and persuading people to go to Holy Scripture. For if another were to do so, who would not have seen it, he would either be feared or disbelieved. But I have worn myself out in this for many years, and I have seen and heard much of it, and I see that it is a search for vanity and perdition.
>
> That is why I warn you all, as far as I can, that you should quickly undertake these studies with the sole aim, not of fixing yourself in them and defending them, but rather as we learn bad things in order to destroy them, and errors in order to refute them victoriously. In the same way, we learn knowledge in order to reject it, or at least to learn the language of those with whom we have to live. It is time, in fact, to give ourselves over to other studies and to learn about Jesus Christ, a crucified Jesus Christ.[19]

In the years 1513–1517 Luther moved away from the philosophical conceptions that he still shared when he commented on the Sentences in 1509. Under the influence of Augustine's anti-Pelagian writings, he distanced himself from the Pelagianism of Gabriel, which led to his theses of 5 September 1517 *contra Gabrielem.*[20]

---

19. *'Ego quidem Credo me debere Domino hoc obsequium latrandi contra philosophiam et suadendi ad Sacram Scripturam. Nam alius forte si faceret, qui ea non vidisset, Vel timeret Vel non crederetur ei. Ego autem in illis detritus multis iam annis et multos itidem expertus et audiens Video, quod sit studium vanitatis et perditionis. Idcirco omnes vos moneo, quantum possum, Ut ea studia cito faciatis Et id solum queratis, non ut ea statuatis et defendatis, Sed potius sicut artes malas discimus, ut destruamus, et errores, ut revincamus. Ita et haec, ut reprobemus, Aut saltem, ut modum loquendi ipsorum, cum quibus conversari necesse est, accipiamus. Tempus est enim, ut aliis studiis mancipemur et Ihesum Christum discamus "et hunc crucifixum"'*, Römerbrief: WA 56:371,17–27; see LW 25:361, on *Romans 8:1* ('For the creation waits').
20. Leif Grane, *Contra Gabrielem. Luthers Auseinandersetzung mit Gabriel Biel in der Disputatio Contra Scholasticam Theologiam*, 1517 (Acta Theol. Danica, IV) (København: Gyldendal, 1962). Biel was a semipelagian in the sense condemned by the Second Council of Orange, teaching preparation for faith and grace by natural forces, says Harry J McSorley: 'Was Gabriel Biel a Semipelagian?' in *Wahrheit und Verkündigung* (Festgabe M Schmaus) (München: Schöningh, 1967), 2,1109–1120. Luther had received this theology at Erfurt, and had even professed it: 'Once, I also understood it in this way' (*Sic enim ego aliquando intellexi*), Römerbrief, WA 56:382; see LW 25:372. Against this suspicion of semi-pelagianism, Alaister E McGrath, 'The Anti-Pelagian Structure of 'Nominalist' Doctrines of Justification', in *Ephem. Theol. Lovan*, 57 (1981): 107–119.

From then on Luther referred only to Scripture and the Fathers, especially St Augustine, insofar as they agree with Scripture. Regarding this rule, asserted in the final conclusion of the *Disputatio* of 4 September 1517[21] and in correspondence throughout 1518,[22] Luther became even more keenly aware in his polemical responses to Eck and Sylvestre Prierias,[23] to Ambrosius Catharinus, then in

21. 'In this we do not wish to say anything and we believe that we have said nothing that does not agree with the Catholic Church and the Doctors of the Church', *Contra scholasticam theologiam*, WA 1:228, (*In his nihil dicere volumus nec dixisse nos credimus, quod non sit catholicae et ecclesiasticis doctoribus consentaneum*). See LW 31:16, *Against Scholastic Theology*.
22. To John Scultatus, 13 February, WABr 1:139, 27–32, 'From now on it is clear that we owe no faith to scholastic doctors and canonists as long as they express their opinions. As the saying goes: It is shameful for a jurist to speak without the support of a text. But it is even more shameful for a theologian, and I am not talking about a text by Aristotle, because they quote him more, a lot, too much, but our text, those of Holy Scripture, the canons, the Fathers of the Church', (*Porro scolasticis doctoribus et canonistís constat nullam deberi a nobis fidem, dum suas opinantur opiniones. Et ut vulgo dicitur: Turpe est Iuristam loqui sine textu. At multo turpius est Theologum loqui sine textu. Non Aristotelis dico, nam hunc plus, valde, nimis, satis loquuntur, sed nostra, id est sacrae Scripturae, Canonum, Ecclesiasticorum patrum*). Canons are councils. To Trutfetter, 9 May, WABr 1:170,36–38, 'I am asking the Lord every day that this be done quickly, that we return to the very pure studies of the Bible and the Holy Fathers' (*adeo procedo, ut cotidie Dominum rogem, quatenus id statim fiat, ut rursum Bibliae et St Patrum purissima studia revocentur*). *Compare* WABr 1:171,75–80); the *Protestatio* at the head of the *Resolutiones disputationum de indulgentiarum virtute* of May 1518, WA 1:529,33f.; see LW 31:83, *Explanations of the Ninety-five Theses*. The Fathers only '*iudice scriptura*', letter to Jérôme Dungersheim, May 1520, WABr 2:113, and June 1520, WABr 2:125,11–14. See *also* KV Selge, *Normen der Christenheit im Streit um Ablass und Kirchenautorität 1518 bis 1521*, (unpublished thesis, 1968).
23. *Ad dialogum Silvestri Prieriatis de potestate papae responsio*, August 1518, see WA 1:648,2–9; WA 1:650,18–20; WA 1:652,34–36; WA 1:658,1f; WA 1:664:40f.; WA 1:670,29–31. But it is also necessary to quote WA 1:662,17–26: 'In the first place you bring the authority of St Thomas and you give him a plural, calling him 'of the saints', perhaps out of reverence, and so that I give him credence you say he is approved by the Roman Church, the rule of faith. I am surprised that among so many Doctors of the Church you do not cite some other or a text of Scripture (. . .) I reject both you and Thomas. For Augustine is more accepted by the Church than St Thomas, and Paul supremely, who is my first foundation. I am surprised, then, that you call the Roman Church the rule of faith. I have always believed that faith was the rule of the Roman Church and of all the Churches' (*Primo autoritatem B. Thomae inducis, cuius sententiam s'anctorum vocas numero plurali, forte reverentiae causa, et ut huic credam, dicis a Romana Ecclesia, regula*

his discussion with Cajetan (October 1518),[24] where he confronted another scholasticism, that of the Thomists: this would be 'his' Thomas, because he seems not to have really known the 'real' Saint Thomas: the few precise references he makes to him suggest this.[25] Luther denied that it was necessary to follow these doctors in order to be a Catholic: it is heresy only if one contradicted Scripture and the Fathers. The rest is debatable opinion.

When Luther appeared before the legate in Augsburg, his convictions were already clear and firm: a reform of the Church depended on the substitution of one theology for another, or more precisely, on the substitution of norms of thought and discipline for the norms in use. He expressed this lucidly to Jodocus Trutfetter, his former teacher, on 9 May 1518. Trutfetter had reproached him for despising dialectic, or even to ignore it, which affected the value of his theology.

Luther had come to explain and justify himself, but his old master had been unable to receive him. So Luther wrote to him. He was not alone: with one exception, the entire fledgling university of Wittenberg thought as he did. As for him, he was convinced:

> I believe quite simply that a reform of the Church is impossible unless the canons, the decretals, scholastic theology, philosophy and logic, as they are currently held, are rooted out, and other studies are instituted. This thought has become so strong in me that I pray the Lord every day that this may

---

fidei, probatum. Miror, quod inter tot Ecclesiae doctores non aliquando alium quoque aut textum scripturae iriducas (. . .) tam te quam Thomam reiicio. Quia et Augustinus receptus est ab ecclesia magis quam St Thomas, Paulus autem maxime, qui fundamentum meum primum est. Secundo miror, quid velis, quod Eeclesiam Romanam fidei regulam vocas. Ego credidi semper, quod fides esset regula Romanae Ecclesiae et omnium Ecclesiarum).

24. The question of the authority of papal decrees was one of the two issues at stake in the confrontation (see above 19n32–33). For Luther, one is a heretic only 'if you deny faith in the word of Christ' (*si neges fidem verbi Christi*), WA 2:18,16, see LW 31:278, *Proceedings at Augsburg*.

25. Link, *Das Ringen Luthers*, 192(n) says: 'The only passage that seems to clearly attest to the work of Thomas is WA 31/2:454,16. But this is the *Summa Angelica*, a collection of *casus conscientiae*, written in 1486 by Angelus Carleti of Chivasso, O.F.M. (+1495)'. See LW 17:250(n2), *Lectures on Isaiah*.

> happen without delay and that we may return to the most pure study of the Bible and the Holy Fathers.[26]

In Wittenberg, these new studies were flourishing. Luther's correspondence bears witness to this progress. On 18 May 1517, he wrote to his colleague and friend in Erfurt, Jean Lang:

> Our theology and St Augustine are happily gaining ground and reigning in our university, thank God. Aristotle is gradually going downhill and is on the verge of final ruin. It is marvellous how disgusted we are with the commentary on the *Sentences*, and no one can hope for listeners if he does not want to present that theology, namely the Bible or St Augustine or another authoritative doctor in the Church.[27]

There is similar testimony in letters to Spalatin, 2 September 1518,[28] and 24 May 1519.[29] The university was a success; Duke Frederick the Wise was understandably keen on it. This is one of the reasons why he protected Luther and ensured that his case was handled in Germany by the legate Cajetan.

This is also one of the reasons for Luther's immense success. From Nuremberg, a man named Scheurl asked him to send him 'something

26. '*Ego simpliciter credo, quod impossibíle sit ecclesiam reformari, nisi funditus canones, decretales, scholastica theologia, philosophia, logica, ut nunc habentur, eradícentur et alia Studia instituantur, atque in ea sententia adeo procedo, ut cotidie Domimum rogem, quatenus id statím fiat, ut rursum Bibliae et St Patrum purissima studía revocentur*'. Letter to Trutfetter (no.74), WABr 1:170,33–38.
27. '*Theologia nostra et St Augustinus prospere procedunt et regnant in nostra universitate Deo operante. Aristoteles descendit paulatim ínclinatus ad ruínam prope futuram sempiternam. Mire fastidíuntur lectiones sententiaríae, nec est ut quis sibi àuditores sperare possit, nisi theologiam hanc, id est bibliam aut St Augustinum aliumve ecclesiasticae autoritatis doctorem velit profiteri.*' Letter no.41: WABr 1:99,8–13, see LW48:41–42, to John Lang. Also letter no.66, to Staupitz, 31 March 1518, WABr 1:160,16.
28. Letter no.90, WABr 1:196,23–29: students want to be exempted from ethics courses. See LW 48:83.
29. Letter no.181, WABr 1:407,9–10: 'The number of students is increasing mightily, it's a real tide!' (*Augescit studentium numerus vehementer sicut aqua inundans*). In fact, Melanchthon, commenting on Romans, had nearly 300 listeners; letter from Luther to Gerard de Listrius, of Zwolle, 28 July 1520: WABr 2:149,6f. Hartmann GRISAR, *Luther*, (Freiburg: Herder, 1924), gives 400 listeners for Luther in 1520, and from 500 to 600 for Melanchthon, 1,370f.

Christian, as you are accustomed to doing'.[30] From Bohemia, J. Poduška congratulated him on having restored the pure theology of the Fathers.[31] According to Jean de Botzheim, he had brought help to a failing theology.[32] And he did this without using great eloquence, using the word of truth, the testimony of the Scriptures, and Christian fervour.[33] It was through his religious writings, often small books with considerable print runs that were distributed by booksellers–some thirty treatises between 1517 and 1520–that Luther had an immense impact.[34] His words were eagerly awaited.

The positions taken by Luther had quite radical consequences for the practice and content of theology. Luther contrasted two realms, that of this world and that of God, just as there were two justices, one *coram hominibus* (in human eyes) and the other *coram Deo* (in God's eyes).[35] Nature, reason, law and statutes belong to what is valid *coram hominibus*; only the word and the promise are valid *coram Deo*.[36] *Theo*-logy could only exist in a discourse made from God's point of view, normed by his Word, that is, in concrete terms, by the Scriptures.

I have already quoted the passage from the 1532 commentary on Psalm 51, 'the proper subject of theology is humanity guilty of sin and lost, and God who justifies and saves the sinful'.[37] Now the terms and the language must correspond to the *subiectum*, i.e. to the reality in question. A new reality requires a new language, a new grammar.[38]

30. 'aliquid christiani, ut soles', letter of 30 September 1517, WABr 1:107,18.
31. Letter of 17 July 1519, WABr 1:417.
32. Letter of 3 March 1520, WABr 2:60–61.
33. Letter from Conrad Pellicanus, Basel, 16 March 1520, WABr 2:67,93-96. Compare also letter from Nicolas Gerbel, 18 May 1521, WABr 2:342.
34. Heinz Dannebauer, *Luther als religiöser Volks-Schriftsteller* (Tübingen, 1930), 38ff, a table of these writings with the dates of their editions; the *Appeal to the Nobility* had twelve editions.
35. A constant theme. See, *for example* WA 40/1:392, a passage from the 1535 *ad Galatas Commentarius* distinguishing between the '*locus politicus*' and the '*locus theologicus*', which is that of *coram Deo*. See LW 26:249.
36. In *Vraie et fausse réforme*, (Paris: Cerf, 1969) 355f., I quoted significant texts from the *Resolutio de potestate papae*, WA 2:239; *Vorlesung über Genesis*, WA 43:385,9–17, see LW 4:345 on Genesis 25:21 (Jacob and Esau); etc.
37. '*Theologica proprium subiectum est homo peccati reus ac perditus et Deus iustificans ac salvator hominis peccatoris*', WA 40/2:328,17; See LW 12:311, *Psalm 51*.
38. From the *Vorlesung über Genesis*, WA 42:195,3–21: 'This is the natural order, as Aristotle himself testifies: words at the service of things, not the other way round.

Luther followed this rule with remarkable fidelity. He also developed a new theology whose meaning was not understood by his opponents or his judges, bound as they were to Scholasticism. I myself, in 1950 (draft form) or 1954 (publication), assessed his Christology too much in the light not only of the dogma of Chalcedon, but also of high scholasticism.[39] Already, in an addendum of 1963, I have

---

And Hilary's idea is well known. The Master quotes it in the Sentences. That words are to be understood according to the subject matter. So, in any explanation, we must first consider this, i.e. see what reality is involved. Once this has been done, the words must be referred to the thing and not the thing to the words. Because the rabbis and those who follow them do not do this (because they have lost touch with reality and are only attached to words), they frequently fall into the most absurd propositions. Indeed, not having thoughts worthy of the spiritual things with which the Holy Letters deal, they depart from reality and draw words to vain and carnal cogitations. It is certain that the Jews have lost Christ. How then can they understand the things of the Gospel or of the law? They do not know what sin, grace, righteousness are; how can they explain such passages correctly? Our sophists are almost the same. What true sense do they have of these things? When you do not know what reality is, it is impossible to hear the words correctly. For if we first have knowledge of words, however, knowledge of realities prevails. Indeed, when realities change, words take on a different meaning and we have a completely new grammar'. (*Porro natura sic ordinatum est, ut verba testante etiam Philosopho debent servire rebus, non res verbis. Et nota est Hilarii sententia, quam etiam Magister in sententiis citat, quod verba intelligi debeant secundum materiam subiectam. Igitur in omni expositione primo subiectum considerari debet, hoc est, videndum est, de qua re agatur. Hoc postquam factum est, deinde verba, si ita fert grammaticae ratio, ad rem ducenda sunt, et non res ad verba. Hoc quia Rabini et qui eos sequuntur, non faciunt (nam res amiserunt, et tantum in verbis herent), saepe in absurdissimas sententias incidunt. Quia enim non habent cogitationes dignas spiritualibus rebus, de quibus sacrae literae tractant, a re aberrant et verba trahunt ad vanas et carnales cogitationes. 'Certum autem est amisisse Iudaeos Christum, quomodo igitur, quae vel Evangelii vel Legis sunt, recte possunt intelligere? Nesciunt, quid sit Peccatum, quid Gratia, quid Iustitia, quomodo igitur huius-modi locos dextre possunt explicare? Similes horum fere sunt Sophistae nostri, quid enim sani de tantis rebus habent? Re igitur non cognita impossibile est, ut verba possint recte intelligi. Etsi enim verborum cognitio ordine prior est, tamen rerum cognitio est potior. Nam mutatis rebus etiam verba mutantur in alium sensum et fit plane nova Grammatica*). See LW 1:263–264 on Genesis 4:7 (Cain and Abel) and compare WA 42:560,14f. (LW 3:16–17); 597,17–31 (LW 3:69); 598,17 and 21 (LW 3:70–71); 599,4–9 (LW 3:71); 600,20–30 and 36–40 (LW 3:72–73).

39. Yves Congar, 'Regards et réflexions sur la christologie de Luther', in *Das Konzil von Chalkedon*, edited by Aloys Grillmeier and H Bacht (Würzburg: Echter, 1954), 3,457–486. Reprinted with an Addendum in *Chrétiens en dialogue* (Paris: Cerf, 1964), 453–489 = *Dialogue Between Christians: Catholic Contributions to Ecumenism* (London: Chapman, 1966).

corrected this approach somewhat. I believe that I have improved it still further since then.[40] But it was only after this new work that I was able to become acquainted with Constantini di Bruno's unpublished thesis on the role of Christ's humanity in the context of Luther's Christology. Leaving aside two remarks about what he attributes to me, I believe that what he shows is correct, namely that, in holding the truth of the dogmas of Ephesus and Chalcedon, Luther was not interested, like Scholasticism, in the ontology of Christ, but in what he is for us in God's plan of salvation, and he spoke accordingly. His Christology, Bruno thinks, is classical, but it is expressed in a new language.[41]

One finds a similar situation in the theology of the sacrament of the body and blood of the Lord. Luther held to a 'real presence', which led to his being accused of papalism. If he personally rejects transubstantiation—he leaves people free to accept it—it is because, he thinks, it uses a philosophical, rational concept, and, what is more, misunderstood Aristotle.[42] It is enough to hold, with the Word of God, 'This is my body'. But it is in Christology that the new language is most clearly affirmed, in particular in two *Christological Disputations*, of 11 January 1539 on John 1:14 and of 28 February 1540, *De divinitate et humanitate Christi*. Here are the first four and the last three theses of 1539:

1. Although it is necessary to hold the maxim 'everything that is true agrees with the truth', nevertheless the same (statement) is not true in different domains.
2. In theology it is true that the Word became flesh; in philosophy it is simply impossible and absurd.

---

40. Yves Congar, 'Nouveaux regards sur la christologie de Luther', in *Revue des Sciences philosophiques et théologiques*, 62 (1982): 180–197. [Editor's note: see 'Study Three' below]
41. Constantini du Bruno, *Le rôle salutaire de Humanité du Christ à la lumière des grands thèmes de la christologie de Luther* (unpublished thesis,1979). See also, Marc Lienhardt, *Luther: Témoin de Jésus-Christ* (Cerf: Paris, 1973) = Luther: Witness to Jesus Christ. Translated Edwin Robertson (Minneapolis: Augsburg, 1982)
42. In Aristotelian logic, the subject and the predicate must designate the same reality. Theologically, this is not so. In *Hoc est corpus meum*, '*Hoc*' designates bread, and bread is the body of Christ while remaining bread.

3. The statement God is man is no less repugnant than if you said: man is an ass.
4. The Sorbonne, the mother of errors, has very misguidedly defined: the same is true in philosophy and theology.
5. It would therefore be more appropriate if we left dialectics or philosophy in their domain and learned to speak new languages in the realm of faith beyond any domain (outside any system).
6. Otherwise it will happen that we put new wine into old wineskins and lose both, as the Sorbonne does.
7. In the articles of faith, it is the believing heart that must be put to work, not the philosophical intelligence. Then we will truly know what it is that the Word became flesh.[43]

The new languages to be spoken are those of the Scriptures and of the Holy Spirit: 'The Holy Spirit has his own grammar'.[44] This applies mainly to the mystery of the Trinity: in theology three are one;[45] and to the incarnation: God is man, a man is God; the word *verbum*, which in philosophy designates only a word, designates in theology a person.[46] But this applies to all the realities of salvation that the

43. *1. Etsi tenendum est quod dicitur. Omne verum vero consonat, tamen idem non est verum in diversis professionibus. 2. In theologia verum est, verbum esse carnem factum, in philosophia simpliciter impossibile et absurdum. 3. Nec minus, imo magis disparata est praedicatio: Deus est homo, quasi dicas: Homo est asinus. 4. Sorbona, mater errorum, pessime definivit: idem esse verum in philosophia et theologia. 40. Rectius ergo fecerimus, si dialectica seu philosophia in sua sphaera relictis discamus loqui novis linguis in regno fidei extra omnem sphaeram. 41. Alioqui futurum est, ut vinum novum in utres ÿeteres mittamus, et utrumque perdamus, ut Sorbona acit. 42. Affectus fidei exercendus est in articulis fidei, non intellectus philosophiae. Tum vere scietur, quid sit. Verbum caro factum est. Disputatio*, WA 39/2:2 and 5. See LW 38:239 and 242, *The Disputation concerning 'The Word Was Made Flesh'*. See also xxi n55 above.
44. '*Spiritus sanctus habet suam grammaticam*', *Disputatio* of 28 February 1540, WA 39/2:104, 22. See LW 73:265, *On the Divinity and Humanity of Christ* (Argument 7, *Against Schwenkfeld*).
45. *Disputatio* of 11 January 1539, WA 39/2:22. See LW 38:255 (Argument 16).
46. *Disputatio* of 1540, WA 39/2:103 (LW 73:264), WA 39/2:121 (LW 73:280) and thesis 20, WA 39/2:94: 'It is certain that all the vocables applied to Christ take on a new meaning, for the same reality signified' (*Certum est tamen, omnia vocabula in Christo novam significationem accipere in eadem re significata*); see LW 73:255. Already in the *Dictata super Psaltarium*: 'That a man should be God is far from all human reason' (*Quod homo sit deus . . . omnis ratio abhorret humana*), WA 4:105,6; see LW 11:258, on *Psalm 95:3*.

Word of God communicates to our faith. Luther often returned to the opposition between the Pauline and Christian meaning of 'God's justice' and the Aristotelian definition of justice, namely, giving to each his due.[47] Aristotle, that 'stinking, rancid philosopher',[48] perverted theology and the truth of the religious relationship with his notion of *habitus*, a reality that would be ours without being attributed to us from outside.[49]

This led Luther to demand a *modus loquendi* for theology, different from the *metaphysicus seu moralis*[50] and to reject the use of dialectics in theology, because theology uses the 'same grammatical terms but in a different way than dialectics',[51] to claim 'a form of expression other than that of nature',[52] 'use of a new language' (*novae linguae usus*),

47. Compare, for example, *Vorlesung über den Galaterbrief, 1516-1517,* edited Hans von Schubert (Heidelberg, 1918), 42; and see WA 57:98,12–18; the *Commentarius* of 1519 (WA 2:562; LW 27:328); and the *Vorrede* (preface) to the 1545 edition of the Latin works, WA 54:185,12–20 (LW 34:336), also Otto Scheel, *Dokumente zu Luthers Entwicklung* (Tübingen: Mohr, 1929), no.511.

48. '*Rancidus philosophus*', *Handbemerkungen zu den Sentenzen* (WA 9:43,5), '*rancidae logicorum regulae*': *Handbemerkungen* (WA 9:47,6). Porphyry shares in Luther's hatred of Aristotle: 'It would have been good for the Church if Porphyry had not been born, with his universals, for the use of theologians', (*Bonum erat ecclesiae si theologis natus non juisset Porphyrus cum suis universalibus*): *Contra Scholasticam Theologiam* (1517), thesis 52, WA 1:226 (see LW 31:13); Letter of 22 February 1518 to Spalatin, WABr 1:150 (see LW 48:59); *Disputatio* of 1539 on John 1:14, WA 39/2:12,3–6. See LW 38:247.

49. Already in the *Handbemerkungen* (WA 9:43,4). Because this makes it possible to attribute a formal justice inherent in the soul: *ad Galatas* of 1531, WA 40/1:225f. See LW 26:127–129, on *Galatians 2:16*.

50. *Scolia* on Romans 7:1 (1516): 'The Apostle does not speak of the law metaphysically or morally, but in a spiritual and theological way' (*Apostolus non metaphysice neque moraliter de lege loquitur, Sed spiritualiter et theologice*); 'The language of the Apostle and the metaphysical or moral language are contrary' (*Modus loquenti Apostoli et modus metaphysicus seu moralis sunt contrarii*): WA 56:334, 3–4 and 14–15; see LW 25:322. *Compare* the *Disputatio* of 1 June 1537, WA 39/1:227,13–15. See Leif Grane, *Modus loquendi theologicus, Luthers Kampf um die Erneuerung der Theologie (1515–1518), Acta Theologica Danica*, XII (Leiden: Schöningh, 1975).

51. '*Eisdem vocabalis grammaticis longe aliter utatur Theologia quam Dialectica*', Letter 61 of 22 February 1518 to Spalatin, WABr 1:150, 24–25. See LW 48:57.

52. '*Aliam formam loqaendi quam est illa nataralis*', *Disputatio de promotion de Palladius et Tileman*, 1 June 1537, WA 39/1:202–257. This little-known text is important; it is one of those in which Luther expresses himself very clearly.

'new terms' (*nova vocabula*),[53] and to be affirmed finally: 'It would be more fitting if we left dialectics or philosophy in their domain and learned to speak new languages in the kingdom of faith, beyond any domain.'[54]

Scholasticism has always recognised what Luther says at the beginning of the *Disputatio* of January 1539 on John 1:14: 'Philosophy and theology differ. Philosophy deals with what is knowable to human reason, theology with objects of faith, with what is accessible to faith.'[55] There is no problem of principle with this distinction between the two fields. The difference seems to me to reside in the fact that the scholastics accepted the use in theology of rational concepts developed in philosophy, and their application to a new given.

This is how Luther saw things: 'When physical terms were transposed to theology, then we had scholastic theology.'[56] Hadn't the Sorbonne defined that the same truth applies to philosophy and theology?[57] This is what Luther could not admit. He admitted the usefulness of dialectic for exercising the mind, as a scholarly and pedagogical utility. He did not posit an absolute heterogeneity between reason exercised on the human level and the same powers, for we have no other, exercised in faith: the same reason operates on the level of creation and redemption.[58] But, in Luther's eyes, the introduction of philosophical concepts with their content betrayed

53. *Disputatio* of 28 February 1540, WA 39/2:94, theses 22,23, see LW 73:255; 'Vocabala nova': WA 39/1:231f., and Luther's speech for the *Promotion of Palladius*, WA 39/1:262,19f.

54. '*Rectius facerimus, si dialectica seu philosophia in sua sphaera relictis, discamas loqui novis lingais in regno fidei extra omnem sphaeram*', Thesis 40 of the *Disputatio* of 11 January 1539 on John 1:14, WA 39/2:5,35–36; see LW 38:242. *Compare* in preceding n52, WA 39/1:231,15.

55. '*Differunt philosophia et theologia. Philosophia versatur circa cognoscibilia ratione humana. Theologia versatur circa credibilia, id est quae fide apprehendantur*', WA 39/2:6,25–28. *Compare* LW 38:244.

56. '*Cum vocabala physica in theologiam translata sunt, facta est inde scholastica quaedam theologia*', *Disputatio* of 1 June 1537: WA 39/1:229,22.

57. Compare thesis 4 of the *Disputatio* of 11 January 1539 on John 1:14 at n97 above, and see LW 38:239; also *Disputatio* of 1 June 1537 (as above n52), WA 39/1:229,27f.

58. This is the conclusion of Bernhard Lohse, *Ratio und Fides. Eine Untersuchung über die ratio in der Theologie Luthers* (Göttingen: Vandenhoeck & Ruprecht, 1957), 155. For the pedagogical utility of dialectic, see the letter of 22 February 1518 to Spalatin, WABr 1:149,11–12, see LW 48:56–59.

the true knowledge of the *quid*, that is, of the original reality of the data of faith.[59]

Of course, Luther reasons. He even proudly claims, against his opponents, that he can do it as well as they can, and even better. He proclaimed that one should not speculate or ask questions out of pure curiosity, but only believe: for example, in the matter of the Eucharist.[60] (94) Yet in spite of everything, Luther did discuss questions philosophically, even when it came to the Eucharist.[61]

Luther had two enemies to bring down, scholastic theology with Aristotle, Porphyry and the Thomists, and papal power demanding adherence to its decretals and canons. He had met these two enemies together when he appeared before the legate Cajetan in October 1518. Cajetan represented the scholastic doctrine of penance and argued for the authority of papal bulls in favour of indulgences. Luther had encountered them in 1519 in the *Disputatio of Leipzig* with John Eck, a scholastic, himself a champion of papal authority. Criticism and struggle excited Luther. From then on, he was to radicalise his positions and his opposition. Luther began to suspect that the antichrist dominated the papal Rome that was trying his case.[62] The outcome would be, after Leo X's bull *Exsurge Domine* (15 June 1520), Luther's publication of the three 'reformation writings',[63] also Luther's response *Adversus execrabilem Antichristi bullam*, and the scene of 10

59. Letter of 22 February 1518 to Spalatin, WABr 1:150,41–42, 'These men are prisoners of Aristotle and Porphyry. They pay attention not to what they say but to the fact that they say' (*Sunt et illi homines Aristoteli et Purphyrio Captivi, Nec Quid, sed quia dicunt, advertunt*). See LW 48:59.
60. To Paul Speratus 13 June 1522, WABr 2:561; *De captivitate Babylonica*, WA 6:510, see LW 36:32–33. The fault of Mûnzer, the Anabaptists, the Sacramentarians, Zwingli and Oecolampadius is that they had allowed themselves to be inflated by the virus of knowledge: *Vorlesung über Genesis* on Genesis 15:1, WA 42:552,9–16. See LW 3:5–6, *Genesis*.
61. Compare: Link, *Das Ringen Luthers*, 165, 206–208, 382; Grane, *Contra Gabrielem*, 380: 'In spite of the struggle against the influence of philosophy on theology, Luther's writings are rich in material of a philosophical nature'. For the Eucharist, see (for example), *De captivitate Babylonica*, WA 6:508f; *compare* LW 36:28–31.
62. Compare his letter of 18 December 1518 to Wenceslas Link, WABr 1:270,11–13.
63. Mid-August 1520, *An den christlichen Adel Deutscher Nation: von des christlichen Standes Besserung* (WA 6:404–469, LW 44:115–217); in October, *De captivitate Babylonica ecclesiae praeludium* (WA 6:497–573, LW 36:3–126); at the same time, backdated to 6 September, *De libertate christiana* (German: WA 7:1–38 and Latin: 42–73, LW 31:327–377).

December 1520 where outside the Elster Gate, Luther publicly burned the papal bull and the books of canon law. He did so in the name of his dual status as a Christian and a sworn doctor of Holy Scripture.[64]

Rome herself condemned him as a heretic. At least from the time of Gregory VII onwards, Rome had considered all those who opposed her decisions to be heretics. Luther did not accept this view. Since one is made a Christian by faith in the Word of God, it is only by contradicting it that one would be a heretic. Far from opposing it, he was faithful to it. He challenged the normative character of papal decisions in the order of faith. For him, it was the papists, 'Thomists' and others who were heretics![65]

64. WA 7:162; see LW 31:383, *Why the Books of the Pope and his Disciples were Burned* (1520).
65. Compare: *Acta Augustana*, WA2:18,14, see LW 31:278, *Proceedings at Augsburg* (1518); letters to Karlstadt, 14 October 1518, WABr 1:217,61f; to Miltitz, 17 May 1519, WABr 1:402,37.

How Luther was a Reformer

His Reform and His Church

That Luther, as a religious and a priest, was committed to the Church, that is, to the Catholic Church, is evident from a large number of passages in the *Dictata super Psalterium* of 1513-1515. This has been shown in various studies.[1] In his letters concerning his appearance before Cajetan, October 1518, Luther says it is for the Church to judge. He seems to be using the word as commonly understood in the sense of 'the authorities', and even as the papal authority.[2] Until 1522, Luther addressed the bishops as any Catholic might do. If, as E. Iserloh has established, Luther did not post the *Ninety-five Theses* but only sent them to the bishops and universities, he followed an ecclesiastically correct procedure. He referred the Bohemians to the

1. For example (from Catholics): W Wagner, 'Die Kirche als Corpus Christi mysticum beim jungen Luther', in *Zeitschrift* für Katholische Theologie, 61 (1937): 29–98; Joseph Lortz, 'Zum Kirchendenken des jungen Luther', in *Wahrheit und Verkündigung: Festgabe M.Schmaus* (München-Paderborn, 1967), 2, 947–986.
2. Thus in his letter of 13 February 1518 to the bishop of Brandenburg (WABr 1:138,16) 'while waiting for the Holy Church to pronounce', (*donec ecclesia sancta statueret*); in that of 18 October to Cajetan, where he announces his departure from Augsburg (WABr 1:223,19), 'as I have deferred all things to the judgment of the Church', (*cum ego omnia in iudicium ecclesiae retulerim*), Ibid, (223,27), 'I am attentive to what the Church will say', (*quid ecclesia dictura sit attendo*), Ibid, (223,40), 'the Church must first condemn', (*damnet ecclesia prius*). See LW48:87–89, *Letter to Cajetan*. Compare the *Resolutiones disputationum de indulgentiarum virtute*, WA 1:573,35 and 619,37 (see LW31:156 and 236): until an official decision (of the council) Luther says the question was debatable.

bishop of Prague.[3] Until the end of 1520, he multiplied his protests of respect and obedience. I am somewhat troubled by this, and wonder what it means when we know the radical nature of his criticism and his positions.[4] But there can be no doubt that Luther would have preferred a reform of the Roman Church to the Gospel, without a schism.

He had formed his doctrine, he had emerged from his spiritual anguish, by finding Christ in Scripture, a Christ who takes away our sins and communicates his justice to us. In his *Vorlesung über den Römerbrief*, in 1516, he expressed his awareness of having to react against what he perceived as evil:

> For my part, I believe I owe it to the Lord in this task: to cry out against philosophy and to promote Sacred Scripture.[5]

3. *An den christlichen Adel,* WA 6:456,31–34; see LW 44:198–199, *To the Christian Nobility of the German Nation.* Luther often distanced himself from the Bohemians and criticised their disobedience. Martin Brecht, *Martin Luther. Sein Weg zur Reformation* (Stuttgart: Calwer, 1981), 473n11, refers for this to WA 1:69,20–24; WA 1:425,35–426,1; WA 3:334;24–29 (LW 10:278–279); WA 4:345,24–27 (LW 11:470); WA 9:188,13–16; WA 31/1:475,30–476,36; WA 56:494,9–17 (LW25:487–488). See Martin Brecht, *Martin Luther. His Road to Reformation.* Translated by James Schaaf (Philadephia: Fortress, 1985), 146n11.
4. At the beginning of 1519, the papal nuncio Miltitz negotiated a settlement in Saxony. Luther declared himself ready to remain silent on the points under discussion (?), and expressed respect and obedience towards the Roman Church: see *Unterricht auff etlich artickell,* WA 2:72–73 (February 1519) and letter of 4 March to Spalatin, WABr 1:356: obedience to a power is of little importance, there is only one important thing, faith in Christ and the Gospel. See also the *Vorrede* of 1545, WA 54:184,26–30; see LW 34:335, *Preface to the Latin Writings.* What can be the meaning of such a paragraph of the letter of 5 or 6 January 1519 to Leo X (WABr 1:292,31–293,48, see LW 48:102), and the letter sent to Leo as the forward of *De libertate christiana,* backdated to 6 September 1520 (WA 7:3–11 or, Latin text, 42–49, see LW 31:334–343)? Did Luther think he could win him over, mixing honey with vitriol? Would this neutralise his Roman opponents? What could the *Erbieten,* the protest addressed to Charles V on 30 August 1520, mean, 'I want to die as a suppliant and obedient son of the holy Catholic Church' (*ut filius supplex et obediens Sanctae Ecclesiae Catholicae . . . mori volo*)? WA 6:482,29–30.
5. '*Ego quidem Credo me debere Domino hoc obsequium latrandi contra philosophiam et suadendi ad Sacram Scripturam*', WA 56:371,17–18; see LW 25:361 *Lectures on Romans.*

> [B]ecause I fulfil the task of teaching by apostolic authority, it is incumbent on me to say whatever I see deviating from the right path, even among those in high places'.[6]

Luther refers to his status as a doctor, conferred by the proper authorities. It played a very large role in his life.[7] He insisted on the fact that he had received a mission from the Church, that he was *vocatus*, a sworn doctor of Scripture.[8]

He stresses the fact that he did not seek it, that he was appointed in spite of himself, *invitus*, which was the sign of a true vocation to office, a vocation from God.[9] He was seized, grabbed. He obeyed like a blind horse being led. He was aware that he had received from heaven and from Jesus Christ a *revelatio evangelii*.[10] From the years following his promotion (1512), Luther was keenly aware that he was a man

6. '*Quia authoritate Apostolica officio docendi fungor, Meum est dicere quecumque videro non recta fieri, etiam in sublimioribus*', WA 56:480,5–7; see LW 25:472.
7. I dealt with this point in *Vraie et fausse réforme* (1950), 510–514; 1969, 455–459. I also drew on Hans Preuss, *Martin Luther, Der Prophet* (Gütersloh: Bertelsmann, 1933), 96–99 and 107–119.
8. 'Vocatus' (*called*): letter of 31 October 1517 sending 95 theses to the Archbishop of Mainz, WABr 1:112; see LW 48:49). 'Geschworner' (*sworn*): *An den christlichen Adel*, WA 6:405,1 (LW 44:124); also *Warum des Papstes Bücher verbrannt sind*, 27 December 1520, WA 7:162,9 (or 23, 'iuratus'), see LW 31:383, *Why the Books of the Pope were Burned*.
9. For example, *Dictata super Psalterium*, WA3:14; see LW 10:8, *Preface to the Scholia*; letter of 22 September 1512 to André Lohr (WA Br1:18, *compare* LW 48:6); letter of 14 January 1520 to Spalatin (WABr 1:611,43f. 'out of obedience', compare LW 48:146); the *Erbieten*, ('protestatio') of 1520 (WA 6,482,13f. and 483,11–12); *Commentary on Psalm 82* (1530): 'I never wished to do this (attack Rome), nor do I wish to do it today. I was first forced and pushed into it when I became a doctor of Sacred Scripture, against my will. Then, as a doctor in a free university by the will of the Pope and the Emperor, I set myself to do what such a doctor undertakes by oath to do: to expound the Scriptures for all the world and to teach all the world. I must stick to this and cannot in good conscience renounce it', (WA 31/1:212, see LW 13:66). Compare also Erwin Iserloh, *Luther zwischen Reform und Reformation*, third edition (Munster: Aschendorff, 1966), 82, who refers to the *Theses* of 1538, WA 39/1:6,9–32, and to WATr 1:n1206. For numerous uses of the verb 'rapi[o]' (*seized*), see Preuss, *Martin Luther*, 110f.
10. Letter of 5 March 1522, to Frederick the Wise, WA Br2:455, see LW 48:390.

providentially chosen, raised up and led by God for an exceptional work.[11]

His superior and friend Staupitz had assured him that he had a mission to fulfil and that God had not raised up a man of his worth and experience for nothing.[12] In Augsburg itself, on the eve of his appearance before the legate, he had encouraged him: 'Remember, brother, that you began all this in the name of our Lord Jesus Christ'.[13]

'All this' was the criticism of 'works' and especially of indulgences; it was the proposal for a new theology and a new preaching in conformity with Scripture and centred on Jesus Christ the Saviour. It was the programme that Luther expressed in his letter of 9 May 1518 to Trutfetter: 'I simply believe that it is impossible to reform the Church until canons, decretals, scholastic theology, philosophy, logic, as they now exist, are thoroughly uprooted, and other studies are established' (see 30n26). Leif Grane correctly writes: 'He became a reformer because, on the basis of his newly acquired vision of how the Bible should be understood, he had to reject the foundations on which theology was practised at the end of the Middle Ages'.[14] In May 1518 Luther wrote his *Resolutiones disputationum de indulgentiarum virtute.* It came off the presses in August, and was known by Cajetan. It reads:

> The Church needs reform; it cannot be the task of one man, the Pontiff, nor of several Cardinals, as the last Council proved, but that of the whole world, indeed of God alone.[15]

---

11. On this compare Karl Holl, 'Luthers Urteil über sich selbst' in *Gesammelte Aufsätze zur Kirchengeschichte* (Tübingen: Mohr Siebeck, 1903), 1,381–419; Preuss, *Martin Luther*, 73ff, 96ff, 119ff; Hans Von Campenhausen, 'Reformatorisches Selbstbewusstsein und reformatorisches Geschichtsbewusstsein bei Luther, 1517–1522', in *Archiv* für *Reformationsgeschichte*, 37 (1940), 128–150, reprinted in *Tradition und Leben*, (Tübingen: Mohr Siebeck, 1960), 318–342.
12. Letter of 1530 to H Weller: O Scheel, *Dokumente zu Luthers Entwicklung*, no.138, 54,4–6.
13. Letter of 14 January 1521 to Staupitz, WABr 2:245–246; see LW 48:191–194.
14. Grane, *Contra Gabrielem*, 321.
15. 'Ecclesia indiget reformatione, quod non est unius hominis Pontificis nec multorum Cardinalium officium, sicut probavit utrumque novissimum concilium, sed totius orbis, immo solius dei', *Resolutiones*, conclusio 89: WA 1:627,27–30; see LW31:250, *Explanations of the Ninety-Five Theses*.

Soon, opposed by Eck, by the University of Louvain, and threatened by Roman censorship, Luther wrote (summer 1519):

> I believe myself to be a Christian theologian and to live in the kingdom of truth, which is why I believe it to be my duty, not only to affirm the truth, but to support and defend it, even at the cost of my blood or death. From now on I want to be free and become the prisoner of no one, of a council, of a power, of the universities or by pontifical authority.[16]

A year later, in his rather cavalier dedication of *De libertate christiana* to Leo X, Luther wrote: 'I do not argue with anyone about morals, but only about the word of truth. On everything else I will yield, but I cannot and will not desert the word (. . .) I do not suffer laws that must interpret the word of God, whereas the word of God should not be bound, it which teaches freedom to all others.'[17]

Already well advanced in his opposition to those who upheld the old Church, very resolute, very sure of himself as a theologian of Scripture, Luther sometimes asked himself, 'Are you alone wise. Were you alone the first to understand the truth?'[18] His opponents reproached him for innovating. He replied that he was protesting against Roman innovations and re-establishing the truth of the origins.[19] His friends advised him to be moderate.[20] He responded by criticising the prudence of the hesitant, all-too-human prudence of Erasmus.[21]

16. *Resolutiones Lutherianae super proposionibus suis Lipsiae disputatis*: WA 2:404,11–15.
17. WA 7:43,36–37 and 47,28–30; see LW31:335 and 341, *The Freedom of a Christian* (1520).
18. *Resolutiones Lutherianae*, WA 2:43,16 f.; *Vom Missbrauch der Messe* (1521), WA 8:482,32 f.; see LW 36:34, *The Misuse of the Mass*; WATr 3:439,6. Other references are in WA 58/1, *Gesamtregister*, 145.
19. Thus in the *Vermahnung an die Geistlichen* (1530), WA 30/2:347f, see LW34:54–58; *Das 16. Kapitel Johannes gepredigt und ausgelegt* (1538), WA 46:62,27f, see LW 24:368, *Sermon on John 16*; *Wider Hans Worst* (1541), WA 51:478,31f., see LW 41:194–195; WA 51:487,18f, see LW41:199, *Against HansWurst*. Compare Preuss, *Martin Luther*, 169*ff*.
20. Thus, in 1518, Christoph Scheurl (WABr 1:274, 275, 279), in 1520 Luther's superior Jean Lang (WA 6:396), and Erasmus (WABr 2:158,22 f.).
21. Thus in letters to Staupitz, 9 February 1521 (WABr 2:264,42f.); on Erasmus, to *Anon*, Leipzig, 28 May 1522 (WABr 2:544–545, see LW 49:7–9), to Oecolampadius, 20 June 1523 (WABr 3:96–97, see LW 49:43–44) and 1 October 1531 (WABr 3:160,34–35), 'May he learn Christ and say farewell to human prudence!' (*discat Christam et valefaciat humanae pradentiae!*).

The choice to be made was radical, it was simply between Christ and Satan![22] He recognised that he was carried away, *irasciblem*.[23] He was harsh. But without that temperament, he would have done nothing.[24] And that did not stop him from feeling weary at times, if not discouraged.[25] And what followed was disappointing: 'Thanks be that God did not show beforehand how many sects would spring up. I would not have dared to begin!'[26]

Luther's whole assurance, like the entire principle of the Reformation, consisted in the Word of God. The Word became flesh. It was Jesus Christ; it was Scripture, of which Jesus Christ is the content. Reforms had indeed been made, but they were only minor reforms, questions of shoes and dress: that was not where we should start, but

---

22. Thus letters to Claus Storm of 15 June 1522 (WABr 2:563); of 27 June to Staupitz (WABr 2:567, see LW 49:12–13); of 18 August to *Anon.* (WABr 2:594). Erasmus and the papists were not aligning themselves with Scripture: 'they lack agreement in faith and doctrine: it is impossible to unite' (*coire nulla concordia in fide et doctrina potest*), *Vorrede zu Antonius Corvinus* (1534), WA 38:278, see LW 60:62.
23. *Vorlesang über Genesis*, WA43:46,11, see LW3:239; Holl, 'Luthers Urteil', 383n4 and 409n3f.; Preuss, *Martin Luther*, 147f.
24. Holl, quoted above: Luther thought he had waited too long to rebel against the Pope: letter of 15 June 1522 to Claus Storm, WABr 2:563,89f. Also *Rationis latomianae confutatio*, WA 8:45, see LW 32:139, *Against Latomus* (1521). In his 1519 *Ad Galatas commentarius,* he wrote: 'You are still biting? I am not biting, but having to shed light on Scripture, I am showing the morals of our century so that we can see where the glory of the Church stands, which Church is true and which is false. To put it bluntly, it's impossible to shed light on Scripture and to reform the other Churches if we don't reform that universal reality, the Roman Curia, as quickly as possible. The Roman Curia cannot listen to the Word of God, nor can it tolerate its pure exposition. And if the word of God is not exposed, it is impossible to help the other Churches' (*Iterum mordes? Non mordeo, sed necessitate scripturae elucidandae nostri saeculi mores commonstro ut videamus, quo pervenerit gloria ecclesiae et quae sit vera aut ficta ecclesia. Et at dicam libere, impossibile est, scripturas posse elucidari et alias ecclesias reformari, nisi universale illad reale, Romana curia, quam primum reformetur. Haec enim verbam dei audire non potes! nec sustinere ut pure tractetur: verbo autem dei non tractato neque ceteris ecclesiis succurri potest*): WA 2:609,8–14, see LW 27:397–398, *Commentary on Galatians.* The prophets 'were biting': letter to Leo X, WA 7:43,22f., see LW 31:335, *The Freedom of a Christian.*
25. Texts in Preuss, *Martin Luther*, 127.
26. *Annotationes in ep. Pauli ad Titam* (winter 1527), WA 25:10,18, see LW 29:8, *Lectures on Titus.*

with teaching![27] In a sermon on the Decalogue in the winter of 1516–1517, Luther developed a whole code of ethics for the use of words, with regard to the precept 'You must not bear false witness against your neighbour'. This applies first and foremost to 'theologians and all those who pass on the faith to their disciples'. The theologians 'sin more grievously than anyone else against this commandment when they pervert Sacred Scripture and the Word of God, explain it falsely and apply it inaccurately' Among them are true heretics, who teach errors. Secondly, there are those who, without teaching falsehoods, fall short of what they should teach, for example—we are before the autumn of 1517—those who, being saved by faith in Christ, teach the righteousness of works and speak more of works than of faith. After the theologians came the jurists. 'They could well be the wretched kind of men who deceive themselves and exhaust themselves with the false title of Aristotle's philosophy, which is misunderstood'.[28] Then come the deceptions of superstition. Luther comments: 'But woe, woe and more woe to such tellers of fables. Here above all we need a reform of the Church, such that nothing but the pious and the good is allowed to be preached, nothing that is not authentic and canonised'.[29]

If the seriousness of what was being preached had been taken to heart, if the false relics had been excluded, if Tetzel had been brought back to the authentic Gospel, the drama that was about to unfold would undoubtedly have been avoided. In the beginning,

27. *Vorlesung über Genesis*, WA 44:170,35 and 171,39. See LW 6:230 and 231–232. In a speech addressed in 1512 to the dean of Leitzkau, Georges Mascov, Luther said that fornication and drinking are considered serious offences, and of course they must be corrected. Many priests consider it a greater fault to have sinned carnally, to have failed to pray, to have made a mistake in the canon than to have failed to preach the word of truth or to have failed to expound it correctly. Yet this is their proper and principal office. This is where the most serious faults should be placed, but what pontiff cares? (WA 1:12–13). [Editor's note: *possibly* from 1515]
28. *Decem praecepta Wittenbergensi praedicata* populo (1517), WA 1:505–510, *variously*.
29. WA 1:509,18–34. Luther relates the example of a woman who had shaved her pubic hair and presented it as the hair of Saint Catherine. It was worshipped and worked miracles! Another example: hay was taken and made to look like Christ had slept on it. For the summary, with its threefold "woe!" (*v[a]e*), see WA 1:509,38–510,2 (*Sed ve, ve atque ve iterum talibus fabulatoribus. Opus hic esset maxime reformatione ecclesiae ut prorsus nihil quantumcumque pium et bonum praedicari permitteretur, nisi quod authenticum et canonisatum esset*).

Luther's reform was just that, a reform of teaching and preaching in conformity with this fundamental truth: Jesus Christ is the Saviour, and he alone. The reformist programme of *An den christlichen Adel* —which Luther elsewhere describes as 'a writing directed at the Pope concerning the reform to be made in the Church'[30]—included the reform of the universities.[31]

The *Vermahnung* written in Coburg for the ecclesiastics gathered at the Diet of Augsburg in 1530 also contains a detailed programme of reform. Luther attributed his attack on the Pope, indulgences and monasticism to his teaching, his *Lehre.*[32] Later still, in his *Vorlesung über Genesis* of 1535–1545, he placed at the forefront the fight against replacing the only Saviour, Jesus Christ, with the saints, and concluded:

> Let us therefore direct our minds and all our concerns to the one God, Father, Son and Holy Spirit, and let us abide in the mediator, Christ. This is the first act of reform (. . .). It is a fine reform to begin by cleansing doctrine.[33]

I will not go into detail about the reforms called for in *An den christlichen Adel* or the *Vermahnung an die Geistlichen*, nor will I list the other uses of the word *reformatio.*[34] What is most important for my research is that, in Luther's eyes, everything depends on doctrinal truth and must begin with the word. For the word (The Word) makes

---

30. 'Libellus in Papam de reformanda ecclesia', *Letter to Wenceslas Link*, Nuremberg, 20 July 1520: WABr 2:146.
31. This is the twenty-fifth point, WA 6:457,28–462,11, see LW 44:200–207; even for the universities Luther speaks of a 'good, strong reformation' (WA 6:457,28; LW 44:200). He adds the teaching of the Gospel and the catechism in schools (WA 6:461,11–23; LW 44:205–206).
32. WA 30/2:278–281; see LW34:14–15, *Exhortation to all Clergy* (1530).
33. '*Referamus igitur mentes nostras et omnia studia ad unum Deum, qui est pater, filius et spiritus sanctus, et maneamus in mediatore Christo. Haec prima est pars reformationis . . .. Haec pulchra reformatio est, qua primum doctrina repurgetur*': *Genesis,* WA 44:170,35f. and WA 44:171,37. See LW 6:230 and 231–232.
34. Note, however: the suppression of the 'Stiften' (religious foundations) and monasteries 'were the best reformation', *Adventpostille* (1522): WA 10/1.2:176,29; see LW 75:162n15. A 'reformatío missae' (reform of the Mass) was needed (*Postille* on John 1:1–14, 25 December 1522: WA 10/1,1:180-246). Other references in WA 58/1, *Gesamtregister*, 43.

the Church. The Church is *creatura verbi divini*.[35] Luther repeats that the Word has done everything; it overthrew the papacy,[36] it will change the world, but not without painful crises.[37]

It is precisely the Papacy, the Roman Curia, which is opposed to any serious reform because it is opposed to the Word, to the Gospel, to Christ. 'They fear reformation' (*Reformari metuit*), said Luther to Leo X.[38]

And, in *Von den Konzíliis und Kirchen*: 'Because the pope refuses to hold a council and does not want to reform the Churches, we are obliged to look elsewhere for advice and help and to seek and ask our Lord Christ for reform.'[39] 'This papacy is contrary to Christ, it is opposed to him and to his Gospel, so it deserves the description of antichrist'.[40] It became, for Luther, the exponent or personification

35. *Resolutiones . . . Lipsiae disputatis*, 1519, WA 2:430,6; Sermon of 15 March 1525 on Matthew 28:10f. (WA 17/1:99,3–100,14). There are innumerable texts with the same meaning, some of which were quoted in my *Vraie et fausse réforme* (second edition, 1969) 365f, nn96,101,102.
36. 'Faith will be born and the necessary reforms will take place if the Word acts freely. Take my example. I opposed the Papists without resorting to violence. I simply put into practice the Word of God (. . .) This Word, while I slept, did everything to weaken the papacy': Sermon of 10 March 1522 (WA 10/3:13–20), in Henri Strohl, *La Substance de l'Évangile selon Luther*, (Paris, 1934), 25. Compare LW 51:77, *Eight sermons at Wittenberg* (The Second Sermon), (1522).
37. *De servo arbitrio*, WA 18:626,26; see LW 33:50–53, *The Bondage of the Will* (1525).
38. WA 7:44,23f. [editor's note: Congar has here, 'Reformari *maluit*'] See LW 33:336. *The Freedom of a Christian.*
39. '*Weil der Papst . . . abschlegt ein Concilium zu halten und die Kirchen nicht Reformiren . . . will, so müssen wir . . . uns anderswo umb rat hülffe umbthun, und zuforderst bey unsern Herrn Christo ein Reformation suchen und bitten*', WA 50:512,13f; see LW 41:11, *On the Councils and the Church*. Luther did not believe that the Papal Church was capable of reform. After having hoped for a 'free' council, he could no longer believe in it: *Von den Konzilíis und Kirchen* (1539), WA 50:511,22f, (see LW 41:9–11); WA 50:512,13f. and 514, (LW 41:12–14). See *also* in WA 50:288 (LW 41:9), etc. In WATr 3:402, no.3551, 19 March 1537, the concession of communion in the chalice and the marriage of priests would be insufficient: 'We want to have an authentic doctrine of faith and justification', (*volumus hebere etiam doctrinam fidei et iustificationis sinceram*). See LW 51:231, *Table Talk*.
40. The idea that the pope was the antichrist first appeared in Luther's writings in 1518, and from 1522 onwards it became an essential part not only of his polemics but also of his theology. It is not a question of this or that pope, but of the papacy itself insofar as it is essentially the claim to the sovereign regulation of the belief, practice and behaviour of the faithful, in place of the sole Word of God and

of the opposite of what he believed and adhered to, hence the name of what he hated. Paul Reiter even says that Luther concretised his psychosis in the figure of the pope.[41]

I have often asked myself, when did the break occur? Joseph Lortz said that it was with the publication of *De captivitate Babylonica*, in October 1520.[42] Luther set out his doctrine on the sacraments, which he reduced to two: baptism and the Lord's Supper. The rejection of the sacrament of Holy Orders would be decisive here. But when Luther wrote 'this sacrament was invented by the Church of the Pope',[43] he was forgetting the orthodox East. In fact, the Lutheran real-life practice (*vecue*), expressed in numerous texts by Luther himself, is more positive than his denials of principle.[44] The new ecclesial communities had to be structured and brought to life.

Luther had wanted nothing more than an evangelical reform of the existing Church. The Church, with its responsible pastors, had not only failed to follow Luther, but had instituted a so-called heresy trial against him, the herald of the true faith, and had excommunicated him. It was not, Luther believed, the authentic Church, the Church of Christ, which had excommunicated him.[45] From the beginning there were two peoples, one from Abel and one from Cain, as Augustine

---

Jesus Christ alone. Since he is opposed to the Gospel, the Pope is, in his claims to authority, the antichrist. See Hans Preuss, *Die Vorstellungen vom Antichrist im späteren Mittelalter, bei Luther und in der konfessionellen Polemik* (Leipzig: Hartmann & Wolf, 1906), 49–63; also Hartmann GRISAR and Franz HAEGE, *Luthers Kampfbilder*, volume 1, *Passionale Christi und Antichristi* (Freiburg: Herder, 1921–23); and Ernst Bizer, *Luther und der Papst* München: Kaiser, 1959.

41. Paul J Reiter, *Martin Luthers Umwelt, Charakter und Psychose*, 2 volumes (Copenhagen: Leven & Munksgaard, 1937 and 1941), 1:385. See 'Study Four' below.
42. Joseph Lortz, 'Zum Kirchendenken des jungen Luther' (see 39n1), 2:953.
43. 'Hoc sacramentum . . . inventumque est ab ecclesia Papae', *De captivitate Babylonica*: WA 6:560,20–21, see LW 36:106.
44. Compare Paul Manns, 'Amt und Eucharistie in der Theologie Martin Luthers', in *Amt und Eucharistie*, edited by P Blàser (Paderborn, 1973), 68–173.
45. Eighteen years after the Event, Luther was still keen to make it clear that he had not been excommunicated by the true Church: *Das XVI. Kapitel St Johannis gepredigt und ausgelegt* (1538): WA 46:8; see LW 24:306, on John 16:2 'they will put you out of synagogues'.

explains.[46] In what we would today call the sociological Church, or the Christian world, there is a true and a false Church, a *vera* and a *ficta*.[47] The true Church is the one which, adhering to the Word, is made up of fideles, true Christians who are such by faith. Texts abound proclaiming this.[48]

As early as the *Dictata super Psalterium*, Luther often speaks of *populus fidelis*.[49] He liked to describe the Church as 'Christendom', 'congregatio sanctorum', the flock of Christ, which recognises and follows his voice. 'The kingdom of Christ is none other than the kingdom of those who believe in God's Word'.[50] The Church is 'an assembly of all believing Christians on earth'.[51] On the other hand, a false Church (here, the Papal Church) is based on reason and human laws:

---

46. *Vorlesung über Genesis*, WA 42:187,13f, (see LW1:252, on Cain and Abel): 'This is where the Church begins to divide itself into a Church which is Church in name but in reality is only a hypocritical and bloodthirsty Church, and another', (*Hic incipit ecclesia dividí: in ecclesiam quae nomine ecclesia est, re nihil est nisi hypocritica et sanguinaria ecclesia, et alteram*). And compare: WA 42:229,37 (LW 1:311); WA 43:38,5 (LW 3:227); WA 44:23,18 (LW 6:32); For Augustine on 'two peoples', see *Wider Hans Worst* (1541), WA 51:477,30 (LW 41:194).
47. *Ad Galatas commentarius* (1519), WA 2:609,10, see LW 27:398; *Von dem Papsttum zu Rom* (1520), WA 6:296,38, see LW 39:70, *On the Papacy in Rome*. Also, Letter of 11 December 1522 to *Wolfgang Stein*, WABr 2:623,63ff.
48. Need references be given? But compare: *De captivitate Babylonica*, WA 6:560–61 (LW 36:106–108); *Von dem Papsttum*, WA 6:292 (LW 39:64–65); *ad Librum Ambrosii Catharini Responsio*, WA 7:742; *Von den Konziliis*, WA 50:624–525 (LW 41:143–144); Luther's two Catechisms; and compare the *Augsburg Confession*, articles VII (*congregatio sanctorum*) and VIII (*congregatio sanctorum et vere credentium*): BK:61–62, see BC:43. See also Melanchthon in 1539: 'The Church is an assembly linked not to succession in the office but to the Word of God. The Church is reborn where God restores doctrine and gives the Holy Spirit' (*De Ecclesia et auctoritate verbi Dei*: CR 23:598).
49. This term, frequent in the *Dictata*, gave its title to Joseph Vercruysse's *Fidelis Populus* (Wiesbaden: Steiner, 1968), an analysis of various ecclesiological themes in the *Dictata*.
50. 'Das Reich christi ist nichts anderes als das Reich des Glaubens im Worte Gottes', *Praelectiones in prophetas minores . . . Ioel* (1524), WA 13:113,32; see LW 18:111, *Lectures on Joel*.
51. 'Eine Versammlung aller Christgläubigen auf Erden', *Von den Papsttum*, WA 6:292,37–38; see LW 39:65, *On the Papacy in Rome*.

> The Pope's Church is not the true Church because it is the Church of the first birth (. . .) The Romans founded the most beautiful juridical structures and laws (. . .) but they are only reason, which is born of the flesh, of woman and man.[52]

Insofar as the Church consists in faith, its reality is hidden, invisible. It belongs to the realm of faith. Luther often says this.[53] The Church does not consist in visible things, but it is not in this world without these visible things. Made within by the Holy Spirit, who sanctifies, the Church depends outside on the three great means or signs which are the preached Gospel, baptism and 'the sacrament' (of the Eucharist).[54]

> The signs by which it can be seen externally where this same Church is in the world are baptism, the sacrament of the altar and the Gospel. Where there is baptism and the Gospel, no one can doubt that there are saints.[55]

Luther endeavoured to create, nurture and organise Churches according to these standards. It is not my intention here to judge the value of this ecclesiology from a theological point of view, nor from a historical point of view, the degree of success and failure, of evangelical ambition and illusion, which in fact came to fruition. I am impressed by the almost superhuman effort that Luther made to preach, advise, intervene, animate and set up (*dresser*, as Calvin

---

52. '*Papistica Ecclesia non est vera ecclesia quia incedunt in prima nativitate (. . .) Romani condiderunt pulcherrima iura et leges (. . .) sed nihil aliud sant quam ratio, quae nata est ex carne, miiliere et viro*', *Vorlesung uber Genesis*, WA 43:386,21f.; see LW 4:347. Compare the *Vermahnung* of 1530, with its astonishing radicalism, addressed as it was to the '*geistlichen*' gathered at the Diet of Augsburg (where Melanchthon presented the Confession and spoke in favour of an agreement). This is where the painful formula is found: 'Alive, I am a pest for you [, Pope]; dead, I will be your death'. WA 30/2:321,30 and 339,33–34; see LW 34:39 and 49, *Exhortation to all Clergy at Augsburg*. In the form of the famous Latin hexameter, this sentence appears on Luther's tombstone, prepared for Wittenberg but preserved only in Halle.
53. References given in my *Vraie et fausse réforme*, second edition (1969), 351n63.
54. *Von dem Papsttum*, WA 6:295,22 and 301,3–10, see LW 39:68 and 75; *Von Abendmahl Christi*, WA 26:505,38–506,12, see LW 37:367–368, *Confession concerning Christ's Supper* (1528).
55. *Von dem Papsttum*, WA 6:301,3–6; see LW 39:75.

would say) the Churches of the Gospel. If the papacy educated the West through its decretals, Luther was like the pope of the new Church born of his reformation. From 1519 onwards, he published either sermons or short treatises to provide guidance in accordance with the Gospel in matters of prayer and piety.

The protagonists of the ancient Church obviously reproached this Church, which was being constituted opposite the other and in opposition to it, for being new. Luther's response, as we have seen, was firstly that he was returning to the forms of the old tradition against medieval innovations, and secondly that God had always reserved for himself a people who would be faithful to sound doctrine.[56]

In my 1947–1950 study of Luther's ecclesiology, I based my reading very largely on the opposition between exterior and interior, with the two series of ideas that are interdependent or equivalent:

> **exterior** = corporeal = visible / reason = nature = first carnal birth = *jura politica, disciplina, leges* = *res, loca, corpora*;
> **interior** = spiritual = invisible = faith = second birth, concerning vocation and the word = Spirit, from God's own being.

It seemed to me that Luther had already dissociated the pure act of God (of the Holy Spirit) internally through faith, and the external means of grace which, taken in themselves, i.e. isolated from faith, are purely human and carnal.[57]

I felt that this made a satisfactory ecclesiology impossible. Now it is true that Luther contrasts the *coram Deo* and the *coram hominibus*, or the reality of the two realms, on which a new study appears almost every year. But, while citing authors who have interpreted Luther in this way, in particular Reinhold Seeberg, I had not taken sufficient account of the fact that, for him, the external means are also from God (from Christ). They require faith, it is true; the adage so often

56. *Vorlesung über Genesis*, WA 42:241,12–35 (LW 1:327–328); 423,19–424,8 (LW 2:229). Compare also *Vermahnung an die Geistlichen*, WA 30/2:345f. (LW 34:54–58); *Wider Hans Worst*, WA 51:476f., 501, (LW 41:193–194 and 207). This was then developed in the theme of the precursors of the Reformation or the 'Reformers before the Reformation': bibliographical references in my *Vraie et fausse réforme*, second edition, 1969, 413n199.

57. Congar, *Vraie et fausse réforme dans l'Eglise* (Paris, 1950,) 382; (second edition, 1969), 345f.

repeated and which Luther calls a 'well-known and widely accepted maxim', *non sacramentum (tantum), sed fides sacramenti* ('not the sacrament [alone], but faith in the sacrament'), runs the risk of making us ignore the proper contribution of the sacrament. Hence Cajetan's reaction and that of the Council of Trent (defining exactly *ex opere operato*). But two facts must be given full weight. Firstly, Luther's very formal rejection of Donatism. Secondly, his frequent appreciation of the Papal Church as 'Church'.

Of course, for Luther this was not the true Church of Christ. However, not only were there still true believers in it—the seven thousand who did not bend the knee to Baal[58] —but this remnant of the faithful was made such by the external means of grace. Here are some explicit texts, in translation.[59]

> We recognise that under the Papacy there exists much Christian good, indeed all Christian good, and that it has even come to us from there. Specifically, we acknowledge that under the Papacy there exists authentic Holy Scripture, authentic Baptism, the authentic Sacrament of the Altar, the authentic keys to the forgiveness of sins, the authentic office of preaching, the authentic catechism, such as the Lord's Prayer and the Ten Commandments, the Articles of Faith (. . .) authentic Christianity.[60]

> The same holy Church is the holy place of abomination. For God has, by his power and by miracle, preserved what has remained under the pope: first, holy baptism; second, in the pulpit, the text of the holy gospel in the language of each country. Thirdly, the holy forgiveness of sins and absolution, both in confession and publicly. Fourthly, the holy sacrament of the altar, which is given to Christians at Easter and throughout the year, even though they have stolen a *species* from it. Fifthly, the vocation or ordination to the office of parish priest, preacher or pastor, to bind or loose sins, and at the time of death and also for some other consolation. For among many the custom has remained of representing

58. *Vom Dolmetschen und Fürbitte der Heiligen* (1530): WA 30/2:645; see LW 35:200, *On Translating.*
59. I owe the references to Preuss, *Martin Luther*, 228, as well as others.
60. *Von der Wiedertauffe* (1528), WA 26:147,13–18 and 25; see LW 40:231–232, *Concerning Rebaptism.*

> to the dying the crucifix, making them remember Christ's passion and entrust themselves to him. Then also prayer, such as the Psalter, the Our Father, the Creed and the Ten Commandments. Also, many excellent hymns and songs in Latin and German. Where such elements have remained, the Church and some of the saints have certainly also remained. For these are all ordinances and fruits of Christ, except that one species has been stolen. Christ is therefore certainly present among his own with his Holy Spirit and has maintained the Christian faith in them.[61]

These texts—and Preuss quotes others in the same vein—lead me to recognise the positive place given by Luther to the external means of grace in the Church, which come from Christ. They also provide a basis for the very important thesis that Luther really did not want to found a new Church, but to purify the existing one: 'We do not want to abolish your Gospel (. . .) but to purify and polish it like a dirty and spoiled mirror'.[62]

What did the 'cleaning and polishing' consist of? They needed to be radical, because in the papacy these Church realities are perverted. Faith in Christ, our only salvation, is perverted by practices and by a clerical structure that stifles the freedom of faith.

Luther's reform programme is spelled out in a large number of texts, but we believe that its essence can be found in these four writings: *An den christlichen Adel Deutscher Nation* and *De captivitate Babylonica* (1520); *Ad librum Catharini responsio* (1521); *Vermahnung an die Geistlichen* (1530). This was followed by the *Smalkald Articles* (1537), etc.[63]

---

61. *Von der Winkelmesse und Pfaffenweihe* (1533), WA 38:221,18–35; see LW 38:177–178, *The Private Mass and the Consecration of Priests.*
62. *Das fünfte Kapital Matthaei gepredigt und ausgelegt* (1530/1532), WA 32:357,8; see LW 21:70 on Matt 5:18. Quoted by Preuss, *Martin Luther*, 229.
63. These articles from Smalcald are particularly important because they were composed by Luther as an official presentation for the Council convened in Mantua. In them, he distinguishes three categories of articles: (1) those on which there is agreement with the Papal Church: Trinity, Incarnation; (2) Those on which no concessions could be made: justification by faith alone, the Mass was not a sacrifice (and with it the rejection of the cult of the saints, indulgences and Purgatory), the abolition of convents and chapters, and the rejection of papal primacy; and (3) Points on which there was room for discussion: Luther includes transubstantiation and communion under both species. See the text of these *Articles* in BK 407–468; BC 297–328.

Of the twenty-seven points developed in the Appeal, one could accept almost everything, were it not for the doctrinal undertones of several items, and the transfer to temporal authority of the regulation of the external life of the Church in a manner reminiscent of Marsilio of Padua. There is a spirit of radical criticism lacking in compassion and a sense of the weight of history. Who would deny that the Pope is above Scripture? Above the Council? Many good theologians denied it. The three-crowned tiara? Where could you find it in the Gospel or in the ancient Church?

Was it possible not to criticise the corruption of the system of benefices, the big business that so many ecclesiastics made a living from, even on the occasion of holy celebrations, pilgrimages, etc.? Who would not have wanted to clean up the practice of celibacy and vows? Wasn't the teaching of Scripture and the sacred sciences in need of renewal? When it came to abuses concerning the Roman Curia and Church pastors, the *Consilium* addressed to Paul III in 1537 by a group of cardinals and prelates included a number of them.[64] Moreover, Luther was aware of it and published it, adding his own remarks.[65]

The response to *Catharinus* and the *Vermahnung* attack everything that Luther criticises in the life of the clergy, the Papal Curia, devotions and practices that have taken the place of faith, masses celebrated for money and without the faithful, the refusal of the chalice to laypeople, the obligation of celibacy that leads to much misery, the teaching of theology in which Aristotle and reason reign instead of the Word of God, canon law, etc. The *Vermahnung* evokes a number of concrete cases of abuse in devotions, and ends with lists, first of devotions, then of practices that Luther criticises or rejects.

There is, in all this, much that indeed called for serious critical revision, much that has since then been revised and changed. Luther is often right. In the *Vermahnung*, he can even boast that he was alone in denouncing abuses and criticising indulgences. But he did so victoriously, and by the sheer force of doctrine and the Word! It was I, Luther, who by my doctrine (alone), destroyed indulgences and the

64. Text annotated in *Concilium Tridentinum*, edited Goerresgesellschaft, XII:131f.

65. *Consilium delectorum cardinalium* (1537 / 1538), WA 50:288–308; see LW 34:235–267, *Counsel of a Committee of Cardinals Concerning the Reform of the Church, with Luther's Preface* (and annotations).

domination of monks![66] Several times, too, he notes that there were novelties: thus Masses celebrated for money and without the faithful, and certain devotions.[67] It is obviously impossible for me to take these point by point and, for each one, to disentangle the exact and the inaccurate, the admissible and the debatable.

The *De captivitate Babylonica* raises more dogmatic questions. After protesting against the denial of the chalice to the laity, in which I readily agree with him, Luther in effect affirms only three sacraments, and even the third, that of penance, disappears by the end. Even the sacrament of the Lord's Supper falls victim to three captivities: that of the suppression of the chalice, that of transubstantiation, which can only be a theory of theology, not a dogma, and lastly that of the Mass seen as a work and a sacrifice. As for baptism, Luther would have nothing to say, but he seized the opportunity to argue that the pope has no power to subject a Christian to the slightest law. To do so is tyrannical!

And Luther also speaks against religious vows if they are undertaken to the detriment of the dignity of baptism. On several occasions Luther expresses his conception of the sacrament: a promise addressed to our faith and accompanied by a sensible sign. He applies this definition to penance. The Pope, on the other hand, has turned it into a work; this is one of his betrayals. Neither confirmation, nor marriage, nor ordination, nor extreme unction are attested in Scripture nor do they satisfy the definition of a sacrament. They are ceremonies accompanied by prayers. There are many ancient testimonies about clerical order, and they are well-regarded, but none of them is worthy of scriptural attestation, and that of Dionysius least

---

66. WA 30/2:278f, see LW 34:14–15, *Exhortation to All Clergy*. Compare Luther's *Vorrede zu Vom Priesterehe des Herrn Stephan Klingebeil* (1528): 'For a long time there was a cry for a council to reform the Church. I think I set up a council and made a reformation that made the papists' ears ring . . . If the Pope has to hold a general council, he won't do as much. Firstly, I hunted down the papists in books, particularly in writing, and I chased out of their place the pagan Aristotle and the somnists with the sophists and their commentary on the Sentences . . . Then I silenced the fair of indulgences, which no council would have touched. Thirdly, I cut off the roads to pilgrimages . . . I also hope that convents and collegiate Churches should hold a single mass': WA 26:530,6–30; see LW 59:223–224, *Preface to Stephan Klingebeil*, 'On Clerical Marriage'.
67. Compare WA 30/2:294–95,302,305; see LW 34:23–27,30, *Exhortation to all Clergy*.

of all![68] In truth, every Christian is a priest. Luther even goes so far as to say that every Christian is a bishop and a pope, which is hardly consistent with the distinction he makes between priestly dignity and ministry or function. This shows that he understands the 'universal priesthood' individually, not corporately and within the framework of the (mystical) Body of Christ the Sovereign Priest.[69] It is true, as we have noted with P. Manns (n. 143), that the lived experience (*vécu*) of pastors is more positive and that Luther's texts are more 'Catholic' in their expression. But it is understandable that J. Lortz should have situated the break at the publication of *De captivitate*.

Luther took Scripture as his normative reference. He accepted the Fathers and the ancient councils insofar as they were in conformity with Scripture. This does not amount to what we and the Orthodox call 'Tradition', which presupposes an awareness of the Church as a mystery, as a union of the visible and the invisible, the earthly and the heavenly. This seems to me to be inadequate in Luther. He saw nature too much as radically corrupt. He had an exceptionally vivid sense of faith and of Christ. He lived it to an extraordinary depth.

But, by concentrating everything on 'sin–justice', and 'wretched-me–Christ my salvation', he reduced his principle of interpretation too much. This was pointed out to him.[70] He wanted to know only Jesus Christ. His theology, as Wilhelm Link noted several times, had the character of a confession of faith.[71] All the same, this reduced the angle of vision of Christianity lived in the Church. With his nervous, volatile temperament, inclined to extremes, convinced that his cause was the very cause of Christ and the Gospel, Luther saw everything as black and white, devil or God, Christ or antichrist. His hatred of the Pope was pathological: in fact, it was an outlet for his neurosis. It could not be a good condition for appreciating the things of the old Church.

Under these conditions, Luther seriously upset the balance of important realities held in organic synthesis by the undivided

68. Manns, 'Amt und Eucharistie', 129n122, gives a large number of references for this denial of the proper sacramentality of the ordained ministry.
69. Every Christian is priest, bishop and pope, WA 6:408,7–25, see LW 44:129, *Appeal to the Christian Nobility.*
70. See his *Die Sieben Busspsalmen* on Psalm 143, the seventh penitential psalm (1517), WA 1:219, 21–27.
71. Link, *Das Ringen Luthers*, 77–78, 208, (Luther's texts on *confessio*).

Church. The balance, that is, the mutual relationship of realities such as Scripture-tradition-Church, *ecclesia* and the authority of ordained pastors, community and its ministers, faith and sacrament, various components of the sacraments (e.g. penance), law (*droit*) and the tyrannical exercise of authority, pope and council. Cajetan may have had prophetic foresight when, referring to the fides *apprehensiva* and its role in the sacrament of penance, he wrote: 'that would be to make another Church' (see 19n33).

* * *

Conclusion

A Need for Reform

As a conclusion to this study, and to the months I have spent in Luther's company, indeed to the half-century I have spent returning to him so often, I would like to say how, today, I see his reform and the Reformation.

1. *Reform was needed.* People had been calling for one for four centuries in the case of lay movements that were more or less anti-institutional, and for two centuries in the case of clerics, especially reform *in capite*. This expression, which has become a classic, was coined by Guillaume Durand the Younger in his treatise published for the Council of Vienna in 1311. The texts express very sharp criticism of the omnipotence assumed by the pope at the juridical level (decretals, *Extravagantes*), through the powers of reservation he had attributed to himself over benefices, annates, etc. A general council should 'limit and set the boundaries for the executive power exercised by the pope' (*limit ac terminet coactivam et usurpatam papalem*, Durand). This abuse was unknown in the first ten centuries; it so scandalised the laity that they considered the ecclesiastical state 'more anti-Christian than Christian' (*apud aliquos magis antichristíanum quam christianum fare purent*, report of the German Nation of 14 September 1417).[1] From 1456 onwards, the *Gravamina Nationís Germanicae* were repeated from Diet to Diet against the

1. Johannnes Haller has compiled a number of testimonies in pages 12–22, 166f., 187f. of *Papsttum und Kirchenreform. Vier Kapitel zur Geschichte des ausgehenden Mittelalters* (Berlin, 1903).

> exactions and encroachments of the Papal Curia. The authority of ecclesiastical laws, and of the letters of Pope Clement, had been increased to such an extent that they were given more importance than the Decalogue.[2] We must return to Christ, the foundation of the faith; the only true reform would be that of faith and doctrine, said an orator at the Council of Constance.[3] 'More Christ and less Church', said Jean Rucherat de Wesel (+1481), who had taught at Erfurt from 1441 to 1457, and even Jean Wessel Gansfort (+1489), whom Luther had read and whose *Farrago rerum theologie* he prefaced, was republished at Wittenberg in 1522.[4]

Wessel proclaims the superiority of Scripture over the Pope: the latter derives his authority from it, not the other way round, and we must only follow him when he believes rightly. Wessel Gansfort even attacked the practice of indulgences, the very existence of a 'treasure of the Church' made up of the merits of Christ and the saints. So Luther was able to write of him: 'This admirable man, of rare intelligence and great spirit . . . if I had read him before, my enemies might have thought that Luther had drawn everything from Wessel, so perfectly do the two of us agree in spirit'.[5]

Aspirations for a religion unencumbered by external observances whose performance risked taking the place of a truly personal piety had emerged in many ways. For example, the young Luther had experienced the simple practices of the Brethren of the Common Life. Certainly, Erasmus wrote that 'it is not ceremonies or papal bulls that give access to the temple, but a duly purified spirit of faith and the exercise of fraternal charity'. He also says, 'Would I do away with

2. Dietrich of Munster at the Council of Constance (Haller, *Papsttum* 14), which specifies: Clement VII. If it were Clement VI, he would be the one whose bull on indulgences Luther was discussing.
3. Haller, *Papsttum* 14, with reference to Christian Walch, *Monimenta medii aevi*, (Göttingen, 1757f.), 1,3,167f.
4. Compare: Reinhold Seeberg, *Das Schriftprinzip der Lutherischen Kirche*, vol. 1: 'Geschichtliche und Dogmatische Untersuchungen; Die Vorgeschichte, das Erbe des Mittelalters' (Leipzig, 1904), 407f. He quotes the words of J Rucherat: 'I despise the Pope, the Church and the Councils. I love Christ. May the word of Christ dwell in you abundantly', (*Contemno Papam, Ecclesiam et concilia. Amo Christum. Verbum Christi habiter in vobis abundanter*). Obviously, Rucherat was condemned.
5. *Vortwort zu Wesseli epistolae*, WA 10/2:317,10–15. Compare LW 59:6–11.

external worship? Not at all. I want to free it from all superstition and restore true piety. I would like to see a return to the sobriety of a religion that is above all interior'.[6]

Some things had been done, but it was too partial or too superficial. There had been spiritual renewals, evangelical movements, but they had not affected the whole system or the structures. The acquired forms were not satisfactory.

All that had been done was to take detailed measures against the life of the clergy: priests' concubines, card-players, canons who failed to perform their office, unpaid taxes. It was lacklustre. Since the Church as a whole was not reforming itself, evangelical aspirations were expressed in a half-hearted way or were contained. Without ignoring the play of less disinterested economic and social causes, it is easy to explain the extent and speed with which the message of the Reformers was accepted. We often find this motivation in the men who accepted their message: 'I have passed over to the Gospel and to the reign of Jesus alone'. Each one wanted to make the Gospel their own. The printing press made it possible to spread the Reformers' message—above all the Holy Scriptures—in a completely new way.

2. *Luther ready for reform*. A man emerged who was much more than the synthesis of these aspirations and the sounding board for so many *gravamína*. In the *Dictata super Psalterium*, Luther expressed many criticisms and complaints about the state of the Church: for example, on Psalm 68.[7] The same is true of the *Vorlesung über den Römerbrief*. Such criticisms and complaints were commonplace at the time, and Luther was by no means a rebel. But the monk Martin Luther had experienced the drama of the salvation of sinful man in ways other than ideas and theses: 'How can I have a favourable God?' We have seen that he had found help in Staupitz, from some of his fellow brothers, and in the 'doctors of conscience', Bernard and Bonaventure, in the mystics of abandonment to God, Tauler and the *Theologia Deutsch*.

6. One of Erasmus' most significant texts, taken from his *Commentary on Psalm 14* (Leiden, 1705), 5:301f., 309. And compare: Augustin Renaudet, *Etudes* érasmiennes (1521–1529) (Paris: Droz, 1939); *Préréforme et Humanisme* (Paris: Champion, 1916, 431f.); Alfons Auer, *Die vollkommene Frömmigkeit des Christen nach dem Enchiridion militis christiani des Erasmus von Rotterdam* (Düsseldorf: Patmos Verlag, 1954).
7. *Dictata super Psalterium*, WA 3:416–418; see LW 10:352–354, on Psalm 68.

> But he could only be satisfied with what he personally felt. He experienced enlightenment, perhaps suddenly, perhaps gradually (*see* Ernst Bizer's thesis in *Fides ex auditu,* vindicating Luther's own account in the famous Preface of 1545). The discovery was that of the meaning of Romans 1:17 and, beyond this text, of the content of Scripture: it is 'Christ-my justice' *coram Deo*, simply by faith. It is the liberating Gospel of 'Christ-my Saviour'. From then on, Luther devoted his life to unfolding and transmitting this Gospel. *Scriptura sola, sola gratia, pro me*, fides Christi, *iustitía Dei, extranea, non domestica* are the instances or names for this liberating discovery.

And then a senseless preaching of indulgences provided an opportunity to express the renewed vision of the salvatory relationship in a theology of the Christian life as *metanoia* (radical reversal) and in dependence on God's grace rather than papal graces. The abuse of indulgences goes back even further. There is ample evidence of it in the Augustinian convents of Erfurt at the time of Luther. It had become a convenient (but unacceptable!) way of obtaining money. Criticism of the abuse of indulgences went much further than criticism of the abuse itself: it led to a renewed—or new—vision of the truth of the religious or salvatory relationship.

3. *Principles of Reform.* Luther's action was therefore based on a reform of theology, teaching and preaching. This entailed a) new norms and a new mode of expression; b) a new, positive content; and c) negatively, it would be against a certain number of things, and these exclusions would be radicalised into serious negations.

3a) New standards. Theoretically, they were not really new. With the exception of a few canonists who increased the Pope's authority in such an outrageous way as to go beyond the limits of Christianity and even of reason, theologians had always affirmed the sovereign normative character of the canonical Scriptures.[8] But Luther's

8. By way of example only, Tancrede, shortly after 1215: 'Of what is just he could do injustice by correcting and changing the law . . . And there is no one who can say to him: 'Why are you doing this?' (*de Iustitia potest facere iniustitiam corrigendo ius et mutando . . . nec est qui dicat ei Cur ita facis?*), (*ad Compilationis* III, 1, V, 3). Occam says he heard a high prelate claim that the pope could change the sacraments or institute new ones: *Breviloquium*, IV, 13. Compare also Brian Tierny, *Foundations of the Conciliar Theory* (Cambridge: University Press, 1955), 53n1; 88n1; 147n4; etc.

application of the scriptural norm was much more active, and also more exclusive.

He really tried to establish definitively (*normer*) all of his affirmations, his judgements, all his counsels, by the texts and the examples of Scripture. We also know the use he made of a rule dear to his master Occam: admit nothing that is not supported by a text of Scripture or drawn from clear reason.[9] As we have seen, Luther knew how to reason and argue; he boasted that he could do so as well as and better than his opponents. But, as we have also seen, he did not want to speak the language of the 'sophists', that is to say of Scholasticism: he wanted to be content with the affirmations of Scripture, beyond and apart from any rational construction. His opponents and judges opposed him with their own language, their own constructions and expressions of doctrine, which Luther had rejected. As did Eck, so also Cajetan, and so did the actors in the Roman trial.[10] I myself have still reacted somewhat in this way. It is difficult for a Catholic theologian trained in the great school of the masters to follow Luther in the sometimes disappointing novelty of his new language, *modus loquendí novus, apostolicus*.

3b) On the positive side, the doctrinal content of this theology, and thus of the Church-community of true believers, will be the Gospel. Luther himself liked to call himself, and perhaps define himself, as *Doctor Martin Luther, unworthy evangelist of Our Lord Jesus*.[11] He often explained what he meant by 'Gospel'. These three texts will be sufficient examples:

> It is the preaching of the Son of God incarnate and given to us without merit for peace and salvation . . .The true glory of God is born of this Gospel when we learn that the law was and is fulfilled in Christ, not by our works but by the grace

9. Thus *Acta Augustana* (1518), WA 2:8,38–39; see LW 31:263; *Proceedings at Augsburg*; also *Ad dialogum Prieriatis responsio* (1518), WA 1:656; and *Auf dem Reichstage zu Worms* (1521), WA 7:876,11–12; see LW 32:112, *At the Diet of Worms*.
10. See, for example, Erwin Iserloh, *Die Eucharistie in der Darstellung des Johannes Eck. Ein Beitrag zur vortridentinischen Theologie*, (Munster: Aschendorff, 1950), 16–17, 57, 350. Eck has misunderstood the reasons for Luther's rejection of the sacrificial character of the Mass, 56–57.
11. *Glose an den vermeinte kaiserliche Edikt* (1531), WA 30/3:366,26 (see LW3 4:91) and compare Preuss, *Martin Luther*, 102.

> of a merciful God, not by working but by believing, not by offering something to God but by receiving and participating in everything from Christ.[12]
>
> The preaching of the Gospel is nothing other than Christ coming to us or leading us to him.[13]
>
> *Evangelion* means nothing other than a preaching and proclamation of the grace and mercy of God, merited and won by the Lord Jesus Christ in his death.[14]

I have already quoted twice the definition of the 'subject' of theology (commentary on Psalm 51, 1532, see 13n15 and 31n37): 'man guilty of sin and lost, and God who justifies and saves sinful man'. But man remains a sinner as long as he is not in the Kingdom, even though he is justified *iustitia aliena* (sc. Christ). Hence the *simul iustus et peccator* ('both righteous and a sinner'). It was in the light of these great fundamental perceptions that Luther applies himself to rethink and formulate the whole of Christianity: faith, Christological-soteriology, sacraments, ministry, Church.

3c) On the negative side, Luther fought with excessive passion against human norms that he linked to the first birth, that of nature and the earth, not that of faith in the Word: philosophical reason (Aristotle, Porphyry, the Scholastics), legal authority claiming to impose itself simply by virtue of its supposed legitimacy (canon law, decrees, the Pope). The value of a rule is judged by its content, not by the alleged formal authority of the person issuing it.

---

12. *Resolutiones disputationum de indulgentiarum virtute* (1518): Conclusio LXII, WA 1:616,20–21 and 39f., see LW 31:231). Thesis 62 states that 'the true treasure of the Church is the holy Gospel of the grace and glory of God' (*verus thesaurus Ecclesiae est sacrosanctum Evangelium gratiae et gloriae dei*).
13. From the introduction to the *Weinachtspostille* (1522), *Was man in den Evangelien suchen und erwarten soll*, WA 10/1/1:13, then included in the *Kirchenpostille* (1540/1542); see LW 35:118, *A brief Instruction on what to look for and expect in the Gospels.* And compare STROHL, *La substance de l'Evangile selon Luther*, 282–287.
14. *Epistel S.Petri gepredigt und ausgelegt* (1523), WA1 2:259,8–10; see LW 30:3 *Sermons on the First Epistle of St Peter.*

This was true of Scripture itself: that which expresses Christ is the Word of God.[15] This is a kind of canon within the canon. When Luther was opposed to patristic texts, the usage of the Church (*factum Ecclesiae*), pontifical decrees and the authority of canonical rules, he replied 'Gospel',[16] and the Scripture that bears witness to it. 'Anything that is not in Scripture is simply an addition by Satan'.[17] Many things were attributed to Satan!

This is where, while recognising the greatness and validity of Luther's intention, I cannot follow him in the way he exercised it. The intention was to establish as a principle of reform the sovereignty of the Word of God. It was applied in the sense of a *Scriptura sola* which I believe we must reject. We cannot accept the divide that an extreme pessimism has made between nature (creation) and grace (redemption). And is Scripture, or rather the Word, the only gift that God has given us for the existence of a Church that is the Body of Christ? The Church as the sacrament of Christ, the sacrament of salvation, is made up of gifts, of instituted means of grace, which have been established as such, without their institution necessarily being attested in Scripture. It is true that this consideration can be abused. The biblical reference has at least a negative value: anything that contravenes it is excluded.

15. WADB 7:384–387; see LW 35:395–398, *Preface to the Epistles of James and Jude* (1522 / 1546); also *Ad Galatas* (1531–1535), WA 40/1:458–459; see LW 26:294–296.
16. *Assertio Omnium Articulorum M. Lutheri per bullam Leonis X novissimam damnatorum*, (1521): 'Let no one oppose to me the authority of the Pope or of any saint (= Church father) without a testimony of Scripture (. . .) I do not want to make myself more learned than everyone else, but let Scripture alone reign', (*Nemo* (. . .) *mihi opponat Papae aut Sancti cuiusvis auctoritatem nisi Scripturis munitam* (. . .) *Nolo Omnium doctior iactari, sed solam Scripturam regnare*), WA 7:99 (compare LW 32:11–12, *Defense and Explanation of All Articles* (1521). Also *Contra Henricum regem Angliae* (1522): 'So I cry out: Gospel, Gospel, Christ, Christ, and they reply: Fathers, Fathers, tradition, tradition, decrees, decrees!' (*Ita fit ut ego clamem: Evangelion, Evangelion, Christus, Christus, ipsi respondeant: Patres, Patres usus, usus, statuta, statuta!*), WA 10/2:182; see LW 61:11, *Against King Henry of England*. For the reference to the 'factum Ecclesiae', *Ad dialogum Prieriatis responsio* (1518), WA 1:656–657; 685,23.
17. 'At quod in scripturis nou habetur, hoc plane Satanae additamentum est', *De abroganda missa privata* (1521), WA 8:418,1–2; *compare* LW 36:142, *The Misuse of the Mass*.

Luther very often joined the Fathers and the ancient Church to the criterion of Scripture. Did he not betray them in his criticism of the sacraments, especially the sacrament of Holy Orders? Did not his sick hatred of the Pope make him attribute to Satan things which, perhaps without belonging to the radical level of divine right, are linked to the historical life of the Church in what it has providentially led? Even Luther's biblicism, remarkable in so many ways, doesn't it lack a historical vision of God's plan in its stages and development?

In short, Luther misunderstood many things that belong to this undivided Church from which we must draw inspiration in our search for unity. My conviction, which my work has only confirmed year after year, is that Luther criticised the characteristic forms of the Western Middle Ages. Did he not touch, to the point of wounding them, things that were essential to this pre-medieval and extra-Western Church? The judgement of the Orthodox is of exceptional value to us here.

4. *No New Church.* Many authors have emphasised the fact that the Reformers did not want to create another Church but only, as Calvin said, to clean up the existing one. In 1519, Luther himself severely condemned the secession of the Bohemians: 'I have never liked it and never will', Luther told Eck at the Leipzig Disputation.[18]

'Nothing excuses it', he continued in his *Ad Galatas commentarius*,[19] and added: 'And we ourselves, who bear the burdens and horrors of the Roman Curia, are we going to run away and separate for that reason? *Absit! absit!* We criticise, we hate, we pray, we warn, but we do not separate . . . knowing that charity is above all'.[20]

Sadly, the break was made, and Luther was excommunicated. Nevertheless, in January 1528 he wrote:

> We confess that there was much Christian good in the papacy, that we received from it. We confess that in the Papacy there is the authentic Holy Scripture, the authentic Baptism, the

18. 'Ein Sermon gepredigt zu Leipzig, am Tage Petri und Pauli, 1519' (29 June, on Matthew 16:13–19), WA 2:244–249; see LW 51:54–60 [reference corrected, ed.].
19. 'No excuse can be given to defend the secession of the Bohemians from the Roman Church' (*Boemorum dissidium a Romana ecclesia nulla possit excusatione defendi*), WA 2:605,13f.; see LW 27:392, *Commentary on Galatians* (1519).
20. WA 2:605,23f; see LW 27:392.

> authentic Sacrament of the Altar, the authentic keys for the remission of sins, the authentic ministry of preaching, an authentic Catechism, such as the Our Father, the Ten Commandments, the Articles of Faith (. . .) We are not like the enlightened ones who reject everything in the Papacy, because then we would be rejecting Christendom itself and everything in it that is of Christ.[21]

However, there could be no illusions: the evangelical communities were another true Church as opposed to that of the Pope; it was in conformity, and therefore in continuity with the true Church; it was 'the true, ancient Church, forming one body with the whole holy Christian Church and a communion of saints'.[22]

If the Reformers, and Luther in particular, did not wish to substitute one Church for another, but only to bring back to the Gospel and to its ancient purity the Church from which they confessed to have received Christianity, do not the Churches which they were forced to set up in opposition to that of the Pope have only a provisional legitimacy, as long as the Catholic Church, which has been perpetuated, has not been thoroughly reformed according to the Gospel? Protestant and Anglican voices have said so.[23]

---

21. *Von der Wiedertaufe*, 1528, WA 26:147,13–18 and 148,5–7; see LW 40:231–232. But the context proclaims that the pope is the antichrist who sits in the temple of God and persecutes the true faithful. See Wolfgang Hohne, 'Luthers Anschauungen über die Kontinuität der Kirche', *Arbeiten zur Geschichte und Theologie des Luthertums*, (Hamburg: Broschiert, 1963), 12.
22. *Wider Hans Wurst* (1541), WA 51:487, 3; see LW 41:199. The purpose of this writing, against Duke Henry of Brunswick-Wolfenbüttel, known as 'Hans Wurst', is to explain where the true Church is to be found. The Pope's Church is that of the devil, the antichrist.
23. See for example Max Thurian, *Chrétiens devant l'Oecuménisme* (Catholicité), 1948, 21, 23; Marc Boegner, *L'exigence œcuménique* (Paris: Albin Michel, 1968), 314 and 316; Fenton JA Hort, speaking of 'parenthetical and temporary' (quoted by Leonard Elliott-Bins, *English Thought 1860–1900. The Theological Aspect* (London: Longmans, 1956), 123); Gregory Dix, *The Question of the Anglican Orders* (Westminster: Dacre Press, 1944), 90 f; Jean-Jacques von Allmen, in *Verbum caro*, 71 (1950); most recently Roger Mehl, *Le protestantisme français dans la société actuelle* (Geneva: Labor et Fides, 1982), 158–159, 'the period opened up by the Reformation is a 'parenthesis' in the history of the Church', and 202, where he quotes Jean Bosc, *Situation de l'œcuménisme en perspective réformée* (Paris: Cerf, 1969), 34, 'One problem would be to know to what extent the Reformed Churches were able to retain the feeling that their existence responded to a provisional situation'.

I do not know exactly in what sense Bengel wrote, 'the Lutheran Church is an interim Church',[24] but the history I have lived through makes it easy to appreciate the words of George A. Lindbeck, a professor at Yale University who was an observer at the Council.[25] He compares the situation of the Roman Church to that of a country occupied by a tyrannical power—France between 1940 and 1944, for example—and the Evangelical Lutheran Church, of which he is a member, to a government in exile like that of General de Gaulle during the same period. But can we talk about tyrannical power when we have John XXIII in front of us? Leaving aside the political aspect, the idea is clear: the Evangelical Church is an interim Church, justified and legitimate as long as the ancient Church, from which it emerged, has not been thoroughly reformed according to the Gospel.

But what if Rome reformed?

5. *Reform of the Catholic Church*. It did so, albeit belatedly, at the Council of Trent and through the great movement that followed it. Trent had nothing against the Reformers. It welcomed the arrival of Protestants, but saw only a small number, in the years 1551–1552. It reaffirmed articles of doctrine denied or ignored by the Reformation. It produced some remarkable texts, for example on justification, but operated with resources derived from scholasticism, which were certainly of great quality, but alien to Luther's dialectical and biblical thinking. It remained in line with the medieval system.

The Second Vatican Council was a council of reform: Karl Barth proclaimed this, not without some feeling.[26] It has also been said, quite rightly, that it marked the end of the Counter-Reformation. Written by men trained in the heritage of scholasticism, it spoke the language of salvation history and the kerygma. It was open to

24. 'Die lutherische Kirche ist eine Interimskirche'. Quoted by Richard Baumann, *Des Petrus Bekenntnis und Schlüssel* (Stuttgart: Schwabenvert, 1960), 202.
25. 'Eine protestantische Ansicht über den ekklesiologischen Status der römisch-katholischen Kirche', in *Una Sancta*, 19 (1964): 101–124, article published simultaneously in English in the *Journal of Ecumenical Studies*, (1964): 2.
26. 'The Second Vatican Council was, if anything, a reform council', (*Das Zweite Vatikanische Konzil war, wenn irgendeines, ein Reformkonzil*), Karl Barth, *Ad limina Apostolorum*, (Zürich: Evz-Verlag, 1967), 19.

ecumenism and to a pluralist world. We ourselves have often noted that its greatest value in this respect lay less in its beautiful decree *Unitatis redintegratio* than in its connection with the spirit of the first millennium, over and above what the second may have developed that was too narrowly medieval-Western.

As I have said, my conviction has grown stronger with time and study: it is these developments that are rejected above all by the reform movement and likewise by the Orthodox. A renowned Lutheran theologian has reproduced, approvingly, this list of the Council's achievements, as those considered favourably by a Protestant:

1. From the ideological vision of the Church as a perfect society to the realistic view of its historical imperfection.
2. From spiritual narrowness to authentic catholicity.
3. From legalism to Christian freedom.
4. From liturgical hardening to liturgical reform.
5. From pontifical centralism and curialism to the Petrine Magisterium of Jesus Christ.
6. From the fear of Scripture to the recommendation to read and study the Bible.
7. From clericalism to God's holy people.
8. From uniformity and Romanisation to Pentecostal pluralism of languages.
9. From the simple condemnation of atheistic socialism to the awareness of one's own responsibility.[27]

That is a lot, and yet Luther would have found it somewhat superficial. So would I. He would have called for more Jesus Christ, more Gospel, more Scripture. So would I. But the song of grace remained powerful in the Church of little Thérèse and, at the Council, there was and is a Christological concentration. At the Council, this was reflected not only in Paul VI's speech for the opening of the second period, 29 September 1963, but everywhere, even in *Gaudium et Spes*. Since the Council, Catholics have experienced this Christological concentration in the sacred liturgy and in the proclamation of the word of God.

27. Kristen Skydsgaard, 'La Réformation en tam qu'événement œcuménique', in Œcumenica, (1969): 230–250 (238).

This is where, however, despite the Council's beautiful and strong declarations on the active sovereignty of Scripture, much remains to be desired.[28] A large number of official texts and declarations by the Pope and the bishops are statements in which the Word of God is not questioned and understood first and foremost as the source and norm, the inspiration and light of what is to be said. Rather, it is often quoted as an illustration. In these conditions, we still need to be challenged by Luther, especially if his voice no longer has the violence of his anti-papal hatred, which is absolutely unacceptable, but rather carries the fraternal accents of dialogue. The character of 'interim' or 'parenthesis' that Hort, Boegner and Lindbeck attribute to the Churches of the Reformation insofar as they are 'separate' also concerns the Catholic Church. Let me even say that it depends primarily on the Catholic Church.

6. *The Unity to Which God Leads Us.* Moreover, there can be no question of a simple 'return'. The Reformers were religious geniuses who expressed original and profound aspects of Christianity. Whatever happens, this is the reality and it will remain. Better still, a form of Christianity has been lived for centuries in ecclesial communities. They have accumulated so many elements of a history of thought, holiness, initiatives and creations. This cannot be abolished. It is part of a history of salvation that goes all the way up to eschatology.

Do we have to wait until then to experience the integration of everything that is of God and for God into a final 'Catholic' unity? In a sense, yes. But history tends towards eschatology, prepares for it and, to some degree, anticipates it. Our ecumenism is faced with the impossible and necessary task of seeking to integrate the divine riches of diversity into a unity that is anything but uniform. I approached this monumental question in *Diversités et Communion* (Paris: Cerf, 1982). I do not have a solution. All we have to do is work, with the light and grace of each day, along the lines of the thought of Rilke, whom I admire greatly.[29] It is about questions without solutions:

28. Tradition seen as the unfolding of the understanding of Scripture rather than as a second source; the 'magisterium' subordinated to Scripture (*Dei verbum*, 10); Scripture as the 'suprema regula' of all theology, catechesis and preaching (*Dv*, 21); etc.

29. Rainer Rilke, *Letters to a Young Poet*, (Letter 4).

'perhaps simply by living them you will one day insensibly enter into the answers'. Provided, of course, that you do not just sleep.

Luther's Reformation remains one of those questions. We are living it. Dare we say, as John Paul II said of the anniversary of the Ausburg Confession: 'I live it very intensely. Someone is living it in me'.[30] For my part, the deeper I dig, the deeper the depths appear to me and I have not yet reached them. So let us live the questions honestly. That is what I have tried to do. Pastor Marc Boegner relates this anecdote:

> A Catholic asked of a Protestant, 'If the Catholic Church had appeared in the sixteenth century as it did at the Council, would you have gone through with the Reformation?' And the Protestant replied: 'But you, would you have driven us out?'[31]

30. Meeting with non-Catholic representatives, Paris, 31 May 1980: *Docum Cathol*, n1788, 15 June 1980, 564n1.
31. Marc Boegner, *L'exigence œcuménique*, 314.

Note

Reform Measures at the Fifth Lateran Council, 1512–1517

Luther alludes (42n15) to this recent council to illustrate the inadequacy of the reforms undertaken, or at least proposed, since it remains to be seen to what extent they were applied. The fact that councils (Basel!) had been repeating the same injunctions for over a century suggests that they were poorly followed. After all, who read the interminable chapters of Basel or Lateran V? *And yet, the Church of that time showed great vitality!*

Here are the reforms advocated by the Fifth Lateran Council, which ended just as Luther was emerging: see *Conciliorum* Œcumenicorum *Decreta*, (Bologna, 1973), 595–655. Cajetan, before whom Luther would appear a year later, was one of the Council Fathers. He was personally a zealot for a very serious discipline of morals and religious functions.

Here are the main reformist chapters of Lateran V:

- For the dignity and suitability of curial cardinals, bishops and abbots: a true mirror of the cardinals, exclusion of luxury, good housekeeping.
- Measures in favor of religious instruction, against blasphemy, to be punished differently according to social standing;
- measures called for by the dignity of clerics' lives and their independence from secular powers.
- Detailed legal and disciplinary sanctions are provided for offenders on all these points.

It returns at length to clerical freedom, exemptions, even inquisition and torture, dignity of life and local synods. Each article includes sanctions. What a litigious, punitive Church this must have been!

- Reform of pawnshops to protect the poor and weak.
- Measures to monitor book printing, always with penalties.

In the XIth session, 19 December, 1516:

- Rules for preaching, against deviations of the word, perversion of the meaning of Scripture,
- Against terrorizing preaching,
- Against preaching errors or uselessness, or fables, or false miracles,
- Against announcing the end of the world,
- Against untimely criticism of ecclesiastical authorities.
- Rules for verifying the quality of preachers and their use of Scripture in accordance with the Church's interpretation.

But if we must not extinguish the Spirit, we must also test the authenticity of what it is supposed to inspire.

- The same session, rules to settle the age-old dispute between religious and parish priests or diocesan priests.

XIIth session, 16 March, 1517:

- Against the violent invasion of the cardinals' house, especially when they are in conclave!
- Imposition of tithes for the fight against the Turks.
- It ends with the granting of a plenary indulgence to the Fathers (and their households) who are about to leave a Council that has lasted almost five years.

Throughout, the aim is to ensure good order in a very clerical Church. Some references to Scripture have little more than an ornamental function. As in Basel, the Council sought to root out the weeds in the Lord's field, using legal sanctions. Luther, on the other hand, wanted to renew the seed. He sought to break away from the clerical system, and its dependency on papal authority, drawing the rules for the Church's own proper functioning from within itself.

Study Two
Theology of the Eucharist

In 1950, to celebrate the centenary of the Council of Chalcedon, I wrote a study on Luther's Christology.[1] This study was intended to be modest: '*Regards et réflexions*'. It has been criticized,[2] but it is also still quoted and approved.[3] I thought that Luther did not recognize the role of Christ's free will in his humanity in the work of our salvation, nor therefore that of a merit of Christ. It is *God* who has worked, in this humanity. My conclusion was: 'Luther, in a word, has the Christology of *Allein-wirksamkeit Gottes*'. I want to return to Luther's Christology from his theology of the Eucharist, for it has long been apparent to me that there is a correspondence between the positions we hold in Christology and those we hold on the Eucharist, and

1. Yves Congar, 'Regards et réflexions sur la christologie de Luther', in *Das Konzil von Chalkedon, Geschichte und Gegenwart*, edited by Alois Grillmeier and einrich. Bacht, (Würzburg: Echter-Verlag, 1954), 3:457–486. Reproduced in *Chrétiens en dialogue*, Unam Sanctam 50 (Paris: Cerf, 1964), 453–489; *Dialogue Between Christians: Catholic Contributions to Ecumenism*, translated by Philip Loretz (London: Chapman, 1966), 372–406.
2. Thus by Wilfried Joest, *Ontologie der Person bei Luther* (Göttingen: Vandenhoeck & Ruprecht, 1967), 22f and 364n6; Wolfhart Pannenburg, in *Theologische Literaturzeitung*, 92 (1967): col. 97–98; Marc Lienhard, *Luther, témoin de Jesus-Christ, les étapes et les thèmes de la christologie du Réformatour*, Cogitatio fidei 73 (Paris: Cerf, 1973); *Luther: Witness to Jesus Christ*, translated Edwin Robertson (Minneapolis: Augsburg, 1982).
3. Thus by: Thomas Satory, *Die* ökumenische *Bewegung und Einheit der Kirche* (Meitingen: Kyrios, 1955), 189s; Otto Pesch, 'Um Christi willen (. . .) Christologie und Rechtfertigunslehre in der katholischen Theologie', in *Catholica*, 35 (1981): 15–57 (n20, 24–25); Theobald Beer, *Der fröhliche Wechsel und Streit, Grundzüge der Theologie Martin Luthers* (Einsiedeln: Johannes Verlag, 1980), 411n97 and 439, but Beer further hardens the interpretation

even in ecclesiology. On the basis of what is certainly a partial and undeveloped investigation, I have written a well-documented note on this subject, which appeared in the *Revue des Sciences philosophiques et théologiques*, 66 (1982): 233–244. It claims to be no more than a documentary essay and a suggestion.

There are many studies on Luther's sacrament of body and blood. I have read many of them, but make no claim to have seen them all! I haven't even read all of Luther's texts on the subject, only the main ones.[4] Luther's theology of the sacrament involves perceptions and subject matter that I make no claim to be familiar with.

Luther was led to his own theology of Christ's presence in the bread and wine only gradually and in opposition to the theses of Cornelius Hoën (Honius), with whom he was probably not directly acquainted, but above all to those of Ulrich Zwingli, after 1520.[5] His early texts and sermons on the Eucharistic sacrament are classic.[6] He speaks of our union with Christ, from a moral and personal perspective rather than a dogmatic one. Generally speaking, this is not very ecclesial, and even in later years, Luther will hardly speak of the Eucharist in relation to the community as such.[7]

4. Thus Albrecht Peters, *Realpräsenz, Luthers Zeugnis von Christi Gegenwart im Abendmahl* (Berlin: Lutherisches Verlagshaus, 1960), not only constitutes a very detailed study, but indicates, 203–205, all the passages which speak of this subject in the Weimar edition, and gives, 206–211, a bibliography of some 200 titles. Theobald SUSS, *La Communion au corps du Christ* (Neuchâtel: Delachaux & Niestle, 1968) is not a historical study, but a dogmatic discussion, itself debatable. I was unable to access Paul Genrich; *Die Christologie Luthers im Abendmahlsstreit* (Königsberg: Vandenhoeck & Ruprecht, 1929).

5. Karl Jaeger, *Luthers religiöses Interesse an seiner Lehre von der Realpräsenz, Eine historisch-dogmatische Studie* (Giessen, 1900). Luther became aware of Cornelius Hoën's theses shortly after 1520: see WA 11:420. The date is 1522, says Süss, *La Communion*, 288. Hoën's letter, published by Zwingli in 1525, appears in Luther's *Briefwechsel* edited by Enders (3:412–425), but not in WABr.

6. He himself says that 'I followed the common usage' (*in usu communi haerebam*). See *De captivitate Babylonica*, WA 6:502,3–4 (compare LW 36:19). For an example, see *Sermo de digna preparatione cordis pro suscipiendo Sacramento Eucharistiae*, Eastertide 1518 (WA 1:329–334), where Luther quotes the Fathers and speaks of trusting obedience to the Church.

7. Comment by Paul Althaus, quoted by Peters, *Realpräsenz*, 156. It is worth noting, however, the explanation given by Luther to his rejection of private masses: the mass requires a community.

Of particular interest is the *Sermon von dem Hochwirdigen Sacrament des Heyligen Waren Leychnams Christi* published in the autumn of 1519. Among its twenty-two points it includes a fourth on the Eucharist's effect of communion and incorporation into a spiritual body, a communion that encompasses even the saints in heaven, the City of God.[8] In the *Operationes in Psalmos* of 1519–1521, the theme is the admirable and joyful exchange between *his* justice and *our* sin. The point of view is more ethical than sacramental. Faith is the means:

> It is indeed faith in Christ that makes him live, move and act in me, just as a healing remedy acts on a sick body. We become one flesh and one body with Christ through the intimate and ineffable transmutation of our sin into his righteousness, as represented by the venerable sacrament of the altar, where bread and wine are transformed into the flesh and blood of Christ.[9]

In 1520, reformatory writings appeared in quick succession: in mid-August, *An den christlichen Adel Deutscher Nation*; in early September, *De libertate christiana*; in October, *De captivitate Babylonica ecclesiae praeludium*. Leaving aside a sermon from the same year, *Von dem neuen Testament, das ist von der heyligen Messe* (WA 6:349–378; LW 35:79–111)— it contributes nothing not found elsewhere—I will consider the *De captivitate* (WA 6:497–573). In it, Luther rejects the Church's common doctrine on the Eucharist and advocates consubstantiation, but without using the word, and without explaining Christ's presence by ubiquity. Luther wants to stick to Scripture. He sets aside John 6, which he says speaks only of faith, and retains the Synoptic accounts

8. WA 2:742–758; LW 35:49–73, *The Blessed Sacrament of the Holy and True Body of Christ* and the Brotherhoods (1519). For the fourth point, on 'communion': WA 2:743,7–26, see LW 35:50–51.
9. '*Fides enim in Christum facit eum in me vivere et moveri et agere, non secus atque salutare unguentum in aegrum corpus agit, efficimurque cum Christo una caro et unum corpus per intimam et ineffabilem transmutationen peccati nostri in illius iustitiam, sicut nobis repraesentat venerabile altaris sacramentum, ubi partis et vinum in Christi carnem et sanguinem transformantur*', *Operationes in Psalmos*: WA 5:311,12–17. Through the Eucharist we become one spiritual body with Christ: *Vom Anbeten des Sakrament*, 1523 (WA 11:440,34–441,17; see LW 36:286, *The Adoration of The Sacrament*); and the second of two 'catechism sermons' on the Lord's Supper, May 30, 1528 (WA 30/1:26,25–31.

of the Last Supper and 1 Corinthians 11. He breaks the first captivity imposed on the sacrament, which is to have removed the communion chalice from the laity. The second captivity consists in imposing the doctrine of transubstantiation as a matter of faith.[10] Even if Luther is called a Wyclifite or a Hussite, he has Cardinal Pierre d'Ailly on his side.[11] He would have preferred to admit the persistence of true bread and wine, were it not for the authority of the Church: obviously the chapter *Firmiter* of Lateran IV. But (he says) what is this Church that has so determined? It is Thomistic, that is, Aristotelian. And St Thomas did not understand Aristotle and parted company with him in this theory of substance and accidents. This is only an opinion, not an article of faith.

Moreover, neither the pope nor a council can make an article of faith: 'for what one affirms without reference to Scripture or assured revelation may well be an opinion but is not required by faith' (*Nam quod sine scripturis asseritur aut revelatíone probata, opinari licet, credi non est necesse*). I allow, says Luther (WA 6:508,27; 512,4–5; *see* LW 36:30 and 35), that one may hold either opinion. There is the Thomistic explanation, but for himself he holds to Scripture. That speaks of bread, 'true' bread not the 'accidents' of bread.[12] The Church has thought this way for 1200 years. Why couldn't Christ's glorious body be in the substance of bread as well as in these accidents, as fire is in red-hot iron? It is said that Christ came forth 'from the womb, respecting its integrity' (*ex utero matris illaeso*) so two substances

---

10. Luther had admitted transubstantiation in the 1519 sermon, *von dem Hochwürdigung Sakrament* (WA 2:749,12; LW 35:59, n27). He was less against transubstantiation *per se* as against making it an article of faith. On the occasion of the Regensburg Colloquy of 1541, where Contarini tried to introduce the very term, Luther said that if we gave in, we would be opening the door to the rest of the papal theses! Compare his letter of May 25, 1541 to Prince George of Anhalt: WABr 9:419–420. Luther is quite radical in his rejection of transubstantiation, in a speech at the table on the following June 10 or 11: WABr 9:443–445. And compare below n16.
11. Luther (WA 6:508,7–11; see LW 36:28–29nn59–60) refers to *Questiones quarti libri sententiarum*. The reference is correct and Luther can rely on d'Ailly's reasoning: see Leif Grane, 'Luthers Kritik an Thomas von Aquin in De captivitate Babylonica', in *Zeitschrift für Kirchengeschichte*, 80 (1969): 1–13.
12. In the margin, WA 6:509,15 refers to Matthew 26:26; Mark 14:22; Luke 22:19; Acts 2:46; 1 Corinthians 11:23. See LW 36:31.

existed together.[13] The same is true when he comes to the apostles with closed doors. This is the beginning of Luther's later discussion of the meaning of *hoc est corpus meum*. 'If', he adds, 'I can't explain how the bread is the body of Christ, I'll simply adhere to his word. It says: "This bread is my body"'. And Luther invokes a parallel comparison with the Incarnation (WA 6:511,34; *see* LW 36:34), where the divine in-dwelling did not require a transubstantiation of Christ's human nature, its accidents alone remaining perceptible: 'but, each nature remaining what it is, one says in all truth: this man is God, this God is man' (*sed integra utraque natura, vere dicitur: Hic homo est deus, hic deus est homo*). Here, then, he represents the Incarnation as the concurrent presence, in a tangible being, of two natures or substances.

Luther then develops his vision of the sacrament. He links it to the term 'testament' used by Christ (Luke 22:20): new testament, new covenant in my blood.

A will is a promise. Here it is the promise of the remission of sins. Promise calls for faith: 'these two things are necessary at the same time, promise and faith: without promise, indeed, nothing could be believed, and without faith the promise is useless' (*haec duo sunt simul necessaria promissio et fides: sine promissione enim credi nihil potest, sine fide autem promissio inutilis est*, WA 6:517,8–9; *see* LW 36:42). God accompanies his promises with a sign. There is the promise, given in the word, which is the main thing, and the sign, which will be the sacrament, the water of baptism, the bread and wine of the Eucharist. The main thing, the indispensable thing, is the word and faith. So the mass can only benefit the one who believes, it cannot be applied to another (6:521; 36:48), they can only be prayed for. We have turned the mass into an artistic performance![14]. We have turned it into a sacrifice to be offered to God! (6:523; 36:51) Luther, on the other hand, places so much value on the promise and announcement of the forgiveness of sins that, as we can foresee, this is what to 'do this in remembrance of me' will consist of for him.

In mid-1522, Luther received information about the spread of the symbolical teaching. A booklet published by the Bohemian

---

13. Grane points out that Luther makes the same argument in *Contra Henricum regem Angliae* (1522): WA 10/2:207,35–208,6; see LW 61:43, *Against Henry, King of England.*

14. This is where the misinterpretation of *opus operatum* begins, and continues to this day! Compare WA 6:520,13f; and see LW 36:47.

Brethren for the education of children taught that Christ present in the sacrament cannot be prayed to or adored. Luther wrote to Paul Speratus, who had informed him of this: one is free to adore and pray to Christ in the sacrament.[15] He himself preached on this adoration on January 4, 1523.[16] He wrote a rather long treatise, *Von Anbeten des Sakraments des heiligen Leichnams Christi* in German to the Bohemians, WA 11:431–456; see LW 35:275–305, *The Adoration of the Sacrament* (1523). What is there in the sacrament is identical to that which was born of Mary and hung on the cross.

'Ist' is not 'bedeutet' (*is* is not *signify*), just as we should say of Christ 'Man is God and God is man' (*Der mensch ist gott und gott ist mensch*) and not 'God signifies man' (*Gott bedeutet den menschen*). Luther stigmatised other errors, the third being that of Thomas Aquinas and the popes, according to whom bread does not remain bread (WA 11:441; see LW 36:287), the fourth is that of making the sacrament a sacrifice and a work. Finally, Luther makes it clear that there can be no purely external worship, and that only the worship of the heart is worthwhile, according to the rule of worship in spirit and in truth.

Luther's thinking gradually became clearer, especially through his opposition to the proponents of a symbolical interpretation. Hoën's symbolist ideas had reached Zurich. Karlstadt had rallied to them. Expelled from Saxony, he took refuge in Strasbourg in 1524, and the Strasbourgeois questioned Luther.[17] He replied on December 14–15, 1524. He too would have liked to be able to say that in the sacrament, there is only bread and wine: that would have given the papacy the

15. Letter of June 13, 1522: WABr 2:560.
16. See the table of his sermons for this period, WA 11:3. In a letter of May 25, 1541 to Prince George of Anhalt, Luther expresses himself on the subject of worship: kneeling to receive communion. But he is against worship [of the elements] outside the Lord's Supper: WABr 9:419–420, with a note by Prince George. And compare Peters, *Realpräsenz*, 93–94.
17. Nicolas Gerbel describes to Luther the disturbance caused by Karlstadt in Strasbourg, November 22, 1524: WABr 3:378–380). The next day, on the same subject, was a letter from the preachers, Capiton, Bucer and others (ibid. 381–387), who raise the question of what 'this is my body' means. Luther's replied on December 14–15, 1524: WA 15:391–397 (LW 40:65–71; see the notes in LW 49:94–96). A little later, on March 23, 1525, Nicolas Gerbel of Strasbourg warns Luther that Zwingli has been influenced by Karlstadt: WABr 3:459–460; and, on March 25, he sends him Zwingli's *Peri eucharistias*, 461–462.

hardest blow. But Luther is bound by the word of God, 'I am a captive and cannot free myself; the text is too powerful'.[18]

A few months later, Luther wrote his voluminous *Wider die himmlischen Propheten von den Bildern und Sakrament* (1525), WA 18:62–125 & 134–214; see LW 40:79–223, *Against the Heavenly Prophets*. Here, my focus is not on the first section on 'images' which Karlstadt wanted to ban, whereas, says Luther, Christ left us free.

For now crucifix and holy images are not only to be tolerated, but to be praised (WA 18:73–74; *see* LW 40:90–91). Moses, it is true, forbade them, but we have moved on to the Gospel (18:76f.; LW 40:92f.). It is noteworthy that Luther does not justify them by the fact of the Incarnation, as the iconophiles of the eighth century had done. As said, our interest is the second part of the treatise (18:134–214; LW 40:144–223).

Karlstadt said he could not admit that Christ was in the sacrament with his size, his bodily form, his length (. . .) But, says Luther, faith surpasses reason! (18:142,34–143,24; LW 40:153) The immense God was contained in Mary's womb. Our reformers do not shine in metaphysics. On the other hand, Luther, with his literary and philological training, discusses at length what is meant by the *hoc* or *hic* of 'this is my body'. It is to be interpreted as a synecdoche, that is an expression designating two items of data together, in this case both the bread and the body-blood of Christ. He would later continue the same discussion with the proponents of transubstantiation[19]: for if *hoc* designates the reality contained in the bread, they are right, but if it designates the bread itself, which we see, Luther can support his

18. *[A]ber ich byn gefangen, kan nicht eraus, der text ist zu* gewaltig, WA 15:394,19; see LW 40:68–71, *Letter to the Christians in Strasbourg* (1524). Lienhard, *Luther temoin*, 197–251, goes into more detail than we do on the writings of the controversy with Karlstadt, Œcolampade and Zwingli; bibliography provided. And compare Eberhard Grötzinger, '*Luther und Zwingli. Die Kritik an der mittelalterlichen Lehre von der Messe als Wurzel des Abendmahlsstreites*', 1980, *Oekumenische. Theologie*, Band 5.
19. It was on this point that Barthélemy Arnoldi d'Usingen, Luther's former teacher at Erfurt, focused his criticism in 1530 in reference to *De captivitate Babylonica*. Compare. the edition of his text by Fr XP Duijnstee, *Polemica de SS. Eucharistiae Sacramento inter Bartholomaeum Amoldi de Usingen, O.E.S.A. ejusque olim in Universitate Erphurdiana Discipulum Martinum Lutherum anno 1530*, (Würzburg: Stahel, 1903). Suss, *La Communion*, 152f, has a lengthy and nuanced discussion of Luther's use of synecdoche.

thesis: it is linked to the word of God. (18:166,10–13; LW 40:176). He discusses Karlstadt's text in detail, criticizing the spiritual, symbolic and allegorical interpretation of the terms. Karlstadt has planned fifteen treatises in response to Luther, with the help of a reason-witch, *Hulda*, a real devil's wife! (18:182,11–13; LW 40:192) But reason is just as baffled by *Mensch ist Gott* as it is by *Brod ist Leyb* ('bread is body', 18:187,3; LW 40:197): note this new parallel between the Incarnation (two natures) and the Sacrament (this is the title Luther uses; Karlstadt would prefer *Abendmahl*).

It helps me, says Luther, 'it soothes my conscience to know that Christ's body and blood are *for me, for me*!' (18:195,35–196,1; LW:206). '(Do this) *in memory of me*' does not mean a mere remembrance kept in the mind, but preaching and confessing in faith the promised forgiveness of sins.[20] The forgiveness of sins is communicated in the sacrament precisely because it is preaching and proclamation.[21] Christ does not leave heaven to be present there, any more than when he descended into his mother's body (18:206,10–13; LW 40:216). Once again, Eucharist and Incarnation are compared, in a climate of realistic, concrete, rather imaginative thinking. Christ is in every place, he fills everything (Ephesians 1:22 is quoted). In the sacrament, he is not bound to a place, neither here nor there (18:211,6–18; LW 40:220).

Thus in 1525 Luther had his explanation of Christ's presence in the sacrament, 'with' and 'in' the wine and bread.[22] He would have to defend it, and clarify it as well. And so,

> Bugenhagen, a pastor in Wittenberg, had attacked Zwingli's position, and Zwingli justified it in October 1525. At the same time, a study by Œcolampadius on the position of the Fathers, that he judged to be more in line with Zwingli's than Luther's,

20. What is 'doing this in memory of me' but preaching and confessing? (WA 18:197,21–32; see LW 40:207–208). See also the *Sermon von der Beichte und dem Sakrament* (1524), WA 15:493–494; see LW 76:442, *Sermon on Confession and the Sacrament* (Church Postil, 1525/1545).
21. WA 18:203,27–204,9–204; see LW 40:213–214. For Luther on the Eucharist and the forgiveness of sins, compare Peters, *Realpräsenz*, 140f.
22. In two sermons preached on Holy Thursday, 28 and 29 March, 1526, Luther simply explains that Christ is everywhere, including the sacrament. He uses comparisons: the soul is everywhere in the body, one word penetrates many ears. *Sermon von dem Sakrament*, WA 19:484,14–493,15.

> provoked a riposte from Brenz (*Syngramma suevicum*), who also sided with Luther. For the time being, the controversy continued just between the friends of the great leaders, who themselves avoided direct confrontation. That only happened in the Spring of 1527. In April of that year, Zwingli addressed an 'Amica exegesis' to Luther, who delivered a scathing reply, *Dass diese Worte 'Das ist mein Leib' noch feststehen. Wider die Schwarmgeister.*[23]

This lengthy polemical treatise involved Luther in a great deal of time and effort, and I will summarise it. WA 23:64–283 has a transcription of Luther's manuscript, together with the published text. For this text see LW 37:3–150, *That these Words of Christ,'This is My Body' Still Stand Firm Against the Fanatics* (1527).

He summarises the position of Zwingli and Œcolampade, writing against them and against Karlstadt. This brings us to what interests us. He explains the meaning of 'at God's right hand' (WA 23:133,19–28; LW 37:57). God is present everywhere and he is personally present in Christ. Christ is in various places on earth: in the womb, in the crib, in the temple, in the desert, in cities, in gardens, at the cross, in the tomb and, at the same time, in heaven in the bosom of the Father. 'Christ is God himself. God and man, one [same] person' (*Christus ist Gott selbst. Gott und Mensch, eine Person*), (23:135,12–140,29; LW 37:59–62). On the other hand, two bodies can be together in the same place: the risen Christ passes through the closed doors; being in heaven bodily, he appears to Stephen, to Paul. He said, 'no one can ascend into heaven except he who descended from heaven, the Son of Man, who is in heaven' (John 3:13; WA 23:147,28–32; LW 37:66). But if he is thus everywhere, united as he is with the Godhead, we must look for him where, according to his word, he gives himself and

23. Henri Strohl, *La Pensée de la Réforme*, Manuels et Précis de Théologie, XXXII, (Neuchâtel et Paris: Delachaux et Niestlé, 1951), 231. Zwingli's *Amica exegesis* is published with rich scholarly notes in *Huldreich Zwinglis Sämtllgche Werke*, V in *Corpus Reformatorum* 92 (Leipzig: Heinsius, 1934), 561–758. Writers of that era were not afraid of length! And they were published more quickly than today. On Brenz, see Otto Fricke, *Die Christologie des Johannes Brenz im Zusammenhang mit der Lehre vom Abendmahl und der Rechtfertigung*, (München: C Kaiser, 1927).

where he can be grasped, eaten.[24] This is the sacrament. Certainly, 'the flesh serves no purpose'; Luther explains himself at length on 'flesh', but he affirms the role of what is corporeal, *leiblich*, in salvation history (23:167–189; LW 37:78–92).

There are two things in the Lord's Supper: the word ('Take and eat, this is my body') and the eating itself. The word is received in the heart (23:179,24f.; LW 37:86); this seemed so important to Luther that he quoted this passage in *Vom Abendmahl Christi Bekenntnis* (1528), (WA 26:296; *see* LW 37:193). *Werk*, which is for the body, must not be separated from *Wort Gottes*, which is for the soul (WA 23:189; LW 37:92). Besides, whether we eat carnally or spiritually, it is always the spiritual flesh of Christ.[25] Luther's critics wrongly invoke Augustine to support their reasoning (23:209,28–210,2; LW 37:104). Müntzer is dead, but his spirit has not been eliminated (23:283; LW 37:150). Luther likewise discusses the texts of Tertullian (23:217,4–16, the meaning of figura, 'form', LW 37:108); St Irenaeus (23:229,21–35, on the 'salvation of the body', LW 37:115–116); St Hilary (23:237–238; LW 37:120–122), St Cyprian (23:239; LW 37:122–123). The word of God accomplishes what it says, (23:255,30–256,2; LW 37:132). Is the Mass a sacrifice? Augustine calls the sacrament a sacrifice because Christ's sacrifice is remembered, as is his resurrection every Easter (23:273,13–33; LW 37:143–144).

Zwingli responded to this treatise with another, *Dass diese Worte: Das ist mein Leib usw. ewiglich den alten Sinn haben werden* (June 20, 1527).[26] Luther then re-intervened with his major work *Vom Abendmahl Christi Bekenntnis* (1528), WA 26:261–509; see LW 37:161–372, *Confession Concerning Christ's Supper.* Its violent polemics were aimed against Zwingli and the sacramentarians Luther

---

24. WA 23:151,25–35; see LW 37:69. Luther would repeat the same answer several times. Certainly, for him, Christ is everywhere, as God. But he is there *for us* wherever his word tells us he is, in order to give himself to us. Compare WA 19:492,4f.; see LW 36:342, *Against the Fanatics.*
25. WA 23:203,31–204,2; see LW 37:100. I haven't found much specifically about the Holy Spirit in relation to the sacrament of the Lord's Supper. Luther's thinking on this article is richer if we consider his overall theology of the Christian life and our union with Christ. Peters insists, however, on the place of the Holy Spirit in the Sacrament, *Realpräsenz*, 46–49, but compare 67n95.
26. Text in *Realpräsenz*, supra, n23, CR 92:805–977. In the very title of the treatise, Luther is accused of joining the Papists!

sometimes calls *significatista* (WA 19:472,1 *Letter to John Herwagen*).[27] But this is where he formulates his position most fully, and where we find the best clarification of the relationship between Eucharist and Christology.

Ist, from 'this *is* my body', cannot signify *deutet*, 'point to'; *ist* is not *bedeutet*, 'means', (WA 26:270f.; LW 37:171f.). And we must not separate this statement from what follows, 'given for you' (26:280; LW 37:177) and 'take and eat'; it is a command, that achieves what it commands (26:283; LW 37:181), it is the 'power (*krafft*) of the word' (26:285,3–13; LW 37:184): *virtute verborum* ('by the power of the word'—this expression is already in *De captivitate*, WA 6: 510,34; see LW 36:33). It is true that Christ didn't say: 'You shall make bread my body', and we don't do that, but he said that the body would be there when, in the person and name of Christ, we pronounce these words 'as in his place and in his name' (*ynn seiner person und namen*), (WA 26:287,22–30; LW 37:187). Note these words carefully. And also note that Christ, on the cross, merited once and for all the remission of sins; he does not cease to distribute these merits everywhere he is, at every hour (26:294,23–36; LW 37:192). This is what he does in the Last Supper when he tells us: 'This is my body which is given to you'. The remission of sins is communicated to us. Christ's body is given to us, not in the same *gestalt* or *weise* as on the cross, (26:298,32–299,21; LW 37:195 and also 301; LW 37:196) not in the same state or manner, but in the same reality and nature (*sondem ynn dem selbigen wesen und natur*). Just because he is in heaven does not mean he is not in the sacrament (26:300,17–22; LW 37:195). When St Paul tells us to look for him on high, he is in heaven. Paul tells us to seek him above, where he sits, at the right hand of God (Colossians 3:1f.), it means not to seek him in an earthly, carnal way (26:305,25–30; LW 37:198); likewise when he says 'we no longer know Christ according to the flesh' (2 Corinthians 5:16–17: 26:308,23–26; LW 37:200). Whether Christ is in heaven *or* in the sacrament, Scripture tells us both (26:314,25 and 421,21–32; LW 37:203 and 260). At the Last Supper, Christ was already seated at table, and yet in the bread! (26:316; LW 37:204–205). God's word is incomprehensible to reason, (*unbegrifflich aller vemunfft*: 26:318,14–18; LW 37:207–208). This is because Christ

27. See WA 26:241f. for the tone of the letters exchanged. These controversies were violent.

is God and man in the same person. It is an inseparable unity. Here we are at the heart of Luther's faith and theology. He attacks the *alloiosis* of Zwingli, who ignored the realism of the communication of properties (*idiomata*), seeing them only as ways of speaking.[28]

For Luther, this is absolutely real, so much so that we have to say that Christ, both God and man, one and the same person, did not suffer only in his human nature. No. The Son of God, and therefore *God himself, suffered* (26:321.19–28; LW 37:210). Scripture is clear: God gave his Son (Jn 3:16; Rom 8:32 and compare Heb 6:6; 1 Cor 2:8). Zwingli's *alloíosis* would result in the positing of two persons (26:324, 25–35; LW 37:212–213). We see the two distinct natures in one person and say 'Gott ist mensch und mensch ist Gott'. But actions are of the person. Without confusing the *wesen* ('essence') of natures, we can (we must) attribute the actions of one nature to the other, because of the unity of the person they form (26:325, 33–35; LW 37:214). If we are talking about presence in bread, there are many ways of being in a place. It can be *localiter* or *circumscriptive*, within the limits of a space; it can be *definitive*, the way of angels or demons; it can be *repletive*, übernatürlich, the way that suits God.[29] We cannot measure God's power (26:330,29–331, 29; 217). We can suggest something by considering the conditions of the risen Christ, or how the son of God is also man in the womb (26:332, 334; LW 37:218–219). They cannot be separated. Humanity is bound to God like skin to flesh, like body to soul. Where God is, there man is too (26:333, 340; LW 37:219, 222). Christ can use three ways of being in relation to a place: according to the third, he is there and everywhere where God is. It is something like a voice entering ten thousand ears, or the same face reflected in a multitude of mirrors (26:335–337; LW 37:223–225).

---

28. WA 23:319,27–40; see LW 37:209–210. Lienhard, *Luther temoin* (209) defines *alloiosis* as follows: 'One speaks of one thing while thinking of another [of human nature while thinking of the divine] or one speaks of two things at once while thinking of only one of them'.
29. WA 26:326,29–329,33; see LW 37:214–216. These distinctions (circumscriptive, definitive, repletive) are by Ockham and Biel: Heiko Oberman, *The Harvest of Medieval Theology, Gabriel Biel and Late Medieval Nominalism* (Cambridge, Mass: Harvard, 1963), 276. They are taken up by the Formula of Concord, *Solida Declaratio* VII, *De Coena Domini*, 93–103 (BK 1005–1008; BC 609–611, Solid Declaration VII, *Concerning the Holy Supper*).

I am ignoring the 'flesh is useless' discussions, the vine comparison (against Œcolampade), and even passing over a criticism of Wyclif. Luther believes that Wyclif sees only pure bread in the sacrament (26:437–438, LW 37:443; 26:294–295, LW 37:301); he does not seem to know Wyclif well, nor to suspect that he is very close to him (26:437n2; LW 37:294n222). Luther, for his part, holds to a realism that Catholic theology criticizes: Angels, or the Holy Spirit, have taken on 'sensible forms'. In the same way, bread is the sensible form of Christ, and by biting into it we bite into Christ (26:441–442, LW 37:300–301). And Luther praises the first, ultrarealistic confession of faith, imposed on Berenger in 1059. This is a text of such material realism, that Thomas Aquinas criticizes it.[30] 'We bite into the sacrament', Aquinas says, 'but that doesn't touch Christ, whose presence, while entirely real, is a different kind of reality'.[31] For Luther, when we say 'This is my body', *this* refers to bread. It's no longer the bread you get at the baker's, it is a 'flesh-bread or body-bread, it is a bread that, with the body of Christ, has become one sacramental reality, or substance' (fleischsbrod *odder leibsbrod, das ist ein brod, so mit dem leibe Christi ein sacramentalisch wesen und ein ding worden ist*), WA 26:445,10–12; LW 37:303.

A little further on we find the formula, not so frequent in Luther, that Christ is 'in, with, and under the bread'.[32] As we know, the Formula of Concord was written thirty years after Luther's death. The *Solida Declaratio* takes up these terms and justifies them as expressions of Christology. Besides, it says, these are the ways in which Christ and Paul speak, namely that the bread at the Last Supper is the body of Christ,

30. WA 26:442,39–443,1; see LW 37:300–301. DSc 690. Compare: Ludwig Hödl, 'Die confessio Berengarii von 1059. Eine Arbeit zum frühscholastischen Eucharistietraktat', in *Scholastik*, 37 (1962) 370–394; Karl-Hermann Kandler, *Die Abendmahlslehre des Kardinals Humbert und ihre Bedeutung für das gegenwärtige Abendmahlsgespräch*. Arbeiten zur Geschichte und Theologie des Luthertums, 24 (Lutherisches Verlaghaus: Berlin-Hamburg, 1971).

31. *Sum theol.* IIIa q 77 a 7 ad 3.

32. 'Im brod, mit brod, unter brod': WA 26:447,18–26; see LW 37:306. In the *Small Catechism*, (*Das Sakrament des Altars*, 2) we read 'unter dem Brot und Wein' (BK 519–520; BC 362, *The Sacrament of the Altar*); in the *Large Catechism* (*Von dem Sakrament des Altars*, 8), 'in und unter' (BK 709; BC 467); in a letter of June 13, 1522 to Paul Speratus, 'sub'; *Augsburg Confession* X,1 has 'unter der Gestalt [*form*] des Brotes' (BK 64; BC 44, *Concerning the Lord's Supper*).

> For example, when we say that the body of Christ is present and is presented under the bread, with the bread, in the bread, we have serious reasons for this. First, we have them to reject papist transubstantiation. Secondly, we want to teach by this means the sacramental union of the unchanged substance of bread and the body of Christ. In a similar way, we say 'The Word became flesh' and we repeat and declare it with equivalent propositions, such as, for example: 'The Word dwelt in us'; 'The fullness of the divinity dwelt corporeally in Christ'; 'God was with him'; 'God was in Christ', etc (. . .)These phrases (. . .) declare that, through the Incarnation, the divine essence was not changed into human nature, but that the two natures were personally united without confusion.[33]

The exposition of the *Larger Catechism* (1528) is built on the distinction of two aspects: the act of God, through the word, that calls for absolute faith (BK 707–725; BC 467–476, *The Sacrament of the Altar*). Before the word and without it, we have the plain elements; with it, we have the presence of Christ's body and blood. On our side, we have the blessing of receiving 'a sure pledge and down payment, better still, the very reality that he has provided against my sins, death and all evil' (*The Sacrament* 22: BK 712, BC 469). Here we find Luther's *pro me*, with an emphasis on the blessing personally received. But as we shall see, the traditional idea of the unity of the Mystical Body is absent.

The *Marburg Colloquy*, 1–3 October, 1529, between Luther and his followers on the one hand, and Zwingli, Oecolampadius and Bucer on the other, however important and interesting it may have been, reveals nothing new. The meaning of various texts was discussed;

33. *'[E]tiam alias loquendi formas usurpamus, verbi gratia cum dicimus sub pane, cum pane, in pane adesse et exhiberi corpus Christi, id non sine gravibus causis facimus. Primum enim his phrasibus ad reiiciendam papisticam transsubstantiationem utimur. Deinde etiam sacramentalem unionem substantiae panis non mutatae et corporis Christi hac ratione docere volumus. Ad eundem enim modum hoc dictum est: Verbum caro factum est, repetitur et declaratur aliis aequipollentibus propositionibus, exempli gratia: Verbum habitavit in nobis; in Christo inhabitat tota plenitudo, divinitatis corporaliter; Deus erat cum eo; Deus erat in Christo; etc. (. . .) Haec phrases (. . .) declarant quod per incarnationem divina essentia non sit in humanam naturam conversa, sed quod duae naturae sine confusione personaliter sint unitae.' Solida Declaratio* VII,35–36 (BK 983; see BC 599).

Luther repeated his conviction and explanations with which we are quite familiar.[34]

After the failure of the *Diet of Augsburg*, Luther wrote his *Vermahnung zum Sakrament des Leibes und Blutes Christi* in September 1530 (WA 30/2:595–626; see LW 38:97–137, *An Admonition concerning the Sacrament of the Body and Blood of our Lord*), which is not only a statement of his theology, but also virulent attack on his opponents. He explains what he means by 'remembering Christ', and sacrifice: 'The commemoration of Christ is preaching, praising and giving thanks for the grace of Christ (. . .) one accomplishes the most beautiful sacrifice by giving thanks, praising God and paying him homage.'[35] Indeed, Catholics do say *Memores offerimus*: memorial and sacrifice go together. If the memorial *truly actualizes* what Christ has done, there can be an offering and celebration, by the Church, of the one sacrifice.[36] The Church does not add to it, except to say that she does it; in this manner she becomes its subject.

Like this, we can recognize that the celebration of the Eucharist has a sacrificial value, based on God's gift of grace. For Christ is

34. For accounts of the Colloquy see: *Marburger Gespräch und Marburger Artikel*: WA 30/3:110–159 (Colloquy) 160–171 (Articles), (Historical background, 92–101, Bibliography, 109), and see LW 38:5–13 (Introduction) 15–84 (Reports) 85–89 (Articles); Walther Kohler, *Zwingli und Luther, ihr Streit über das Abendmahl nach seinen politischen und religiösen Beziehungen*, 2 volumes (Leipzig: Verein für Reformationsgeschichte, 1924); Heinrich Bornkamm, *Der grosse Abendmahlsstreit*, chap. XIX, 443–488, from *Martin Luther in der Mitte seines Lebens* (Göttingen: Vandenhoeck & Ruprecht, 1979). On the Marburg symposium see Bornkamm, 561–577 = *Martin Luther in Mid-Career*, translated E. Theodore Bachmann (Philadelphia: Fortress Press, 1983), 633–652.

35. '*Christi Gedechtnis, das ist das predigen, loben und danken für die gnade Christi (. . .) Mit dem dancken, loben und ehren gegen Gott thut er das schonest opfer. . .nemlich ein Danckopfer*', WA 30/2:606,13–34; LW 38:111–112. See also *Sermon von der Beichte und Sakrament* (Palm Sunday, 1524), WA 15:493,33–494,19; see LW 76:444, *Sermon on Confession and the Sacrament*. What is it to 'do this in remembrance of me?' It is preaching and confessing Christ. This is not just for priests, but for all Christians.

36. See Josef Jungmann, 'Das Gedächtnis der Herrn in der Eucharistie', in *Theologische Quartalschrift* 133 (1953), 385–399; Odo Casel, 'Das Mysteriumgedächtnis der Messliturgie im Lichte der Tradition' (especially the Antiochians), in *Jahrbuch für Liturgiewissenschaft*, 6 (1926), 113–204 (compare 151–152). See also the contribution by Erwin lserloh in *Confessio Augustana, Bekenntnis des einen Glaubens*, Gemeinsame Untersuchung lutherischer und katholischer Theologen, Hrsg. v. H. Meyer u. H Schütte, Paderborn-Frankfurt, 1980.

not only the giver of the Lord's Supper, he is also the Head of the community which, through him, with him and in him, presents itself as an offering to the Father. Luther, on the other hand, was obsessed with fighting 'works'. Hence his indignant criticism of the pope and monks' mass (WA 30/2:609–613; LW 38:114–118). They want to offer the sacrifice of Jesus Christ instead of simply giving thanks for it. They thus make it a work and a merit before God. The sacrament is one thing, a pure gift *from God*. Another thing is the *Gedechtnis*, which consists in 'teaching, preaching and giving thanks' (*leren, predigen und dancken*), a sacrifice of thanksgiving rising *from us* to God.[37] Here and in WA 30/2:622,31–623,4; (see LW 38:133), Luther distinguishes two movements and two things to the point of opposing them: what we receive from God as grace and consolation, and our thanksgiving to God. He does not feel that the genius of the liturgy is any less schematic.

We should not forget, however, the very great realism that Luther puts into what he calls *fides Christi*: in the faith that responds to the proclamation or preaching, there takes place that actualisation of redemption through the cross that the Catholic tradition of East and West sees realised sacramentally in the liturgical celebration of the Eucharist.

Yet I am struck by the lack of expression of the sacrament's properly ecclesial fruit. With the exception of the *Sermon von dem Hochwirdigen Sacrament* of Autumn 1519, the traditional theme

37. 'Doing this in memory' is interpreted morally in the *Hebräervorlesung* (1517–1518): 'This oblation of the New Testament is perfect and has totally ceased with regard to the Head of the Church, Christ; but the oblation of his body, which is the Church, is offered day by day through continual death with Christ and the celebration of the mystical passover, namely the passage from this world to future glory by mortifying concupiscence' (*oblatio haec novi testamenti quoad caput Ecclesiae, qui Christus est, perfecta est et cessavit omnino, spiritualis autem corporis sui, quod est Ecclesia, offertur de die in diem, dum assidue moritur cum Christo et phase mysticum celebrat, scilicet concupiscentiis mortificatis ad futuram gloriam transiens ex hoc mundo*): WA 57/3:218,5–9; see LW 29:220, *Lectures on Hebrews*. This is not the sacramental 'memorial'! The reference to John Chrysostom (PG 63,349) given here is erroneous, because, for Chrysostom, in making memorial we offer the unique sacrifice of Christ! At the Marburg Colloquy in October 1529, Luther quoted Fulgentius, 'offering the body and blood of Christ at the Last Supper' (corpus et sanguinem domini in coena offeri), and Zwingli accused him of 'establishing again the sacrifice of the mass' (*missae sacrificium denuo instaurare*): WA 30/3:140; see LW 38:50–51.

of the unity of the Mystical Body is not even mentioned. Luther is well aware that the Church is the bride of Christ and his spiritual body.[38] And yet, even where he is most explicit about the fruits of the Sacrament, Luther speaks only of us, of 'me', of the individual believer.[39] And when he comments on 'the vine and the branches' (John 15), even then he does not speak of the Mystical Body.[40]

At the Diet and Colloquy of Regensburg in 1541, Lutherans and Catholics agreed on a formula that expressed the Real and Substantial Presence under the sacramental species, without specifying the mode.[41] But Cardinal Contarini, the Papal Legate, had added 'being transformed and transubstantiated' (*transmutatis et transsubstantiatis*).

From Wittenberg, Luther had reacted to this agreement (letter of May 25 to Prince George of Anhalt). On June 10 or 11, over a meal, he spoke out in full.[42] Transubstantiation meant, he said, the annihilation of bread (Thomas Aquinas did not admit this!). Moreover, Aristotle ruled that, in an affirmative proposition, the subject and predicate must refer to the same reality (*praedicatio identica*). So if *hoc*, in *Hoc est corpus meum*, refers to the body of Christ, and not to the reality of bread, it would be tantamount to saying 'My body is my body'. This word must designate the reality of bread, which we affirm, based on the word of Christ, is the body of Christ. Similarly, when we say of Christ *Homo est Deus*—in German *Mensch und Got ist ein*

38. WA 2:742–748; LW 35:45–73, *The Blessed Sacrament*, see n8 above. For 'Bride of Christ' see the *Vom Abendmahl Christi, Bekenntnis* (1528): WA 26:506,30–32; see LW 37:367. Luther was obviously familiar with Augustine's texts: see e.g. the glosses given to Melanchthon in December 1534: *Glossae super sententias patrem de controversia coenae*, WA 38:298.
39. Thus in the *Large Catechism* V, *Vom dem Sakrament des Altars*, 23–32 (BK 712–714; BC 469–470); *Vermahnung zum Sakrament des Leibes und Blutes Christi* (1530), WA 30/2:615,29–616,5; see LW 38:124
40. *Vom Abendmahl Christi, Bekenntnis*: WA 26:379f; see LW 38:252–253.
41. Here's the formula, from the *Regensburg Book*: 'The sacrament of the Eucharist has a word, which is the almighty word of Christ, by virtue of which this sacrament is performed and by which, after consecration, the true body and true blood of the Lord are truly and substantially present and are given to the faithful under the species of bread and wine' (*Eucharistiae Sacramentum verbum habet, quod est omnipotens Christi sermo, cuius virtute hoc Sacramentum conficitur et quo fit, ut post consecrationem verum corpus et verus sanguis domini vere et substantialiter adsint et fidelibus sub specie panis et vini distribuantur*).
42. WABr 9:443–445 [No LW].

ding—the truth of the man Jesus remains, without being annihilated (transubstantiated) to become God! Luther often uses this analogy. Eucharist and Incarnation share the same realism. As late as 1544, Luther wrote against the Zwinglians asking, why believe in the Incarnation if you don't believe in the Real Presence?[43]

43. WA 54:157,25-34, see LW 38:306, *Brief Confession concerning the Holy Sacrament*.

Study Three
New Insights into Luther's Christology

A study of some of Luther's major texts on the sacrament of the Lord's body and blood has given me a renewed understanding of Luther's Christological convictions. In the first place, two things become clear: his rejection of scholasticism and his 'discovery'of *fides Christi.*

1° Luther's reaction to scholastic theology was decisive. His *Disputatio contra Scholasticam Theologiam* of September 4, 1517, is perhaps more important than the famous *95 Theses*. In the midst of theses against the latent Pelagianism of later Scholasticism, Luther introduces a dozen theses against the use of Aristotle and dialectics in theology. They arise from his study of Pierre d'Ailly and Gabriel Biel.[1] And these are his clear-cut positions:

> Thesis 43. It is a mistake to say that you can not become a theologian without Aristotle.
> 44. Better still: you do not become a theologian if you do not become one without Aristotle.
> 47. No form of syllogism holds in the realm of divine things.

---

1. See WA 1:224–228; LW 31:3–16, *The Disputation against Scholastic Theology* (1517). Leif Grane, *Contra Gabrielem. Luthers Auseinandersetzung mit Gabriel Biel in der Disputatio Contra Scholasticam Theologiam*, 1517 (Acta Theol. Danica, IV) (København: Gyldendal, 1962).; Leif Grane, *Modus loquendi theologicus, Luthers Kampf um die Erneuerung der Theologie (1515–1518)*, Acta Theologica Danica, XII (Leiden: Schöningh, 1975); Yves Confar, 'Novo et miro vocabulo, et theologico. Luther reformateur de la theologie', in *Rev. d'Hist. et de Phil. Religieuses* 63 (1983).

> 50. In short: the whole of Aristotle, for theology, is darkness in relation to light.[2]

For Luther, this was a profound conviction: the language of theology is different from that of philosophy. Thus, glossing Peter Lombard's *Sentences* in 1509–1510, he wrote:

> What is Christ? The logician will answer: a person, etc. The theologian, on the other hand, answers: a stone, the cornerstone, etc.[3]

Theology will therefore speak a language other than logic and reason, mainly in relation to the mystery of Christ, which is the wisdom of God and outside of which St Paul declares he wants to know nothing.[4] Without fail, Luther will strive to speak another language, to conceive and express the mysteries of faith in the categories, not of scholasticism, but of Scripture, the place of absolute truth surpassing the demands and resources of reason. In the *Disputatio* of February 28, 1540, *De divínitate et humanitate Christi* (against Schwenckfeld), he proclaims:

> Thesis 20: But it is certain that, in Christ, all vocables receive a new meaning, applied to the same reality.
> 21: *Creature*, according to the ancient language and for other realities, means a reality infinitely separated from divinity.
> 22: According to the new languages, it signifies a reality inseparably and ineffably united with the divinity, making one person.
> 23: So it is necessary to see that these words: man, humanity, suffered, etc, and all that is said about Christ are new words.[5]

---

2. '43. Error est dicere: sine Aristotele non fit theologus. 44. Imo theologus non fit nisi id fiat sine Aristotele. 47. Nulla forma syllogistica tenet in terminis divinis. 50. Breviter: totus Aristoteles ad theologiam est tenebrae ad lucem', WA 1:226; see LW 31:12.
3. 'Quid est Christus? Respondet logicus: est persona, etc. Theologus autem: est petra, lapis angularis, etc.': WA 9:91,23f.
4. Luther cites these texts (Colossians 2:3; 1 Corinthians 2:2) and John 14:26 (the Holy Spirit is given to us only to know and confess Christ), *Von den Konziliis und Kirchen* (1539), WA 50:606,10–20; LW 41:122, *On the Councils*.
5. Thesis 20: *Certum est tamen, omnia vocabula in Christo novam significationem accipere in eadem re significata.* 21: *Nam* creatura *veteris linguae usu et in aliis*

What was the old language that Luther abandoned and criticised? It was the language of later Scholasticism, in which he had immersed himself in his formative years, that of Gabriel Biel, a follower of the Ockhamist movement. As we shall see, their Christology is fundamentally correct.[6] Luther, for his part, left behind the concepts of scholasticism, but seems not to have found any others that were fully satisfactory.

2° Luther is driven by an unsurpassable faith in Christ–my Saviour. We must never lose sight of the realism with which, for Luther, Christ is in me through faith. That is the *fides Christi*.[7] In this phrase, analogous to the expressions 'work of God', 'strength of God', 'wisdom of God', the genitive signifies both the origin and the content of faith. It is faith, absolute openness to Christ, that makes Christ present in us through his sovereign action. Christ is the whole of Christianity; faith makes him ours. Marc Lienhard begins his *Luther, témoin de Jesus-Christ* by quoting these beautiful texts:

> In my heart only one article reigns: it is the *fides Christi*. This is where all my theological mediation comes from, this is where it passes through, and this is where it emerges day and night in its flow and its reflux, without my having managed to grasp more than a few fragile and poor first-fruits of crumbs from a wisdom so high, so wide and so deep.[8]

---

rebus significat rem a divinitate separatàm infinitis modis. 22: *Novae linguae usu significat rem cum divinitate inseparabiliter in eandem personam ineffabilibus modis coniunctam*. 23: *Ita necesse est, vocabula: homo, humanitas, passus, etc, et omnia de Christo dicta nova esse vocabula*, WA 30/2:94; see LW 73:255. Luther alludes to Mark 16:18 (Vg), 'you shall speak in new tongues' (*linguís loquentur novis*).

6. See Oberman, *Harvest of Medieval Theology*, 249–280, and especially Reinhard Schwarz, 'Gott ist Mensch. Zu Luthers Lehre von der Person Christi bei den Ockhamisten und bei Luther', in *Zeitschrift für Theologie und Kirche*, 63 (1966), 289–351 (293–301).
7. Thus, among many other testimonies, including the *Dictata super Psalterium*, WA 3:349,15, 'Christus seu fides Christi', see LW 10:296, and in an often equivalent way, the *Ad Galatas Commentarius* (1531/35), WA 40/1:228,33(ff.); see LW 26:129. Joest, *Ontologie der Person bei Luther*, has collected a number of texts on this 'fides Christi, fides apprehensiva Christum', taken in particular from the theses *De fide* of 1535 (WA 39/1:44–48; see LW 34:109–114, *Theses concerning the law and faith*), and further from the *Ad Galatas Commentarius* etc.
8. Lienhard, *Luther, témoin de Jesus-Christ* = ET, *Luther: Witness to Jesus Christ*, translated by Edwin Robertson (Minneapolis: Augsburg, 1982). Quotation from *Ad Galatas Commentarius* (1531/35), WA 40/1:33,7–11; see LW 27:145.

> To have Christ is to have everything: if Christ remains with me, everything remains with me and can be found.[9]

When it comes more specifically to our knowledge of God, and thus theology, Luther never ceases to say that he neither knows nor wishes to honour any other God but [Christ] himself. As he affirmed at the Marburg Colloquy in 1529: 'he neither wanted to know nor honour any other God except the one who became human; he wanted to have no other. For there is no other, except this one, who can save'.[10] Ten years later he says, 'Apart from Christ, there is no other God'.[11] For Luther, there is no God other than God *the Saviour*! It is in Christology, then, that we can best hear the new language Luther spoke.

It will be helpful to recognise and appreciate the major categories for this.

First and foremost, there is the notion of the person, which leads us to raise the question of the 'support' *(suppôt,* 'supplicant') or 'hypostasis'. I can find almost nothing on our theme in Wilfried Joest, *Ontologie der Person bei Luther.* The person in question is that of a human being; it is formed in him by the faith that puts Christ in him and makes him active. Interesting for Luther's religious anthropology and soteriology, this study barely touches on his Trinitarian and Christological theology. Joest acknowledges (391–392) that Luther did not delve deeply into Trinitarian ontology.

In matters of the Trinity, Luther multiplied the classical professions of faith, often by simply reproducing the traditional symbols with barely a gloss.[12] He didn't speculate on the Trinity.

---

9. *Dass diese Worte Christi* (1527), WA 23:207,27; see LW 37:103, *That these words of Christ . . . stand firm against the fanatics.*

10. '*nullum enim deum vel scire se, vel colere praeter eum qui homo sit factus, praeter hunc salvare possit.*' WA 30/3:132–133; see LW 38:46 *The Marburg Colloquy.* Compare *Ad Galatas Commentarius* 1531/35, WA 40/1:76–77; LW 26:28–29. This is indeed the only point by which God has touched us, as a tangent touches a sphere: WA 39/2:255; see LW 73:410, *Disputation on the Unity of the Divine Essence.*

11. 'Extra Christum non est Deus alius'. *Disputatio in John 1:14* (January 1539): WA 39/2:25,18; see LW 38:258 (*Argument 23*).

12. Examples are in *Dass diese Worte Christi* (1527) at the beginning, WA 23:65 (LW 37:3); in the *Bekenntnis* concluding *Vom Abendmahl Christi,* (1528), WA 26:500 (LW 37:361); *Die Schwabacher Artikel,* (1529), 1 (BK 52); *Large Catechism* (1529) Preface, 2 (BK 555–556 [but see also 646–647], BC 384 [also 431–432]); *Smalcald Articles* (1537) Part 1, (BK 414–415; BC 300), etc.

Speaking of the Word made flesh, he also says 'divine nature' or 'divinity'. Lienhard makes it clear that Luther offers little explanation of the meaning of *persona*; he quotes only this definition, that would apply equally well to substance: 'a thing existing by itself' (*res per se existens*).[13] Luther obviously holds that the person of the Word pre-existed his Incarnation.[14] But he abhors Nestorianism more than anything else, which is why he comments on the theology of the Council of Ephesus of 431 even more carefully than that of Nicaea, Constantinople (381) or Chalcedon. He is opposed to a Christology *of homo assumptus*: 'If one were to say: the divine Person assumed a man, namely a human person, that would make two persons, which is unacceptable'.[15] It is absolutely essential that there be only one person, and that this person be God: otherwise we would not be saved. We shall see that this leads Luther to argue passionately that God suffered, died for the redemption of our sins.

So Pilate and the Jews are deicides, *Gottes creuziger und mörder.*[16] Luther is not interested in the eternal Person of the Word. That would concern a *theologia gloriae*, whereas Luther only wants to know and practice the *theologia crucis*. This leads him to introduce the humanity of Christ into the notion of unity of person (salvation), and

---

13. Lienhard, *Luther temoin*, 340 (ET 330); compare 240ff (ET 230ff). The text is from the *Disputatio de divinitate et humanitate Christi*, February 28, 1540, WA, 39/2:117,33; see LW 73:276, *Disputation on the Divinity and Humanity of Christ*), quoted as '*Disp. de div. et hum*'. For 'Word' = divine nature, divinity, compare, Ibid, 119; LW 73:278, *Arguments* 30, 30c. For our purposes, this is a privileged text.
14. *Marginal glosses on Lombard's Sentences*: 'Unde sicut verbum persona deorsum est et cum humanitate eandem personam constituit, ita anima est persona seorsum et tamen cum corpore quod ipsa sustentat eadem est persona', WA 9:84,38–40; *Disp. de div. et hum. Argument* 2: '*Sed illa persona est Deus et Homo, est una persona et eadem, uae est ante mundum creatum (. . .) filius Dei erat, qui nunc est homo*': WA 39/2:101; LW 73:263. Compare *Argument* 14B. 110; LW 73:270. And compare Lienhard, *Luther temoin*, 241–242; *Luther: Witness*, 231–232).
15. '*Si diceretur: Persona divina suscepit hominem, id est humanam personam, sequeretur quod essent duae personae, sed hoc non est ferendum*', *Disp. de div. et hum. Argument* 25, Ibid,116,6ff; LW 73:275. Compare *Argument* 27, 118, 3–4, '*Humanitas enim in Christo significat naturam humanam assumptam, non subsistentem. Sed homo significat personam subsistentem*', see LW 73:276.
16. *Von den Konziliis* (1539), WA 50:590,30; LW 41:104, *On the Councils.*

thus to see this person as the union of (the) two natures.[17] The texts are innumerable; these are just a few of them:

> *Vorlesung über den I. Johannesbrief*, 1527: 'one person is formed from two natures' (*unam personam constitutam ex duabus naturis*, WA 20:603).
> *Vom Abendmahl Christi Bekenntnis*, 1528: 'We blend the two distinct natures into one person, and say *Gott ist mensch und mensch ist Gott*', (WA 26:324,4–5; compare LW 37:211). 'Where you place God for me, you must place humanity with him. You can not separate them. [He] has become one person' (*Es ist eine person worden*), (ibid. 333, 6–8; compare LW 37:219). 'And this man truly became God as a single eternal person made inseparably of God and man' (*als eine ewige unzertrennliche person aus Gott und mensch worden*), (ibid. 501,10–12; compare LW 37:362).
> *Preaching* of November 22, 1537 *on Colossians 1:18–20*: 'The *Communatio idiomatum* is spoken of when one unites and mixes (*vermischt*) the properties of natures in Christ just as one unites and mixes natures, God and man, in one person' (WA 45:297, from Lienhard, *Luther temoin* 357; *Luther: Witness* 344).
> *Von den Konziliis und Kirchen*, 1539: 'From God and man one person has come', (*Denn es ist eine person worden aus Gott und mensch*, WA 50:590,3; LW 41:103); 'when the man dies, who with God is one substance or one person', (*wenn der mensch stirbt der mit Gott ein ding oder eine person ist*, 50:590,21–22; LW 41:104).
> *Disputatio de divinitate et humanitate Christi*, 28 February 1540. *Preface*: 'It is incomprehensible (. . .) that two natures should be in one person (. . .) the two natures are united in one person in such a way that what is done by one is also said to be done by the divine, and vice versa' (*Est res incomprehensibilis (. . .) quod duae naturae in una persona unitae sunt (. . .) duae naturae unitae sunt in una persona sic, ut quod ab una natura fit, dicatur etiam fieri a divina, et econtra*: WA

17. It is unlikely that Luther depended on John Huss. The fourth of the propositions condemned by the Council of Constance, is '*Duae naturae, divinitas et humanitas, sunt unus Christus*', (DSch 1204). This is taken from Huss' *De Ecclesia*, c. 4 (ed. St Harrison Thomson, 1956, 21). This statement, as A Michel, says (DTC VII, 542), could either be well understood, or misunderstood, in a Nestorian sense.

> 39/2:98,18 f.; LW 73:261). *Argument* 1: 'humanity and divinity in Christ constitute a [single] person' (*humanitas et divinitas in Christo constituunt unam personam*: 39/2:100,18; LW 73:263). *Argument* 24: 'The person of Christ exists through two united natures'(*Christi persona constat duabus naturis unitis*: 39/2:114,17–18; LW 73:273). *Argument* 33: 'We join or unite distinct natures in one person' (*Nos distinctas naturas coniungimus vel unimur in unam personam*: 39/2:121,3–4; LW 73:279).

The accusative following the preposition 'in' raises questions: it is as if the two natures had to meet and unite to make one person. Clearly, Luther's intention and faith are those of traditional, Catholic dogma, with a passionate insistence on the unity of two natures. The commentary on the Council of Ephesus in the *Von den Konziliis*, and the *Disputatio de divinitate et humanitate Christi*, are full of such statements. But as Luther is interested only in 'Christ-my *Saviour*', he sees only the end, the result and the perfection of the union between divinity and humanity; he is not concerned with the mode of union. I believe that Luther's avoidance of philosophical terms and reasoning led to a theologically blurred, insufficiently precise formulation. His use of terms like 'mixture', *Ding* or *Wesen* is a sign of this. Marc Lienhard agrees:

> It must be admitted that Luther sometimes lacks precision in his vocabulary. He uses the term *Wesen* both in the sense of essence or nature and in the sense of being. 'We do not mix the two natures in one being (*Wesen*)', he writes (WA 26:324,6 *see* LW 37:211; *Lienhard,* 239; ET 230); 'Often he replaces the term *communicatio* with expressions such as 'communion', 'mix', 'confuse', 'share', etc. (*Lienhard*, 357; ET 344).

One wonders whether the 'person' is not the mixture or union of natures; it would then appear as constituted *from them*, whereas St Leo and Chalcedon were keen to affirm the unity *in*, not *ex*, *duabus naturis*.[18]

It is a fact, extensively studied by Reinhard Schwarz (*supra*, n5), that Luther criticized the Christology of those he calls *Moderni* or

18. But Luther also has '*in duabus naturis*': *Von den letzen Worten Davids* (1543), WA 54:89,35–90,19, see LW 15:340, *Treatise on the Last Words of David.*

Sophistae, and which Schwarz calls Ockhamist Christology (Ockham, Oresme, Pierre d'Ailly, Biel). But this is, on the point at issue at least, only traditional Christology. It is the affirmation that an individuated human nature is supported and personalised by the supplicant or hypostasis of the second Person, the Word. Admittedly, this scholasticism is very unsatisfactory in style and development.[19] But it was developing authentic dogmatics. Luther recognised that the intention of these *Moderni* was correct and catholic, but he wanted to express himself differently, in this new language that he felt was closer to that of Scripture. Once again, from the *Disputatio de divinitate et humanitate Christi*:

> 47: These (*Moderni*) say that human nature is carried and sustained in being by the divine nature or the divine agent (*Hi (Moderni) dicunt, humanam naturam sustentari seu suppositari a divina natura, seu supposito divina*).
> 48: This is quite pretentious and almost obliges God to bear and take charge of [a] humanity. (*Hoc et portentose dicitur et cogit pene Deum velut portare vel gestare humanitatem*).
> 49: But all of them have a just and catholic meaning, so we must dispense with their unfortunate expression (*Sed omnes illi recte et catholice sapiunt, ideo condonanda est illis incommoda locutio*).
> 50: Because they wanted to express something ineffable, subsequently all analogy goes awry and never runs, as they say, on its four feet (*Quia rem ineffabilem volebant effari, deinde omnis similitudo claudicat nec unquam (ut dicunt) currit quatuor pedibus*).
> 52: On the same subject the learned man has a duty to speak differently, and as simply as possible (*In eandem rem variis modis eloqui doctus iubeatur quam potest simplicissime loqui*)'.[20]

Invited by University regulations to conduct *Disputationes*, Luther had placed the one held on January 11, 1539 under the heading of

19. Reasoning about words; treating the mystery of hypostatic union as a theorem of metaphysics or logic (it could unite a stone or a donkey to the Person of the Word: Ockham and Biel, from Schwarz, 'Gott ist Mensch. . .', n5, 298); considering what God could do '*de potentia absoluta*'. What would become of Christ's human nature if God withdrew the support of hypostatic union?
20. WA 39/2:95–96; see LW 73:258. For these theses no discussion was published.

John 1:14. The forty–two theses, against the Sorbonne, are a radical assertion of the difference, even incompatibility, between what is said in philosophy and what must be said in theology. The Trinitarian, and above all Christological, statements are illustrative. For example:

> A philosophical term simply becomes new in theology: thus 'human', in philosophy, is a subsistent person, but in theology it is a certain divinity in Christ.[21]

Presiding over a Doctoral Promotion Disputation on 12 December, 1544, Luther once again asserted the obligation to speak another language and have another anthropology when it comes to Christ. For 'he makes all things new' (*nova facit omnia*).[22] When it comes to the Trinity, we can use the old terms and speak of *hypostasis*: we may even have to, to be understood by the weak, and for teaching purposes. But,

> if you want to use other terms, do so, as long as you respect and express the essence of the thing (. . .) we must preserve the essence (*res*); we may express it using terms as we wish.[23]

Luther wanted to express the same *res*, i.e. the Catholic faith of the great councils, especially that of Ephesus against Nestorius (*redivivivus* in Zwingli!), in another language, that of the non-philosophical affirmations of Scripture. He does not start from the eternal Person of the Word, taken as a 'supplicant' or support for the humanity of Jesus. In fact, he completely dispenses with the concept of a supplicant. Theobald Beer has even argued that he ignores this notion and replaces it with various *ersatz* notions.[24] The theology of the wonderful, joyful exchange between my sin and Christ's righteousness would have

21. 'Vox philosophica in theologia plane fit nova, ut homo in philosophia est persona subsistens, sed in theologia est quaedam divinitas in Christo', WA 39/2:3–33. Here, from *Argumentum* 12, WA 39/2:19,7–9, see LW 38:252.
22. WA 39/2:303–304; see LW 73:487, *Disputation on the Mystery of the Holy Trinity and the Incarnation of the Son.*
23. 'Wiltu ein ander vocabulum gebrauchen, so thue es, modo ut rei proprietatem serves et exprimas (. . .) 'Rem' mussen wir behalten wir redens mit Vocabln, wie wir wöllen'. WA 39/2:305,18–23; see LW 73:489.
24. Theobald Beer, *Der fröhliche Wechsel und Streit*, especially chapter 4, 323f., and particularly 382f.

led to this absence of a fundamental concept. Luther, according to Beer (393), would thus contradict the Councils. I cannot accept this conclusion. Luther simply affirms the unity of the two natures in one person.[25] That this is another conceptualisation than the traditional one, Luther himself proclaims and claims. That the intention or aim of this conceptualisation can be criticized is another matter. All this becomes clearer in the Lutheran thesis of the communication of attributes or properties.

The Lutheran understanding of this classic chapter of theology is linked to the Lutheran way of seeing the person of Christ as the unity of the two natures; it is also the basis of the Lutheran explanation of the real presence of Christ in the sacrament of the Lord's Supper.

The communication of attributes is an immediate consequence of hypostatic union; it is even just another formula for it.[26] The correct expression of the doctrine was fixed in Luther's day, even though the question had been the subject of discussion in the nominalist tradition.[27]

This is the attribution to the single subject of acts or properties realised according to one or the other nature. If we speak of divinity or humanity in the abstract, we cannot make this attribution. We can if we speak to the concrete. This distinction, already made, for example, by Gregory of Nyssa, is known to Luther.[28] Luther, however, is hampered by the theology of the person of Christ that I have just outlined: a theology that dispenses with the notion of the supplicant and is based on the intimate union of the two natures. This is why Luther's notion of the communication of properties is sometimes irreproachable, and sometimes questionable and, in my view, incorrect. It seems to me that statements like these are correct:

---

25. Johannes Brenz (+ 1570) was one of Luther's supporters of this theology and of the Real Presence in the Eucharist: positions he defended against the reformed theologians. See Fricke, *Die Christologie des Johannes Brenz.*

26. As Albert Michel, states in his article ('Incarnation') in DCT VII, col. 595–602, referring to his own article 'Hypostatique' (Union), col. 542ff.

27. See Ernst Borchert, *Der Einfluss des Nominalismus auf die Christologie der Spätscholastik nach dem Traktat de communicatione idiomatum des Nicolaus Oresme*, Beiträge zur Geschichte der Philosophie des Mittelalters 35, 4/ 5 (Münster, 1940 - alas, inaccessible: 1940!) For the classical position, see St Thomas, *Sum. theol.* IIIa q16.

28. Thus in WA 40/3:707,22–27; 709,24–26, *Esaiai 53.* See Lienhard, *Luther temoin,* 350n110. (*Luther: Witness,* 339n110).

> The same and unique person of Christ is both dead and alive, both suffering and blessed, both active and inactive, etc., because of the communication of attributes, even if nothing that is proper to the one nature returns to the other.[29]

And again, from the 22 November 1537 sermon on Colossians 1:18–20:

> Because God and man are one person, it must be said that the person of Christ includes the properties of both natures (. . .) We must therefore attribute to the whole person what belongs individually to one of the two natures (. . .) Because God and man are one person in Christ, one Jesus, one Son of God and Mary, and not two persons, not two Christs, not two Jesuses, not two Sons, it follows that the properties of the two natures in Christ must be attributed to the person in the same way.[30]

But, in the same sermon, Luther had said, ominously: '*Communatio idiomatum* is spoken of when one unites and mixes (*vermischt*) the properties of natures in Christ, just as one unites and mixes natures, God and man, in one person' (WA 45:297).

What is thus announced is clearer and, this time, I believe, incorrect, in the *Disp. de div. et hum.* of February 28, 1540 and in the *Von den Konziliis und Kirchen* of 1539. Let's start with the *Disputatio.* Emphasised in italics are the words where I feel a shift is taking place:

> There are not two sons, nor two judges, nor two persons, nor two Jesus, but there is communication of properties by reason of the assembled conjunction and unity of the two natures, so that what is attributed to one nature is attributed to the other, because there is one person (. . .) It is incomprehensible (. . .) that two natures are united in one person. Therefore, so that we can understand in some measure, God has given us rules of expression, that Christ is man and God in one person and that there are not two persons, but two natures united in one

29. Lienhard, *Luther temoin*, 63 (*Luther:* Witness, 54): *Römervorlesung* (1516), WA 56:343,20–22. See LW 25:332, *Lectures on Romans*,

30. WA 45:300,37f. and 301,21–25; from Lienhard, *Luther temoin*, 349 (*Luther: Witness*, 338).

> person in such a way *that what is done by the human nature is said to be also done by the divine, and vice versa.*[31]
> Being crucified is a property of human nature, but because the two natures are united in one person, it is attributed to both *natures.*[32]
> This unity of two natures in one person is the closest, so that they are equal for what is said, that *they communicate properties to each other* as if there were only God or only man.[33]

It is striking that Luther had an extremely strong sense of the unity of God and man in the person of Christ, but, conceiving the unity of the person as the closest possible uníon of the two natures, he spoke in terms of natures of the communication of properties founded in and demanded by the unity of the person. He developed this against Zwingli and in connection with the Eucharistic question.[34] Zwingli had criticized him for confusing the two natures, whereas the attribution of properties from one to the other is a matter of *alloiosis*, a mere manner of speaking.[35] But it is above all in his discussion of Ephesus and Chalcedon in the *Von den Konziliis* that Luther explains himself. Nestorius, says Luther, admitted the duality of natures and

31. '*Non sunt duo filii, non duo iudices, non duae personae, non duo Iesus, sed propter unitam coniunctionem et unitatem duarum naturarum fit communicatio idiomatum, ut, quid uni naturae tribuitur, tribuitur et alteri, quia fit una persona (. . .) Est res incomprehensibilis (. . .) quod duae naturae in una persona unitae sunt. Ideo ut capere aliquo modo possimus, dedit Deus nobis formulas loquendi, quod Christus sit Deus et homo in una persona, et non sunt duae personae, sed duae naturae unitae sunt in una persona sic, ut quod ab humana natura fit, dicatur etiam fieri a divina, et econtra*.' *Praefatio*: WA 39/2:98,7f,18f; see LW 73:260–261.
32. '*Crucifigi est unum idioma naturae humanae sed quia duae naturae sunt in una persona unitae, tribuitur utrique* naturae'. Argument 3, WA 39/2:102,34f; LW 73:264.
33. '*Maxima est illa unitas duarum naturarum in una persona, ut pares sint in praedicatione, communicant sibi idiomata, quasi vel solum esset Deus vel solum homo*'. Argument 17, 111,14f; LW 73:271
34. Already *Vom Abendmahl Christi* (1528), WA 26:332–333; see LW 37:218–219, and WA 26:440,34–441,8; see LW 37:297–298, *Confession concerning Christ's Supper*.
35. In Zwingli's *Amica exegesis* (CR 92), 564; in pompous and verbose humanist Latin!

their union in one person.[36] Even when he says that Mary is the mother of Christ as far as humanity is concerned, this is not false: she is not the mother of the divinity.

But that does not mean she isn't the 'mother of God': a woman doesn't give her soul to her child, and yet she is the mother of that child, of that person.[37] Nestorius' error was to ignore the communication of attributes (*idiomata*).[38] Nestorius lives again in Zwingli.[39] But the Papists also reject the consequence of the communication of attributes that Luther insists on, namely that God suffered. Moreover, when Luther discusses Chalcedon, it is to denounce the same error in Eutyches as in Nestorius, but applied in reverse. Nestorius missed the transition from humanity to divinity, and denied Mary the title of Mother *of God*. Eutyches and Apollinaris missed the transition from divinity to humanity, and denied to the latter the properties of the former.[40] This whole world admits the antecedent (two natures, one person), but forgets the consequence, the communication of what is proper to one nature to the other. This is the crux of Luther's theology, to which he attaches certain theses of great importance: *The explanation of Christ's presence in the sacrament of the Lord's Supper*. This explanation stems from the fact that the property of ubiquity possessed by the divinity is communicated to Christ. Christ 'sits at the right hand of God', and God is everywhere. St Paul says he was exalted to fill all things.

Obviously, this explanation drew criticism, not only from Catholics,[41] but also from Zwingli, Oecolampadius and other minor figures, such as Hans Mohr, who accused Luther of making the creature the Creator, and whom Luther asked Prince Elector John to silence.[42]

36. WA 50:581–586; see LW 41:93–99, *On the Councils*.
37. WA 50:586,20–22; see LW 41:99. This justification is already found in St Cyril of Alexandria, *Letter to the Monks*, I,12.
38. WA 50:587,29; LW 41:100. At this point, ibid. 591,1–8; 104, Luther has a correct expression of this communication, which refers *to the* unique *person*.
39. 'Denn ich wol auch fur mir habe Nestorianos gehabt', WA 591,9–21; 105.
40. WA. 587,19–34; 100–101. 589,21–590,4; 103. For Nestoríus; WA 50:595; 602.26–29; 609.20f, for Eutyches. See LW 108–118 *passim*.
41. See DCT VII, 543f.
42. Letter of January 19, 1528: WABr 4:349.

Calvin rejected this: the body of Christ occupies a *place*; to see it as immense is contrary to so many facts attested by Scripture, where Christ is present in a place, and ends up resurrecting Marcion's error.[43]

God suffered, God died.[44] Scripture says that the Lord of glory was crucified (1 Corinthians 2:8). We also say this. St Cyril of Alexandria and St John Damascene also said so, but by application to the single subject, and noting that the divinity as such did not suffer.[45] For Luther, it is essential to recognize that God died on the cross, because God alone, present in Christ, could redeem our sins by bearing them himself,[46] and defeat the devil by being swallowed up by him (the image of the hook swallowed up with the worm).[47] We are here at the heart of the Lutheran vision of Christology as soteriology through the exchange between my sin and Christ's righteousness. I'll return to this shortly.

It is undeniable that the Lutheran conception of the *communicatio idiomata* evokes statements of a monophysitic flavour. Luther, whose Alexandrian inspiration has struck me often, over many years, is very

43. *Inst. chr.* (1536), c. 4 (CR 29, 121–122), text taken up again in the edition of 1559: IV, 17, no. 17 (CR 30, 1015–1016). The same accusation is made by Zwingli in his June 1527 treatise addressed to Luther, *Dass diese Worte Das ist mein Leib, etc. ewiglich den alten Sinn haben werden*: Zwingli, Werke, V (CR 92) 912,6f.; 918,6f.; 942,1; 958,13f. The Formula of Concord of 1577 (*Epitome* VIII:23, *De Persona Christi:* BK 809; BC 512) rejects this accusation of Marcionism. As had Luther himself: *Vom Abendmahl Christi*, WA 26:339,14; see LW 37:227.
44. Against Zwingli: *Vom Abendmahl Christi*: WA 26:319,29f. (LW 37:209); 321,19f. (210); 324,25f.(212); *Predig uber Exodus 3* (Easter 1526), WA 20:358–359; *Schwabacher Artikel* (1529), WA 30/3:87,16 (BK 55); *Von den Konziliis*: WA 50:590,18–19 see LW 41:104; ibid. 601,15 see 116 .
45. St Cyril; see DCT VII, 599 and his twelfth anathema (DSch 263). St John of Damascus, who calls for perichoresis between the two natures: DCT VII, 600. It must be acknowledged, however, that these two Fathers come close to Luther's formulas.
46. 'Indeed, to overcome in oneself the sin of the world, death, the curse and the wrath of God is not the work of any creature, but of divine power. Therefore he who has conquered these things in himself must be God truly and by nature' (*Vincere enim peccatum mundi, mortem, maledictionem et iram Dei in semetipso non est ullius creaturae, sed divinae potentiae opus. Igitur necesse est illum qui in seipso ista vicit, vere et natura Deum esse*): *Ad Galatas Commentarius*, 1531/35, WA 40/1:441,16–19 (the rest is for you to read!) See LW 26:282.
47. On this subject, Beer, *Der fröhliche Wesel*, 339–351.

close to St Cyril of Alexandria.[48] Also in his affirmation that *God* suffered.[49]

This question of the communication of attributes in its Lutheran understanding and application was the subject of much discussion. Even Chemnitz had some difficulty with the omnipresence of Christ's flesh. Is this why the *Solida Declaratio* of the Formula of Concord, in whose elaboration he participated, rather than omnipresence speaks of *Multivolipräsenz*, presence 'when and where he wills' (*wenn und wie er will*).[50] The *Solida Declaratio* takes up this question of the communication of attributes at length (*De Persona Christi* VIII 17–96: BK 1022–1049; BC 619–634), showing that it feels the need to explain and justify full conformity with the ancient Church (VIII 61: BK 1036; BC 627).

The intention is not to confuse a 'physical communication or a mixture of essences' (*physica communicatio vel essentialis transfusio*, *De Persona Christi* VIII, 63, BK 1037; BC 628), and yet to go beyond the simple verbal attribution based on the unity of the 'support' or hypostasis (*cf De Persona Christi* VIII, 38: BK 1029; BC 623). These terms do not appear. Instead, we speak of hypostatic union, which

48. Georges-Matthieu de Durand writes (*Cyrille d'Alexandrie. Deux dialogues christologiques*, Sources chrétiennes, 97 (Paris: Cerf, 1964), introduction 117): 'The behavior of Jesus Christ as described by the Gospels indicates that he considers his humanity as penetrated by his divinity, elevated by it and made capable of a properly divine action. Thus, he gives his Spirit through a physical breath (706 d), directing faith towards the visible man he is in the world of men (703 c–704 a). Cyril, moreover, interweaves the two lines of argument in a way that is quite significative. For him, especially at this time, there is no clear distinction between the fact that we can say: Jesus of Nazareth is eternal, or: the Word was born of Mary, and the fact that God incarnate uses his human being and action to produce superhuman effects. The danger of a certain confusion between logical order and physical order seems, to say the least, quite close'. We can even compare St Gregory of Nyssa, *Antirrheticus adv. Apoll.*: 'If a drop of vinegar is poured into the sea, the drop becomes the sea (. . .) The flesh, from its own nature of flesh, has been transformed into the sea of incorruptibility (. . .) the mixture with the divinity has raised the humility of the carnal nature to divine properties' (PG, 45, 1221 D-1224 A); comp. *Ad Theophilum* (45, 1276 C).

49. Compare DCT VII, 598–599.

50. Compare the *Solida Declaratio* VII:106 (BK 1009; BC 611), VIII:64 (BK 1038; 628) VIII:92 (BK 1048; 633–634).

is a correct, traditional formulation.[51] But we continue to speak of the person representing the union of the two natures, the union of humanity with divinity. The explanations and justifications given are interesting. The divine power communicated to Christ is different from that found in the saints, who also performed miracles (cf. ibid., 70). It does not simply pass through him by way of act, it is inherent in him, it qualifies him in his very humanity: this is saving, life-giving (ibid., 59, 60, 76). This is very close to an Alexandrian sense of mystery and, like Luther, I can invoke the Council of Ephesus, i.e. the eleventh *anathema* of St Cyril.[52] I hope that a doctoral thesis in theology will one day apply itself to a sympathetic and critical study of chapter VIII of the *Solida Declaratio* and its appendix, the 'Catalogue of Testimonies', *Catalogus testimoniorum*.

We can now attempt to form an idea of what belongs to God and what belongs to the humanity of Christ in the work of Redemption. In a sense, and by virtue of all we have seen, this question makes no sense to Luther. He would accuse me of Nestorianism. It does make sense to me, and I'll try to answer it using Luther's own texts. This answer will be divided into two paragraphs.

1° Christ saves us *because he is God*

> What is it that gives us life, salvation, peace, righteousness, redemption, power and wisdom, things we don't have on our own? It is Christ - not Christ the man, but Christ the Son of God become man.[53]

The 1531/35 *Ad Galatas Commentarius*, where Luther most fully expresses the heart of his theology, is full of such statements:

---

51. Thus, 'since Christ according to the Godhead is the second person in the holy Trinity': Ibid,73. (BK 1041; BC 630). And compare *Catalogus testimoniorum* V (BK 1123–1128) and VIII (BK 1131–1132).
52. See *Catalogus testimoniorum*, BK 1119, 36–38 (DSch 262), and several other texts in this rich collection.
53. Postils and sermons of 1522 (WA 10/1:126), cited by Lienhard, *Luther temoin*, 162 (*Luther: Witness*, 160).

> To give grace, peace, eternal life, to forgive sins, to justify, to quicken, to free from death and the devil are the work of no creature, but of the one and only Majesty.[54]

Maiestas is God as God. The fact that Christ is victorious over sin and death proves that he is God.[55] Denying Christ`s divinity, Arius necessarily denied the article of Redemption:

> Indeed, overcoming the sin of the world, death, the curse and the wrath of God is not the work of any creature, but of divine power. He who has overcome these things in himself must therefore be God truly and by nature.[56]

> If I believed that only the human nature suffered for me, Christ would be a very inadequate saviour![57]

Luther explains this role of the divinity in Christ's humanity most clearly in his *Ad Galatas Commentarius* on 3:10, a treatise in its own right.[58] The text is: 'All who claim to practice the law incur a curse'. Luther makes a radical distinction between 'political', earthly, natural, corporal justice, and spiritual justice *coram Deo*. The latter is aimed at by the promise made to Abraham, to which faith responds. It is offered to us through and in Christ. It is one thing to perform deeds according to the law, which would obtain justice according to the law and starting from us; it is quite another to first perform faith, the *fides Christi* that puts a goodness in a person's heart that does not come from him or her, but enables them to perform good deeds, just as

---

54. '*Dare autem gratiam, pacem, vitam aeternam, remittere peccata, iustificare, vivificare, liberare a morte et diabolo, non sunt ullius creaturae opera, sed unius et solius Maiestatis*': WA 40/1:81,16–19; 404,32 see LW 26:31; 257.
55. WA 40/1:441,31–33 see LW 26:283, *Galatians.*
56. '*Vincere enim peccatum mundi, mortem, maledictionem et iram Dei in semetipso non est ullius creaturae, sed divinae potentiae opus. Igitur necesse est illum qui in seipso ista vicit, vere et natura Deum esse*': LW 16–19 see LW 26:282. Compare, *Introduction*, WA 40/1:27,9–24.
57. *Vom Abendmahl Christi*: WA 26:319,37–38, see LW 37:209; *Schwabacher Artikel*: WA 30/3:87, (BK 55); *Hohe Christmesse*, 25 Dec.1522 on John 1,1–14 (WA 10/1/1:148,23–24; LW 75:258-259). It is necessary that it be God who dies on the cross: *Von den Konziliis*: WA 50:601,19 see LW 41:116.
58. WA 40/1:391–420 see LW 26:248–268, *Galatians.*

a good tree can bear good fruit.[59] So we attribute to God what can only come from him, while by claiming to produce acts of justice of our own accord, we put ourselves in the place of God and Christ: this is what the monks and the Pope do, who thus proves to be the antichrist.[60] This 'hypocrisy' makes herself creator and justifier by her works, despising the blessing promised and given to Abraham and his believing sons'.[61] Faith, on the other hand, gives divinity pride of place. But it can be seen either in naked faith, that which receives the gift of Christ's justice, or in faith *concreta, composita seu incarnata*.[62]

These words are followed by an application to Christ, to me very interesting: 'Christ, if we consider him according to his outward appearance, seems a pure man. And yet Scripture speaks sometimes of Christ as God, sometimes of Christ composite and incarnate'. (*Ut Christus si inspiciatur secundum externam speciem, videtur purus homo; Et tamen Scriptura loquitur aliquando de Christo ut Deo, aliquando ut de composito et incarnato*). And, a little further on:

> Why should Scripture not speak variously of faith as it speaks variously of Christ God and man, namely sometimes of the whole person, sometimes of his two natures separately, either the divine or the human (. . .) Here I speak of man; but 'man', in this proposition, is a completely new term and, as the Sophists themselves say, it is used for divinity [= the subject it covers is divinity], i.e. the God who became man created all things. Here creation is attributed to the divinity alone, because humanity does not create, and yet it is rightly said: man created, because the divinity, which alone creates, is incarnate with humanity and thus humanity participates in

59. LW 26. 402; 409,30–414,23, where Luther takes up the idea that we find again in his Christology, that theology uses a new and completely different language, see LW 26:255–256; 260–264.

60. '*Quare omnes Hypocritae et idololatrae ea ofera facere conantur quae proprie ad divinitatem pertinent et uni so ique Christo competunt*', LW 26. 406,17s. see LW 26:258–259.

61. '*[F]acit seipsam Creatricem et Iustificatricem per opera sua, aspernans benedictionem promissam et datam Abrahae et filiis eius credentibus*', LW 26. 407,18–19 see LW 26:259.

62. LW 26.. 414.24–415,11; see LW 26:264–265. And compare Paul Manns, '*Fides absoluta-Fides incarnata*', zur Rechtfertigungslehre Luthers im Grossem Galater-Kommentar, in *Reformata Reformanda*, Festgabe H Jedin (Münster: Aschendorff, 1965), I:265–312.

> the properties of what has been said (. . .) Everything, here, is attributed to man because of the divinity.[63]

Just as, in the Christian who does good works from faith, 'justification comes from faith, just as creation comes from the divinity' (*iustificatio solius fidei est ut Creatio divinitatis*), but all that is good in works comes from the faith that has become incarnate in them: so it is the divinity that works salvation in Christ through his humanity, 'ut divinitas per humanitatem in Christo'.[64]

The analogous connections:

$$\frac{\text{God's action – faith}}{\text{good works}} = \frac{\text{divinity in Christ}}{\text{action of his humanity}} \quad \text{continues:}$$

> So that faith, generally, is the divinity in the work, the person and the members, as the sole cause of the justification which, then, is attributed even to matter by reason of form, namely to the work by reason of faith. Just as the reign of the divinity is given to the man Christ by reason, not of humanity, but of divinity. Indeed, the divinity alone created all things, humanity having no part in them.[65]

---

63. '*Quidni ita varie loqueretur Scriptura de fide, cum etiam de Christo Deo et homine varie loquatur, scilicet iam de tota persona, iam de duabus naturis ipsius seorsim, aut divina aut humana (. . .). Hic loquor de homine; Sed homo in ista propositione est plane novum vocabulum et, ut Sophistae ipsi aiunt, supponit pro divinitate, id est, Iste Deus qui factus est homo, creavit omnia. Ibi creatio tribuitur soli divinitati, quia humanitas non creat, et tamen recte dicitur: Homo creavit, uia divinitas quae sola creat, est incarnata cum humanitate ideoque humanitas participat proprietatibus praedicatorum (. . .). Ibi omnia tribuuntur homini propter divinitatem*'. WA 40/1:415,26–29 and 416,10–17 *compare* 427 (see LW 26:265, *compare* 272–273). Note, in this passage, the ambiguity signalled regarding the communication of attributes, the person seen as the concrete reality made of the union of the two natures, again the debatable expression that speaks in this way of the Incarnation, '*divinitas incarnata cum humanitate*'.
64. WA 40/1:417,13–17, see LW 26:266.
65. '*Ut fides in universum sit divinitas in opere, persona et membris, ut unica causa iustificationis quae postea etiam tribuitur materiae propter formam, hoc est operi propter fidem. Ut regnum divinitatis traditur Christo homini non propter humanitatem sed divinitatem. Sola enim divinitas creavit omnia humanitate nihil cooperante*', WA. 417,26–30; LW 26:267. Compare *Von den Konziliis*: WA 50:597,16–21 see LW 41:111–112.

And Luther goes on to use an image familiar to him, that of Christ`s humanity compared to the worm at the end of the hook: the demon-Leviathan swallowed it, but was thus caught and defeated; and he continues: 'Thus humanity alone would have done nothing; divinity alone acted joined to humanity, and humanity because of divinity'.[66]

The parallel that Luther draws between Christ's divinity—'the deeds of his humanity, and faith in the promise'—[and] our works, is precious to him. He no longer explicitly includes the theme, so frequent in his early commentaries on the Psalter, that Christ's destiny is tropologically ours, but this scheme of thought can be found as an underpinning. Simply, in Christ, divinity and humanity are united to the point of being blended into a single being, which is not the case with faith and works in us.

2° Christ *is human*. While being God's, forming a single person with the divinity, his humanity has its own activities: not only sleeping, eating, etc., but suffering on the cross.

Luther is obviously talking about Christ's obedience;[67] he is talking about Christ's merit. The Christ-Spirit, he says, makes the merit of Christ effective in us so that it exists and is not preached in vain. Through him, we become partakers of that merit.[68] Christ once merited forgiveness of sins on the cross.[69] Christ saved us from God's wrath with his innocent blood, he paid for us with his sufferings, and he continually stands for us, priest and bishop of our souls, as a merciful mediator.[70] The 1535 *Commentary on Galatians* (WA 40) is full of statements such as: Christ satisfies (WA 40:232,31–233,15; *see* LW 26:132), he has reconciled us to God (WA 40:261,18–19; LW 26:151), he is our mediator with God (40:299,21; LW 26:178. 40:423,27; LW 26:270. 40:502; LW 26:324), he bears our sins (40:433f.

66. '*Itaque sola humanitas nihil effecisset, sed ciivinitas humanitati coniuncta sola fecit, et humanitas propter divinitatem*', WA 40/1:417,30–35; see LW 26:267. Beer, *Der fröhliche Wesel*, comments on this image, 341–351. He believes it reflects a theology of *Alleinwirksamkeit Gottes*: 338f., 439.

67. '*Oratio Christi offerentis se ad oboedientiam patris*' (*The prayer of Christ offering himself in obedience to his Father*): *Dictata super Psalterium* (WA 3:224,9); '*Christus oboedientissimus fuit*' (*Christ was supremely obedient*), (WA 3: 225,26). *Glosses*, but see LW 10:188 (Psalm 40).

68. *Vom Anbeten des Sakraments des heiligen Leichnams Christi* (1523), WA 11:451,6–17, see LW 36:298, *The Adoration of the Sacrament.*

69. *Vom Abendmahl Christi Bekenntnis* (1528), WA 26:294,25–36, see LW 37:192.

70. WA 26:502,30–34, see LW 37:362.

442. 445. 448. 454; *see* LW 26:277–292 *variously*), he prays for us in heaven.[71]

Luther's *Lieder* offer no new insights. Very often translated from Latin hymns and psalms, they sing of the Lord descending from heaven and obeying his Father's will.[72]

All of this is appropriate to Christ's humanity, but, according to the theology set out above, this is because of its union, its blending with the divinity. We cannot isolate something in Christ that is not of God.[73]

After Luther's death, a controversy arose: is Christ our justice according to his divine nature—so Osiander (+ 1552)—or according to his human nature: so Fr Stancarus (+ 1574)? The dispute was settled by the *Formula of Concord* of 1577: like Luther and Melanchthon, the *Solida Declaratio* (SD) attributes our redemption to Christ's obedience and merit, which are inseparably linked to his human and divine natures:

> This righteousness before God, which is that of faith or which is imputed by pure grace to believers, is the obedience, passion and resurrection of Christ, by which he satisfied the law for

71. On prayer: *The Smalcald Articles* (1537), *De invocatione sanctorum*, BK 424; BC 305. On merit: 'The Son of God, our Lord and redeemer Jesus Christ merited, by his passion, not only remission of sins and reconciliation' (*Meruit Filius Dei, Dominus ac redemptor noster Jesus Christus, non solum remissionem peccatorum sua passione et reconciliationem*), WA 40/3:727, *Enarratio 53 capitis Esaiae*, (1544); *Der CX.Psalm, Gepredigt und Ausgelegt*, Christ is offered as a sacrifice out of obedience, and he prays (WA 41:185–187 and 189; see LW 13:318–322, *Commentary on Psalm 110*, 1539
72. See Klaus Burba, *Die Christologie in Luthers Liedern*, Schriften des Vereins für Reformationsgeschichte, 175 (Gütersloh: Bertelsmann, 1956).
73. Citing and distancing himself from my interpretation of Luther's Christology as *Alleinwirksamkeit Gottes* in 1950–1953, Wilfried Joest, speaks of the 'Faktizität der Person Jesu Christi als Träger der Heilsgegenwart Gottes' (*The fact of the person of Jesus Christ as bearer of God's saving presence*), but does not provide a text that speaks of a saving activity of Christ's humanity as such: *Ontologie der Person bei Luther*, 364. According to Lienhard, *Luther temoin*, 388 (*Luther Witness*, 382), Luther accepted in Christ a human will that translates, in the conditions of human existence, the divine will of the Son. On the other hand, I know only from Daniel Olivier's review (in *Nouvelles de l'Institut Catholique*, October 1979, 40–43) of Constantino di Bruino's unpublished thesis, *Le rôle salutaire de l'humanité du Christ â la lumière des grands thèmes de la christologie de Luther*.

us and atoned for our sins (*iustitia illa, quae coram Deo fidei aut credentibus ex mera gratia imputatur, est obedientia, passio et resurrectio Christi, quibus ille legi nostra causa satisfecit et peccata nostra expiavit.* SD III, 14: BK 918; BC 564)

(. . .) because of the obedience of Christ which he presented for us to his Father from his birth to the most ignominious death of the cross. (*propter obedientiam Christi quam Christus inde a nativitate sua usque ad ignominiosissimam crucis mortem pro nobís patri prestitit.* SD III, 22: BK 921; BC 565–566)

(. . .) that our justice rests neither in the divine nor in the human nature but in his total person, that is to say, that he is our justice as God and man in his one, total and sovereignly perfect obedience. (*quod iustitia nostra neque in divina neque in humana natura, sed in tota ipsius persona consistet, quippe qui ut Deus et homo in sola sua tota et perfectissima obedientía est nostra iustitia.* SD III 55: BK 933; BC 572)

Because this obedience of Christ is not of a single nature, but of the total person, it is an absolutely perfect satisfaction and atonement for the human race, by which the eternal and immutable divine justice has been satisfied. (*Cum autem obedientia illa Christi non sit unius dumtaxat naturae, sed totius personae, ideo ea est perfectissima pro humano genere satiåfactio et expiatio, qua aeternae et immutabili iustitiae ivinae (quae in lege revelata est) satis est factum.* SD III 57: BK 934; BC 572).

This union of natures was based on the Councils of Ephesus and Chalcedon, to which Luther subscribed. But Chalcedon had been concluded in 680–681, by the Third Council of Constantinople against Monothelitism.[74] Yet Luther, who knew and used Crabbe's collection of councils (Cologne 1538), never refers to this council. His *Von den Konziliis* stops at Chalcedon, but nowhere do we find the

74. I have found only one allusion to Monothelitism, in a writing of the 'Philippist' tendency (followers of Melanchthon), *Grundfest von der Person und Menschwerdung . . . Christi* (1571), whose full title reads 'Wider die newen Marcioniten, Samosatener, Sabellianer, Arianer, Nestorianer, Eutychianer und Monotheleten unter dem Flacianischen hauffen'. Quoted at BK 1019n1; see BC 616nn247–249 (*Solida Declaratio*, VIII, 4).

slightest mention of a free act of Christ's human will, although Luther attributes to him a complete humanity, with intelligence and will.

But for Luther, to attribute something to Christ's human will would not be God's will in him, it would be to speak of Christ's humanity as our own, which he rejects.[75] For in 'Deus-homo', *homo* is something other than what we are, mere humans. There is nothing in Christ that is not divine.[76] To speak otherwise would be Nestorian and would amount to positing two persons. Werner Elert, a precise interpreter of Luther, writes:

> The will of the Son of God is the same that determined the man Jesus to fulfill the law even in suffering and death. For Luther, therefore, the revelation of God in Christ in no way means merely that God acted in such and such a way with the man Jesus, that he caused him to die and then resurrected him. The works of Christ are, strictly speaking, the works of God. 'Therefore I must believe that he is true God, as high, mighty and eternal as the Father'.[77]

This explanation can be illustrated by this text from the commentary on Romans (12:2) where Luther, after speaking of Peter who both wills and will not (compare John 21:18), continues,

> Thus, in his agony, Christ brings his will to the perfection of the greatest fervour. This is how God acts in all the saints, to make them do, by the highest will, that very thing they do not want.[78]

To conclude, I will qualify my study of the 1950 (redaction)–1953 (publication) period. Luther makes room for an activity of Christ in his humanity, through acts that are proper to that humanity. But his sense

---

75. See *Disputatio* of January 1539 on John 1:14, WA 39/2:10,24f.; 11; 16,23–24. See LW 38:245–250.
76. *Disputatio.* of February 28, 1540: WA 39/2:107; see LW 73:268, *On the Divinity and Humanity of Christ*, Argument 11.
77. Werner Elert, *Morphologie des Luthertums*, (München, 1952), 1:197–198 = *The Structure of Lutheranism.* Translated by Walter Hansen (St Louis: Concordia, 1962), 224. Quotation is from WA 37:41,1–2, (Sermon on the *Apostles' Creed*, April 1533, at Torgau).
78. '*Sic Christus in agone sua voluntatem suam [. . .] ferventissima voluntate perfecit. Ita enim in omnibus sanctis agit deus, ut faciat eos summa voluntate facere quae summe nolunt*'. WA 56:447,16–19; see LW 25:439 *Romans* (1516).

of union with the divinity and of the unity of the person thus constituted is so strong, so dominant, that he does not distinguish a contribution of the man-Jesus to the work of salvation. It would be a 'monoenergism' if he didn't assert so strongly that, in this theandric operation, humanity's action remained its own. But what is proper to mankind would, if we were to consider it separately (which Luther, of course, would never do!), belong to the external, earthly realm. This is the whole idea of the two *kingdoms*, *realms*. In the realm of salvation, of what is *coram Deo*, God alone works effectively in Christ, who is inseparably God.

Thomas Aquinas built his Christology and Soteriology with both philosophical and traditional conceptual tools, which Luther was unfamiliar with and could only reject. The philosophical notions concern anthropology, the relationship between nature and person, and causality; those of Tradition come mainly from the Greeks, St Cyril of Alexandria and St John of Damascus.[79] Thomas knew a little of St Maximus the Confessor and the Acts of the Sixth Ecumenical Council against Monothelitism: just a dozen quotations in his mature works.[80] He obviously recognizes Christ's full humanity, intelligence and free will. He attributes to him the absolute fullness of created grace, a fullness called forth by the grace of hypostatic union. From then on, he sees Christ as an instrument of the divinity, but *a joint* instrument, an 'organ', like the hand joined to our body, and an intelligent and free instrument.[81] In this respect, all grace and salvation is an act of Christ's holy freedom. And the acquisition of universal salvation at the cross depends on Jesus' free, loving obedience to his Father.

As you can see, this is a different theology from that of Luther. But Luther, who knew him well, didn't appreciate Thomas, and even doubted that he was a saint. On the other hand, he knew and esteemed St Augustine. Can Luther's Christology claim him as its inspiration?

In reproducing our 1950–1954 study of Luther's Christology, I added a few remarks. Having studied Augustine's Christology to some extent, and having read the all-too-rare monographs on

79. See Ignaz Backes, *Die Christologie des hl. Thomas und die griechischen Kirchenväter* (Paderborn: Schöningh, 1931); Theophil TSCHIPKE, *Die Menschheit Christi als Heilsorgan der Gottheit, unter besonderer Berücksichtigung der Lehre des hl. Thomas v. Aquin* (Freiburg in Breisgau: Herder, 1940); Witmar METZGER, *Der Organongedanke in der Christologie der griechischen Kirchenväter* (Münsterschwarzach, 1968).

80. Backes, 32; Tschipke, 114, 143.

81. See *Sum. theol.* IIIa q 7a1; q 19a1c. *and* ad 1; q 64 a 3.

the subject,[82] it appeared to me that, on several points, Luther was closer to it, having deliberately and passionately bypassed the Middle Ages. However, he does not refer specifically to Augustine for his Christology, except in his early works, for the idea that weaknesses and complaints are put by the psalms into the mouth of Christ for his Body that we are. Augustine often uses the formulas *homo Deus*, *Deus homo*.[83] He speaks of *mors Dei* at the cross.[84] And here's what he wrote in 418 against the Arians:

> In saying (son) *of man*, he did not separate God, who assumed man, because, as I said - and this is very important—he is a single person. Indeed, the same and unique Christ is always Son of God by nature and Son of man, assumed in time, by grace: assumed, not in the sense that he first existed, then was assumed, but he was created in the very fact of being assumed. Thus, because of this unity of person which must be seen in both natures, the Son of Man is said to have descended from heaven, although he was assumed from this Virgin who was on earth, and the Son of God is said to have been crucified and buried, although he suffered this in his human nature and weakness, not in the divinity by which he is called the 'only-begotten' of the Father, eternal like him (. . .). This unity of Christ Jesus, our Lord, is made up of the one and the other nature, the divine and the human, in such a way that any one of the two communicates to the other its attribute, the divine to the human, the human to the divine.[85]

We seem to be close to the idea that a person is born of the union of the two natures[86] and a communication of the properties of one to

82. Otto Scheel, *Die Anschauung Augustins über Christi Person und Werk unter Berücksichtigung ihrer verschiedenen Entwicklungsstufen und ihrer dogmengeschichtlichen Stellung* (Tübingen: Mohr, 1901). Scheel is somewhat tendentious, and pushes Augustine in the Alexandrian direction; Eug. SCHILTZ, 'Aux sources de la théologie du mystère de l'Incarnation. La christologie de St Augustin', in *Nouvelle Revue théologique* 63 (1936), 689–713; TJ van Bavel, *Recherches sur la Christologie de saint Augustin*, Paradosis 10 (Fribourg: Editions universitaires, 1954).
83. References in van Bavel, 19n21, 25, 43n44.
84. Van Bavel, 57.
85. *Contra sermonem Arianorum*, c. 8 (PL 42, 688).
86. Other texts that express themselves in this way: *In Ioan. Ev. tr.* 99, 1 (PL, 35, 1885); *De Trin.* XIII, 17, 22, '*sic Deo coniungi potuit humana natara, ut ex duabus*

the other. But on the first point, texts abound, at least in Augustine's mature period, where the union of human nature is with the pre-existing person of the Word.[87] As for the communication of attributes, Augustine has an authentic idea of this, linked to that of the assuming Person, without any physical communication from one nature to another. The text we have quoted merely seeks to justify Scripture's application of the attributes of the other to one of them.[88] Augustine does not admit the ubiquity of Christ's human nature.[89]

As for the role played by Christ *as a man* in our redemption, let's confess to being a little unclear. Augustine speaks constantly of the Mediator, and never tires of repeating that the same subject exists 'in forma Dei' and 'in forma servi'. So we are saved 'by the blood of the only-begotten Son of God', (*sanguine unici Filii Dei*).[90] Christ, both priest and victim, thus in his humanity, 'redeemed us by the shedding of the Creator's blood', (*redemit nos fuso sanguine Creatoris*).[91] Augustine insists that Christ died because he wanted to and when he wanted to.[92] But Augustine's insistence on *sed quia voluit* stems from his affirmation of Christ's perfection in his humanity. Otherwise, his perfection as Incarnate Word would dominate. And since what Christ freely assumes is done in obedience to the Father's will, Augustine sees the Son involved in what Christ declares.[93] But he attributes to his human will the obedient prayer of the Agony in the Garden, which St Maximus the Confessor will argue against monothelitism.[94]

---

substantiis fieret una persona' ('human nature could be conjoined with God so that, from the two realities there came one person') [PL, 42, 1031].

87. Scheel quotes, 247f, 255, and criticizes Dorner for referring to *Christ* incarnate, not the eternal Person. Van Bavel also quotes some very formal ones: *op. cit.* 21; 23n39; 178.
88. See Scheel, 257–268; Van Bavel, 58, 60.
89. See *Epist.* 187, 3, 10 (PL, 33, 835–836); *In Ioan. Ev.* tr. 20, 1, '*Corpus enim Domini, in quo resurrexit, uno loco esse potes:*' ('The Lord's resurrection body can only be in one (single) place') [PL, 35, 1632]; other references given by VAN BAVEL, 59, n157. But Christ's divinity is always everywhere: 71.
90. *En. in. Ps* 147, 16 (PL, 37, 1925).
91. *Sermo* 242, 1 (PL, 39, 1591). And see n37 above.
92. *In Ioan. Ev. tr.* 43,9 (PL 35, 1709); 49, 18 (col. 1754–55) with the repetition of 'sed quia voluit' *De Trin.* IV, 13, 16 (42,898); *Sermo* 218, 1 (38,10 4); *Enchiridion* 33 (40, 248). Also Scheel, 235.
93. Van Bavel, 65, 108.
94. See *En.in Ps* 93,19 (PL 37, 1206–1207); *En. 2 sermo I in Ps* 32,2 (36, 277–278); *En.in Ps* 31,II, 26 (36, 274). Van Bavel, 135n52.

Study Four
'Luther's Anguish'

It is often said that Luther's discovery of what became the source and the soul of his doctrine was linked to his experience and his personal crisis. That is said, without claiming to reduce this doctrine to be only an expression of this crisis and experience. It is fairly well known, and it seems certain to me, that Luther suffered from neurosis during the Catholic period of his life, and that he experienced severe bouts of depression and anguish to the end of his life. The description of the crisis of 1527 by Justus Jonas and Johannes Bugenhagen is as impressive as it is revealing.

Dr Paul J Reiter of Copenhagen has studied all this in two large volumes.[1] It is impossible to analyse them here; I can only indicate the main conclusions. Reiter is not a psychoanalyst but a psychiatrist, and he takes a keen interest in the environment in which Luther grew up: a neurotic relationship with his father, a harsh family and school environment, a sense of guilt, the portrayal of God and Christ as harsh judges, and so on.

But Reiter was mainly interested in a psychosomatic illness, an 'endogenous' anguish. He ruled out syphilis, alcoholism, schizophrenia, epilepsy and even neurasthenia. Reiter proposes that Luther suffered from a manic-depressive psychosis that produced

1. Dr Paul J Reiter, *Martin Luthers Umwelt, Charakter und Psychose, sowie die Bedeutung dieser Faktoren* für seine *Entwicklung und Lehre.* 2 volumes (Copenhagen: Ejnar Munksgaard 1937 and 1941). Before his death, Reiter revised his books and corrected certain points: U Becke, 'Ein unterlassene psychiatrische Studie Paul Johann Reiters über Luther', in *Zeitschrift für Kirchengeschichte*, 90 (1979), 83–95.

attacks of varying length—he counted twelve—following episodes of extreme agitation that, especially later in life, exploded into anger.

Erik Erikson is an internationally-recognised psychoanalyst, but his personal interests have led him to studies that combine psychoanalysis and history.[2] He is interested in the crisis through which a young man discovers who he is and, if he has this dimension, his place in history. This was the case, for example, of Alfred Loisy and Sigmund Freud, to whom Erikson emphatically compares Luther. Erikson does not seek, as Preserved Smith did, to apply to Luther the more or less authentically Freudian schemas of the infantile sexual complex.[3] He refers to the *schema* he has developed for the successive critical stages to be overcome in order to become oneself, but does not attempt a psychoanalysis of Martin Luther's problems.

In the case of young Martin, his brutal father beat him and had ambitions for his son's place in society, and directed his studies to that end. For Martin, this conflicted with his joyful attachment to his mother, arousing feelings of guilt.[4]

Then, caught in a violent thunderstorm (2 July, 1505), Martin promised to enter a monastery. He did so against the wishes of his father who, at his son's first Mass in April or May 1507, declared that it might be under the inspiration of Satan that Martin became a monk, recklessly committing himself to celibacy!

Erikson attaches extreme importance to Luther's reaction to the story of the the deaf and dumb man (Mk 9: 17–24). Hearing this reading, Luther fell to the ground shouting *Non sum, non sum!* Erikson translates—not as one should obviously do, 'I am not that one!'— but as 'I am not', thus meaning: I am not what my father claims I am, namely inspired by the devil. But is it fair to attribute so much to this episode, which Luther never mentioned, when he

2. Erik H Erikson, *Young Man Luther* (London: Faber, 1958) = *Luther avant Luther, psychanalyse et histoire*, translated Nina Godneff (Paris: Flammarion, 1968). For a critique of Erikson, *Psychohistory and Religion. The Case of Young Man Luther*, edited Roger A Johnson (Philadelphia: Fortress Press, 1977).
3. Preserved Smith, 'Luther's Early Development in the Light of Psychoanalysis', in *American Journal of Psychology*, 24 (1913), 362f.
4. In fact, Erikson assumes this attachment, for which there is no direct testimony. Luther barely mentions his mother, except to inform us that she once whipped him until he bled, for taking a nut. Erikson notes this absence of the mother (63, 68–69) and observes (202) that Luther found a mother in the Bible because he did not recognise her in the Church or locate her in Mary.

recounted more than once the day of his first Mass and the difficulties of his religious life?

According to Erikson, through the spiritual and physical trials of this life, at the end of a period of 'latency' during which Brother Martin was the theatre for a struggle between destructive and constructive forces, Luther found his identity by returning to the confidence and security of his half-happy, half-unhappy childhood in other ways.

On the one hand, he fulfilled his attachment to his mother through poetry, music, and a strong and popular message *(la parole forte et populaire).*

On the other hand, he satisfied paternal values by acknowledging that his entry into the convent had perhaps been inspired by Satan, that the sexual impulse was irrepressible, and by effectively becoming a social leader. Luther had rescued himself on the basis of the biblical text through a liberating discovery of faith, that the justice of Jesus Christ replaces that which we ourselves could not achieve. Luther brought all his capacity for obedience back to God alone, turning against the Pope with a vicious challenge, an eruption of obscenity which, says Erikson (291), expressed the needs of his manic-depressive nature. A new religious individual was born, responding to the demands of the time and the new dimensions of humanity.

For someone who, like me, is interested in Luther's theological positions, knowing, moreover, that they are linked to his personal destiny and experience, Erikson's work is somewhat disappointing.

Without ignoring Luther's theological discoveries (see especially chapter six: 'The Meaning of *Meaning It*'), Erikson gives, if not an explanation, at least a psychological transcription. This is in keeping his competence and his perspective, and I have not ignored this. But I have other interests that have their own importance and value. So I read with eagerness Roland Dalbiez's study, *Luther's Anguish.*[5]

Erikson analysed Luther's psychogenesis from the point of view of the young Martin by interpreting his deep feelings and his reactions conditioned by his relationships with his father, his mother, and his family and then the monastic environment. Dalbiez proposes an explanation of the psychogenesis of Luther's doctrine distinct from

5. Roland Dalbiez, *l'Angoisse de Luther*, preface by Dr Lamache (Paris: Téqui, 1974). Dalbiez was one of the first Catholic philosophers to study psychoanalysis, in *La Méthode psychanalytique et la doctrine freudienne*, 2 volumes (Paris: de Brouwer, 1936).

classical Catholic doctrine, by analysing a decisive element of Luther's anguish and of the theology of faith through which he emerged from it. This is how he himself summarises the conclusions of his research:

> The conclusions I have reached are as follows: On the historical level, I believe that, if Luther's morbid anguish of guilt depends his innate constitution at the time, on the education he received in his family and then at school, his suffering as a scrupulous man was brought to a climax by the theological doctrine of the guilt of natural temptation that Peter Lombard had succeeded in having accepted by the greatest doctors of Scholasticism. For the Master of the Sentences, the temptation coming from the the devil is only guilty if one consents to it, but this is not the case with temptation which arises from one's nature. This is always a sin, undoubtedly venial, the most venial of all, but nevertheless a sin properly so called, in the strictest sense of the word, even if we do not consent to it (. . .) My second conclusion is psychopathological. In the grip of an extremely strong, morbid sense of guilt, Luther was at risk of suicide. He escaped death by making his own justification the object of his faith.

This is what Dalbiez calls 'special faith': Christ is my salvation, I am saved. Let's leave this second point for the moment. As for the first, what has Roland Dalbiez proved? How can we assess his contribution as an explanation of the genesis of Luther's 'reforming' doctrine?

Dalbiez is correct when he writes, 'There is no doubt that Saint Augustine is extremely pessimistic with regard to *original* sin, but when it comes to *actual* sin, it is absolutely crucial to note that he makes it begin only with consent' (52). This is correct, and we regret that Malcolm Alflatt, in articles that Dalbiez could not have known, did not sufficiently distinguish in his category of 'Involuntary Sin', the sin of which we were all guilty in Adam (because *omnes fuimus ille unus* ['we were all that one'], *De civ. Dei*, XIII, 14) and our present sins.[6] However, if Augustine holds that concupiscence, which remains among Christians, is not sin if we do not allow it to reign by

6. Malcolm E Alflatt, 'The Development of the Idea of Involuntary Sin in St Augustine', in *Revue d' Etudes Augustiniennes Et Patristiques*, 20 (1974): 113–134; 'The Responsibility for Involuntary Sin in St Augustine', in *Recherches Augustiniennes*, 10 (1975): 171–186.

consenting to its appeals, he also says that it is called 'sin' because it comes from sin and that it causes sin if we give in to it.[7]

But certain medieval disciples of Augustine, whom Luther read, qualified as sins the impulses of concupiscence outside of our consent.

These are mortal sins in the non-baptized, according to St Anselm, that maintain these impulses with the disorder of our nature, that which, according to him, original sin consists in us; so that they are venial sins even among Christians, according to Peter Lombard, prior to any consent or if there is temporary tolerance without true consent.

Full consent would make them mortal sins. It seems that Luther fed his scrupulous anguish from this theology. All the same, it is rather curious that *his* authors, Ockham, Nicolas de Lyre, Gabriel Biel, were *against* this debatable theology. It is true that Luther often reproached them for a certain Pelagianism. He himself was a hyper-Augustinian. Nevertheless, this raises the question of whether this thesis was really the determining factor in Luther's moral drama and the psychogenesis of his doctrine.

Roland Dalbiez honestly acknowledges the limits of his argument:

> (Lutherans) will refuse to acknowledge that my psychopathological explanation of Luther's evolution is *total*, but they will not be able to say that it is *null* (332).

I am not a Lutheran, hardly even an occasional or modest Lutheran. I think that Roland Dalbiez provides valuable insights into Luther's anguish and its outcome. He could have, in the very line of his research, exposed other aspects, for example the theology of contrition, linked to the ideal of God's perfect love, which I will consider later.[8]

7. Compare *In Ioan. Ev*, tr. XLI, 12 (PL 35, 1968) where Augustine calls the spontaneous movement of anger not followed by an act, *peccatum*; if one allows it, it reigns. *De nuptiis et concupiscentia*, I, 23, 25 (44, 428): '*Nam ipsa quidem concupiscentia jam non est peccatum in regeneratis quando illi ad illicitaopera non consentitur (. . .) Sed quia modo quodam loquendi peccatum vocatur, quod et peccato facta est et peccatum, si vicerit, facit*'.
8. In Erfurt, Paltz (+1511) taught the contritionist thesis. Luther said that he had never been sure that he had experienced true contrition; he thought that it must be very rare. See the texts indicated by Scheel in the tables of his *Dokumente zu Luzhers Entwicklung*, s. v. contritio; Henri Strohl, *L'évolution religieuse de Luther jusqu'en 1515*, (Strasbourg & Paris: Istra, 1922), 49, 86–88; Reiter, *Martin Luthers Umwelt*, 2:27f, 285–289.

The conviction of the guilt of involuntary inclinations, while provisionally admitted in the texts quoted by Dalbiez, represents only a small part of what Luther says (before 1517) about the sin that dwells within us. To give it the predominant importance that Dalbiez does, doesn't that assume that Luther followed a theological thesis? And yet Luther 'took things seriously', as he did the monastic life (*ego serio rem agebam*), *Vorrede zum seiner lateinischen Schriften* (March 1545), WA 54:179,31–32; see LW 34:328, *Preface to Luther's Latin Writings*).

He used and quoted the texts of the Fathers and Doctors, sometimes to build on them, sometimes to criticise them, but he was not a scholastic who was bound by the arguments of the schools. What Roland Dalbiez says about his inaptitude for metaphysics and abstract thought, and about the predominance in him of affectivity and emotionalism is correct and must be confirmed (44–47, 278, etc.). But it is even more necessary to recognise the positive light in which Luther worked.

His purpose, his effort, consisted precisely in replacing scholastic concepts, categories and terms with biblical concepts, categories and terms, and therefore, above all, Christological ones. This is what he often calls speaking 'theologically' not 'physically' or 'metaphysically'. It is a pity that Dalbiez did not quote the commentary on the *Epistle to the Romans* at all (the allusion on page 313 is not a quotation). He has read it, but states,

> I have looked in vain for something original, either in content or even just in form, compared with Luther's other works from the same period, on the neuralgic point of the guilt of the first inpulses (159).

But what if the statements about sin sheds light on what Luther says about this guilt and on the very texts that R Dalbiez quotes on this subject?

I have re-read carefully these texts by Luther, taken for the most part from sermons, which R Dalbiez quotes on pages 136–181. In *none of them* does Luther refer to the thesis of certain scholastics concerning the culpability of involuntary disordered acts. All of them express, *with reference to Scripture and experience*, that (#1) we do not fulfil the requirements of the Law ('you shall not covet'—*non concupisces*) especially as urged by the Sermon on the Mount:

concupiscence cannot be eliminated; (#2) there exists within us a struggle between our spiritual and carnal natures; (#3) we must therefore take refuge under Christ, and in Christ, who alone has fulfilled the inner demands of the Law. In several of these texts (cf. 163, 168, 176, 179). Luther quotes Romans 7:7, 18, 24–25. In fact, following Augustine and Thomas Aquinas, Luther holds that Paul speaks in Romans 7:7–25 of his own condition and experience as a baptized Christian.[9]

Now Luther groups together and cites a series of texts from the Old and New Testaments that call these impulses from concupiscence 'sins', or that speak of a radical sin prior to explicit and consensual acts.[10] Luther claims the right to speak as Scripture does, even if the Fathers and Doctors have done otherwise: this is particularly true in his reply to the Lovanist Latomus, who had already made most of the objections and criticisms articulated by Dalbiez.[11] It is also important to consider Luther's concept of sin. He cites a definition by St Ambrose: 'sin is disobeying divine commands',[12] which is extremely extensive and does not make explicit the note of voluntary consent. And he himself often repeats 'sin is none other than that which is not according to God's law'[13] a

9. Histoire de l'exégèse: Otto Kuss, « Zur Geschichte der Auslegung von Röm. 7, 7–25 », in Der Römerbrief, Regensburg, 1975, p.462–485. S. Augustin avait d'abord tenu que Paul parlait de l'homme avant la grâce. C'est au cours de sa discussion avec le manichéen Fortunatus, 28–29 avril 392, qu'il a reconnu qu°en 7, 19, Paul parle du chrétien sous la grâce: cf. Acta contra Fortunatum, 22 (PL., 42, 124–126); Retract., I, 15, 2 (32, 608); - A. de Veer, « L'exégèse de Rom. VII et ses variations », in Bibl. August., t. 33, Paris, 1974, p. 770–778. Contre W. G. Kummel (Römer 7 und die Bekehrung des Paulus, Leipzig, 1929), James D. G. Dunn a montré récemment qu'il s'agit bien de Paul chrétien, la condition du chrétien ici-bas étant la lutte entre lui comme sarx et lui comme pneuma: « Rom. 7, 14–25 in the Theology of Paul », in Theol. Zeitschr., 31 (1975), 257–273.

10. Such lists can be found in the *Römervorlesung*, 1515–1516 (WA 56:287–288; see LW 25:275–276); extensively in the important *Rationis Latomianae confutatio*, 1521 (*e.g.* WA 8:55, *etc.* and see LW 32:145–146, *Against Latomus*).

11. See *l'Angoisse de Luther*, 52, 95, 100, 103 (better to drink from the spring than from the stream), 108, 127.

12. '*Peccatum est inoboedientia celestium mandatorum*', St Ambrose, *De paradiso*, 8, 39 (PL 14, 309), quoted in *Römervorlesung*, WA 56:186; see LW 25:168.

13. '*Peccatum nihil aliud quam quod non est secundum legem Dei*'. See *Rationis Latomianae confutatio*: WA 8:83,28, (see LW32:194), see 104,27f. (LW 32:224), 113,31f. (LW 32:238), 117,28 (LW 32:244), 125,25f. (LW 32:255).

definition which calls for the same remarks. The will, he also says, freely quoting St Augustine, is guilty (*rea*), a sinner (*peccatrix*), if we do the works of the Law to the letter, for fear of punishment, while deep down we retain a contrary will and would do evil if we were not afraid.[14]

It is true that Luther appealed to St Augustine: however, not only did he retain only those texts that supported his understanding, but he sometimes changed a term in the text: thus where St Augustine said 'concupiscence is forgiven in baptism, not that it no longer exists, but that sin is no longer imputed'.[15] Luther writes 'sin or concupiscence',[16] or even *universum peccatum*.[17] Obviously, he can defend himself with the text of Romans 7:7 as it was sometimes read in the Middle Ages (Dalbiez, 275), namely that *concupiscentiam nesciebam esse peccatum*. Moreover, a certain Augustinian school had identified concupiscence with original ('universal') sin.

So it is not surprising that Luther calls the inner 'spark' (*fomes*), 'sin'.[18] Even in the justified baptized there remains a 'radical sin'.[19] Dalbiez rightly notes that Luther does not think only of the sexual impulse, although in his monastic environment attention was readily fixed on this point,[20] but Luther always cites anger, pride, hatred, jealousy, unbelief, and finally the fact of being 'turned in upon

14. *Römervorlesung*: WA 56:191; *see* LW 25:174.
15. *'Dimitti concupiscentiam carnis in baptismo, non ut non sit, sed ut peccatum non imputetur'*, Augustine, *De nuptiis et concupiscentia*, I, 25, 28 (PL 44, 430).
16. *'peccati concupiscentiam'*, *Römervorlesung*: WA 56:273; see LW 25:261. And *infra* n18.
17. *Rationis Latomianae confutatio*: WA 8:93,7–8 (compare LW 32:208).
18. Thus *Römervorlesung*, WA 56:271 on Romans 4:7, '*Non tantum hic loquitur de peccatis in opere, verbo et cogitatione factis sed et de fomite, ut infra 7, Non ego, sed quod habitat in me peccatum (. . .) Ergo actuale (sicut a theologis vocatur) verius est peccatum, id est opus et fructus peccati, peccatum autem ipsa passio fomes et concupiscentia sive pronitas ad malμm et difficultas ad bonum, sicut infra, Concupiscentiam nesciebam esse peccatum (. . .) Peccatum meum contra me est semper.*' See LW 25:259, 'sin itself is the passion, spark, and concupiscence'; Compare WA 56:281, 286, 332; see LW 25: 268, 274, 320.
19. *Römervorlesung*, WA 56:284, see LW 25:272; also *Rationis Latomianae confutatio*, '*radicale illud fermentum*', WA 8:104,6, see LW 32:224.
20. 'We thought there was no sin except lust' (*Putabamus nullum esse peccatum praeter libidinem*), WATr I:53, no126.

ourselves' (*incurvatus in se*).[21] It is an inherent disorder, soaked into our tissues. But it is up to us whether it reigns in us, or not.[22]

At this exact point, Luther reproaches the scholastics, Scotus, Ockham and Biel, as well as his critics including Latomus, for not seeing the depths to which we are inhabited by sin, for reducing it to a few acts or impulses.[23] It is much more serious, it is everything in us that is not in conformity with God, who is loved for himself in a total and absolute way.[24] This is why sin, like God's justice, can only be known in faith.[25]

Therefore I could not write, as Roland Dalbiez does (182, 136 and elsewhere): 'The texts of Luther that we have quoted are sufficient to establish that the Reformer built the three stages of his theological system starting from the necessary guilt of natural temptation'. No. He built them from his experience as an anguished and scrupulous

21. Thus *Römervorlesung*, WA 56:258 (LW 25:245), 356 (LW 25:345–346), 361 (LW 25:351); also variously in *ad Galatas*, 1535 (Strohl, 87).
22. Luther gives consent a role: '*concupiscentia iam non est peccatum in regeneratis quando illi non consentitur*', (WA 56:353; see LW 25:342, *Romans*). It is according to whether one consents or does not consent that sin is said to reign or not to reign: '*regnare peccatum* et *obedire peccato* est consentire et facere que peccatum cupit. Quod peccatum? Actuale? Non, sed originale' (*Gloss* on Romans 6:12: WA 56:60); 'Lutherus nunquam de regnante peccato dixit quod in sanctis esset' (WA 8:94, see LW 32:210, *Against Latomus*) and, to Latomus objecting to Augustine's word, 'non esse peccatum nisi consentiatur' (*De Civ. Dei*, I, 25 and III, 2), Luther replies: 'Quis non videt Augustinum hic loqui de mortali peccato quod fit eonsensu in concupiscentias peccati, non tamen negat istos motus esse venialia peccata' (WA 8:113–114, see LW 32:238–239). It would be necessary, moreover, to specify what Luther, following St Augustine, means by *venialia peccata*.
23. *Römervorlesung*, WA 56:273: (against Scotus, Ockham, Biel) '*qui originale totum auferri somniant sicut et actuale; quasi sint quedam amovibilia in ictu oculi, sicut tenebre per lucem, cum Antiqui sancti paires Augustinus, Ambrosius multum aliter sint locuti ad modum Scripture, illi autem ad modum Arlstotelis in Ethicorum . . .*' (see LW 25:261, *Romans*); WA 56:275: '*venerunt quod peccatum, quid esset ignoraverunt, nec quid remissio, quia peccatum artaverunt us ue ad minutissimum quendam motum animi sicut et iustitiam et huius parvulum motum in Deum (quem naturaliter potest) illi somniant esse actum diligendi Dem super omnia*' (see LW 25:262). See also the *95 Theses* on indulgences, 1517.
24. In addition to the last quoted text, see *Römervorlesung*, WA 56:191 (LW 25:174), 200 (LW 25:183–184), 281 (LW 25:269), 361 (LW 25:350–351).
25. Compare: WA 56:226,18 (LW 25:211), 229,11 (LW 25:213), 231,8–10 (LW 25:215).

man whose conscience was not appeased by the search for virtuous action and perfection.

He had found in Scripture, and in St Paul in particular, that the law imposes an impossible perfection but that Christ has accomplished everything and that it is therefore necessary, but also sufficient, to apply his justice to us by faith. As Luther wrote to Spenlein on 8 April 1516, 'You will only find peace in [Christ] through a 'confident despair' in yourself and in your works'.[26]

So, *what about* forensic justification, by purely legal imputation? Dalbiez obviously mentions it (compare: 218f, 267, 272f, 283). He considers it to have been both the consequence of and the solution to the extreme anguish caused in Luther's soul by the thesis of the inevitability of sin and the guilt of the involuntary inclination to concupiscence: 'Luther's whole theology will be founded on this notion of *peccatum nolentis* (undesired sin)' (94). I believe that the Lutheran doctrine of justification coincides neither with Catholic doctrine nor even, as many Protestant exegetes acknowledge, with the thought of St Paul.[27] It must also be admitted that some of Luther's expressions are ambiguous and do not make it easy to understand his position. But to see Luther's position as nothing more than the affirmation of a purely juridical imputation is to fail to understand the realism of what he is asserting.

Luther's conviction and affirmation is that through faith in Christ-my Saviour, the justice of Christ *becomes ours*. Christ remains the subject, and for Luther there is ever only one subject of holiness,

---

26. '*Non nisi in illo, per fiducialem desperationem tui et operum tuorum, pacem invenies*', WABr I:35, see LW 48:13, *Letter to Spenlein*.
27. By way of example (there are many more): Wilhelm Heitmuller, *Luthers Stellung in der Religionsgeschichte des Christentums* (Marburg: Elwert, 1917), 19, 21f.; Otto Dibelius, *Bericht von der Kirche* (Berlin: Furche, 1941), 106; F Refoulé, 'Problèmes luthériens vus de Suède', in *Istina* (1958), 333–360. Particularly on the *simul iustus et peccator*, Alfons Kirchgássner gives several references, *Erlösung und Sünde im Neuen Testament*, (Freiburg: Herder, 1950); Wilhelm Joest, 'Paulus und das lutherische Simul justus et peccator', in *Kerygma und Dogma* 1 (1955), 269–320; Nils Dahl, 'In welchem Sinne ist nach dem Neuen Testament der Getaufte gerecht und Sünder zugleich?' in *Lutherische Rundschau,* 12 (1962): 289–295. Catholic doctrine always sees justification from the perspective of incorporation into Christ: *Council of Trent*, session VI, chapter 16; Emile Mersch, *Le Corps mystique du Christ, études de théologie historique*, DDB, second edition (Paris: Brouwer, 1936), 2:265f.

Christ. But what is true of him becomes tropologically true of us, by this transfer from Christ to us, this 'exchange' of which Luther never ceases to speak.[28] Sometimes he even terms borrowed from classical theology, such as 'infusion'.[29] But we know that he wanted to avoid scholastic terminology ('quality', 'form', 'habitus', etc.); he abhorred the idea of charity as the '*form* of the virtues' and that of 'faith *informed* by love'.

He saw the danger of reintroducing the justice of works and replacing Christ with a virtue. Hence the texts quoted by Dalbiez (193–196, 292). And it is quite true that a Catholic cannot subscribe to them, but it would also be wrong to think that Luther gives no place to the love of God—precisely, it is a sin not to love God for himself and above all else!—nor does Luther deny the struggle against the 'flesh', against sin, and towards growth into a life for which Christ is *exemplum*.

Roland Dalbiez cites authentic texts whose 'unacceptable meaning' he very carefully notes. But there is an abundance of other texts by Luther; I am thinking of the theme of double justice, on which there are not only the two sermons of 1518/1519 (WA 2:43–47, *de triplici*

28. For example, *Römervorlesung*, WA 56:218, (LW 25:204); *Dictata super Psalterium*, 1513–1516: '*Quidquid de domino Ihesu Christo in persona sua ad litteram dicitur, hic ipsum allegorice de adiutorio sibi simili et ecclesia sibi in omnibus conformi debet intelligi. Idemque simul tropologice debet intelligi de quolibet spirituali et interiore homine, contra suam carnem et exteriorem hominem*', WA 3:13,14–17, see LW 10:7; and *compare* 167, 20f. (LW 10:39), 299,35 (LW 10:247–248). The ecclesiological allegory is indeed Augustinian, the tropology is specifically Lutheran. Also see Beer, *Der fröhliche Wechsel*.
29. Thus in the *Sermo de duplici iusticia* (1518, edited in 1519): '*Igitur per fidem in Christum fit iusticia Christi nostra iusticia et omnia quae sunt ipsius, immo ipsemet noster fit (. . .) qui credit in Christo haeret in Christo, estque unum cum Christo, habens eandem iusticiam cum ipso. Ideo impossibile est quod in eo maneat peccatum. Et haec iusticia est prima, fundamentum, causa, origo omnis iusticiae propriae seu actualis; quia vere ipsa datur pro originali iusticia in Adam perdita et operatur id, immo maius quam illa iusticia originalis fuisset operata (. . .) Haec igitur iusticia aliena et sine actibus nostris per solam gratiam infusa nobis, trahente intus scilicet patre nos ad Christum opponitur peccato originali, quod alienum similiter et sine nostris actibus per solam generationem nobis cognatum et contractum. Et ita Christus expellit Adam de die in diem magis et magis, secundum quod crescit illa fides et cognitio Christi. Non enim tota simul infunditur, sed incipit proficit et perficitur tandem in fine per mortem*', WA 2:146, see LW 31:299, *Sermon on Two-Fold Righteousness*.

iustitia; 145–152, *de duplici iustitia*, LW 31:297–306) but which Luther maintained to the end, emphasising only more strongly that works are of value in faith.[30] I am thinking of the theme of faith that is concrete and incarnate, that is to say, faith that produces works.[31]

I am also thinking of the double theme of *gratia-donum*, and of Christ *sacramentum-exemplum*: a Christological pairing that Luther found in St Augustine (*De Trin.*, IV, 3.6) but to which he gives a breadth of application that goes far beyond Augustine's text.[32] I am thinking here of the difference Luther makes between our total justification through Christ for which he speaks of imputation, and our justification through the purification that the Holy Spirit works through our lives and works.[33] These are all important themes that very significantly diminish the difference or opposition between Luther and Catholicism. To develop them would be to write a study that this is not the place to undertake. Our purpose here is limited to attempting an assessment of Dalbiez's construction, which is rigorous and serious within its limits, but inadequate as an explanation of Luther's path to his break with the ancient Church, and of the foundations of Lutheran doctrine.

Are there inconsistencies in Luther's teaching? Maintaining the necessity of 'special faith', why did he keep the baptism of new-born infants? And if, as Roland Dalbiez says, the necessary guilt of natural temptation is the cornerstone of Luther's formation, why are the medieval proponents of the same thesis anything other than

30. Studies on this theme in Beer, *Der fröhliche Wechsel*; Walther von Loewnich, *Duplex iustitia, Luthers Stellung zu einer Unionsformel des 16, Jahrhunderts* (Wiesbaden: Steiner, 1972).

31. Compare Paul Manns, 'Fides absoluta-Fides incarnata. Zur Rechtfertigunslehre Luthers im grossem Galater-Kommentar', in *Reformata reformanda*, Festgabe Hubert Jedin (Münster: Aschendorff, 1965), I:265–312.

32. In addition to Beer (as above) see Erwin Iserloh, 'Gratia und Donum. Rechtfertigung und Heiligung nach Luthers Schrift Wider den Löwener Theologen Latomus (1521)', in *Catholica*, 24 (1970): 67–83 (reproduced in *Luther und die Reformation* [Aschaffenburg, 1974], 88–105); 'Sacramentum et exemplum. Ein augustinisches Thema lutherischer Theologie', in *Reformata reformanda*, 1:247–264. For this pairing in St Augustine and St Leo, see Basil Studer, 'Sacramentum et exemplum chez St Augustin', in *Recherches augustiniennes* 10 (1975): 87–141.

33. *Disputatio* of 1538: WA 39/1:434, see LW 73:127; compare WA 39/1 383,3f. (LW 73:86), 431,8f. (LW 73:125), 491,23f. (LW 73:164).

Lutheran? In his theology of gratia-donum, and of double justice, Luther makes favourable statements about human cooperation with God, and about merit itself. Is this inconsistency?

Or will Luther, however great he may be, remain an example of the danger of moving, without self-criticism or serious elaboration, from simple existential affirmations or spiritual attitudes to an objective theory or doctrine? Luther is speaking spiritually, he is interested in our innermost being *coram Deo*. What is needed is to live the relationship of the forgiven sinner: pardoned precisely because he confesses himself to be a sinner, justified because he confesses himself to be wretched. 'Only the sheep that was lost is sought, only the captive is set free, only the poor is enriched, only the weak is strengthened, only the humble is exalted, it is what is empty that is filled, only what was not, that is built'.[34] This admirable text reveals the whole of Luther's search for an evangelical *ethos*. It expresses a truth about spiritual attitude that could only be translated into objective doctrine by means of some clarification, just like its counter-value: it is when we are unjust in this way that God is (confessed to be) just. Luther's thought is constantly dialectical and paradoxical.

Conclusion

Roland Dalbiez's study is new. No one has combined expertise in metaphysics and theology as he has. He sheds light on decisive theological aspects of Luther's anguish and the theological solution that the Reformer found for this, and thus also on decisive aspects of the link between Lutheran doctrine and Luther's personal destiny or drama.

But for me, it does not seem to do justice to Luther's thought. Dalbiez has constantly, lucidly and rigorously, assessed it in the light of and against the yardstick of Catholic doctrine and even Thomistic theology. His questions and insights are invaluable. But he did not place himself within the genuine perspective and true inspiration of Luther's thought. Even if 'special faith' is what he says it is, for justification it is more debatable. It does not originate in the Scholastic thesis of the guilt of involuntary impulses or temptations. What Luther has to say on this matter comes from another context:

34. *Römervorlesung*, WA 56:218; see LW 25:204.

biblical, Pauline, Augustinian, as well as from his own exacerbated experience. All in all, there are other aspects to Luther's thought that have not found a place in Dalbiez's analysis.

Added in 1982

I have discussed Roland Dalbiez's thesis within the framework of theological texts and positions. And also by proposing the existence of a particular 'anguish' in Luther as a young man. Admittedly, the late texts in which he speaks of this are largely reconstructed, in order to condemn works-righteousness. But there also facts such as frequent, sometimes daily confession, etc. Daniel Olivier (*la Foi de Luther. La cause de l'Évangile dans l'Église* (Paris: Beauchesne, 1978), 139–152 = *Luther's Faith* (St Louis: Concordia, 1982), 94–103) refuses to accept that there was any 'anguish' in Luther. He sees in him the victory of faith, 'special faith' being none other than faith in the word of God personally experienced: 'it is a matter of *my* justification because faith is always *someone's* faith'. Olivier refutes Dalbiez by radically rejecting his position on the question and what arises from it. I have commented on 'special faith' (see above 19–21). The question should be taken up again in depth.

More recently, I have read the magnificent *Martin Luther* published by Peter Manns, disciple and successor of Joseph Lortz (Freiberg: Herder, 1982). For Manns, Luther's 'anguish' concerned confession, perfect contriteness and God's absolute love for himself. The concupiscence that dwells in us and makes humans *incurvatus in seipsum* means that sin continues to dwell in us. What are our works worth if there is no perfect love of God, even though the law says, you shall not covet? I acknowledge that this explanation accords well with what Luther says in his *Römervorlesung* of 1515–1516.

* * *

www.ingramcontent.com/pod-product-compliance
Lightning Source LLC
Chambersburg PA
CBHW031121150826
49772CB00004B/146